How the Law Works

THIRD EDITION

GARY SLAPPER

LLB (UCL), LLM (UCL), PhD (LSE), PGCE (Law) (Manc)
Global Professor, New York University
Director, New York University, London
Door Tenant, 36 Bedford Row
Visiting Professor of Law,
The Chinese University of Hong Kong;
The Open University, UK

Routledge
Taylor & Francis Group

LONDON AND NEW YORK

Third edition published 2014
by Routledge
2 Park Square, Milton Park, Abingdon, Oxon OX14 4RN

and by Routledge
711 Third Avenue, New York, NY 10017

Routledge is an imprint of the Taylor & Francis Group, an informa business

© 2014 Gary Slapper

First edition published by Collins in 2007
Second edition published by Routledge in 2011

British Library Cataloguing in Publication Data
A catalogue record for this book is available from the British Library

Library of Congress Cataloging in Publication Data
A catalog record for this book has been requested

ISBN: 978–0–415–81634–2 (hbk)
ISBN: 978–0–415–81633–5 (pbk)
ISBN: 978–1–315–86977–3 (ebk)

Typeset in Vectora LH
by RefineCatch Ltd, Bungay, Suffolk

MIX
Paper from
responsible sources
FSC   FSC® C013056
www.fsc.org

Printed and bound in Great Britain by
TJ International Ltd, Padstow, Cornwall

Contents

Preface   ix
Acknowledgements   xi

1   The Importance of Law   1
The nature of law   4
The rule of law   7
Clear and accessible law   12
The golden metwand   15
Law and social change   17
The law and democracy   24
Further reading   26

2   Judges   27
Profile of the judiciary   28
Types of judge   30
Judicial appointments   33
Judicial animation of the law   35
Battle of the law-makers   37
The judiciary and the administration of the courts   41
Judges and communicating with the public   43
The training of judges   43
Judicial independence   45
Judicial impartiality   46
Removal of judges from office   51
Magistrates   53
Magistrates and popular justice   55
Further reading   58

3   Lawyers   59
The legal profession   61
Lawyers and fees   64
A fusion of the professions   65
Solicitors   66
New forms of organisation for lawyers   69
The Institute of Legal Executives   71

Barristers	72
Other help in the courtroom	77
Legal claims against lawyers	77
The proliferation of lawyers	80
Further reading	82

4   Cases and the Courts   **83**

Cases that changed the law	83
The common law system	88
The hierarchy of the courts	92
Human rights	103
Further reading	106

5   Case Technique   **107**

Titles	107
Ratio decidendi	108
Obiter dictum	109
Overruling	112
Distinguishing	113
Judicial development of the law	117
Dissenting judgments	120
Law reporting	121
Law online	124
News reporting	125
Judging the system of precedent	126
Further reading	127

6   Interpreting Acts of Parliament   **129**

A danger due to the state of the premises	131
The rules of interpretation	133
Other aids to interpretation	138
Human rights and interpreting UK law	143
The European context	146
Statutory interpretation, justice and truth	150
Further reading	156

7   Types of Law   **157**

Common law and civil law	158
Common law and equity	159
Common law and statute law	162

Public law and private law   163
Criminal law and civil law   166
Further reading   182

8   The Jury   **183**
The law of juries   185
When juries are used   186
Majority verdicts   191
Judges as jurors   192
Tale 1: The seancer's tale   194
Tale 2: The astrologer's tale   196
Tale 3: The peace campaigner's tale   197
Tale 4: The recusant's tale   199
Tale 5: The madame's tale   200
Tale 6: The avenger's tale   201
Tale 7: The expert's tale   202
Tale 8: The bonded juror's tale   204
Tale 9: The cougher's tale   204
Tale 10: The smoker's tale   205
Tale 11: The crime fighters' tale   206
Tale 12: The optimist's tale   208
A verdict   208
Further reading   210

9   Language and Law   **211**
Latin and the law   213
Punctuation   217
Legal words that have become common   219
Names   220
Profane language   224
Conciseness   226
Arcane legal words and phrases   227
Further reading   230

10   Miscellany   **231**
Ten legal literary classics   231
Ten remarkable witnesses   235
Ten great lawyers   238
Ten great places to experience law live   241
Ten great films for those interested in law   244

Ten classic law school witticisms   249
Ten classic judgment openings   252
Ten classic legal mistakes   255
Ten remarkable pieces of evidence   257

Glossary of Terms   261
Notes   273
Bibliography   283
Table of Cases   287
Table of Legislation   293
Index   297

Preface

Today law is a popular subject at universities and colleges. Although people who study subjects like mathematics, music, biology or history will have studied them before while at high school, and know something of the elements and methods of their chosen subject, that is not true of those who study law as a specialist subject. This book is aimed at introducing the subject to newcomers. It has also been written to be of use as a continuing companion to legal study, and of being helpful, I hope, to other citizens.

The number and range of law books, law reports and legislative volumes in the library has grown considerably over the years. In his inaugural lecture at Oxford on 21 April 1883, the distinguished constitutional lawyer A.V. Dicey noted that even until well into the nineteenth century it was possible for a person to read the entirety of English law within the compass of an ordinary adult life. It could be contained in fewer than 200 volumes. Today, an earnest reader would probably need to live for over 600 years to read all law and regulations applicable in the United Kingdom. Whether that would be the most edifying way to spend a 600-year life is another matter.

This book is about both the hardware and software of law. It is about the tangible parts of the enterprise, like lawyers, judges, the dramas of courtrooms, and juries – the hardware. It is also about the theories inexplicitly, and thus invisibly, relied on in law when, for example, cases are analysed or legislation is interpreted and applied – the software.

In 1846, a parliamentary committee on legal education urged in a report that law be taught more animatedly and more widely. But five years after it published that report, another committee discovered that not only had no one done anything about the proposal, no one had even read the report! There was dust on the pages whose obscured writing complained that law was a dusty subject.

Law continued to be seen widely as a subject of limited importance and as something for a social elite. In 1948, in his inspiring Presidential Address to the Society of Public Teachers of Law, W.T.S. Stallybrass accepted that law was a fit subject to be studied at universities. He made many perceptive suggestions, some very advanced for the time, about how best legal education should be carried out.

However, he accepted the then prevailing notion that a law faculty should provide the sort of liberal education equated with 'a gentleman's knowledge'. He did not accept that the subject should include any analysis or criticism of the policies embodied in legal doctrines or in the operation of legal principles. He also did not want it to cover 'those branches of the Law which depend on Statute'.

By contrast, today, legal education seeks to equip students with a wider knowledge and more contextual appreciation of law. Critical technique is important, and today all taught branches of the law suspend a spectacular array of legislative fruit. To those who embark on the study of law for whatever reason, or who are contemplating such study, or who simply want to know how the law works, it is hoped that this book will be of use.

Acknowledgements

I am, as ever, immeasurably indebted to Suzanne, Hannah, Emily and Charlotte for their enduring support and encouragement.

I owe particular thanks to Fiona Briden, Senior Publisher at Routledge, for her enlivening interest in and abiding encouragement of this book. I am greatly indebted to rising star of the Bar, Martha Spurrier, for her superb work on legal developments throughout the text. I am also very grateful to Damian Mitchell, Editorial Assistant at Routledge, for his editorial management. I am indebted to Mel Dyer at RefineCatch for his professionalism, and Jackie Day for production management at Routledge. For having read and commented upon earlier drafts, and providing immensely useful guidance, I thank Helen Zhou, David Holt, David Jeffreys QC, Professor Tony Lentin, Ben Fitzpatrick, Alexis Longshaw, Dr Ray Arthur, Fiona Tucker, HH Judge Lynn Tayton QC, Vicki Scoble, Carol Howells, Professor Michael Furmston, and the later, and missed Jane Goodey.

Many others have been extraordinarily generous as educators, iridescent sources of inspiration, and stimulating friends. I thank Doreen and Ivor Slapper, Clifford, Maxine, Pav, Anish, the late Raie Schwartz, David and Julie Whight, Lulu Phillips, Carolyn Bracknell, Abigail Carr, Jock Williamson, Dr Hetty Henderson, Professor Stephen Coleman, Professor Michael Freeman, Professor Robert Reiner, Hugh McLaughlan, Keren Bright, Ben Fitzpatrick, Professor Sir Jeffrey Jowell QC, Professor Ian Dennis, Lady Jacqueline Dyson, Professor Dame Hazel Genn QC, Professor Andrew Lewis, Natasha Phillips of Researching Reform, Frances Thomas, Mandy Winter, Eric Sneddon, Professor Matthew Weait, Ken Shaw, Robert Zimmerman, Patrick Whight, Dr David Kelly, Clare Hogan, Frances Gibb, Lord Justice Sedley and Lord Woolf.

The Importance of Law

Law is all-pervasive. It exists in every cell of life. It affects everyone virtually all of the time. It governs everything in life and even what happens to us after life. It applies to everything from the embryo to exhumation. It governs the air we breathe, the food and drink that we consume, our travel, sexuality, family relationships, and our property. It applies at the bottom of the ocean and in space. It regulates the world of sport, science, employment, business, political liberty, education, health services; everything, in fact, from neighbour disputes to war.

The law in the United Kingdom has evolved over a long period. It has, over the centuries, successfully adapted itself through a great variety of social settings and types of government. Today it contains elements that are ancient, such as the coroner's courts, which have an 800-year history, and elements that are very modern, such as electronic law reports and judges using laptop computers. Law has also become much more widely recognised as the standard by which behaviour needs to be judged. A very telling change in recent history is the way in which the law has permeated all parts of social life. The universal standard of whether something is socially acceptable is progressively becoming whether it is legal. In earlier times, most people were illiterate and did not have the vote. They were ruled, in effect, by what we would call tyranny. And this was not just in 1250. That state of affairs still existed in the UK in 1850. Today, by contrast, most people are literate and have the vote. Parliamentary democracy is our system of government. So, it is quite possible and desirable for people in general to take an interest in law. A widely esteemed jurist, A.V. Dicey, said that:

> Where the public has influence, the development of law must of necessity be governed by public opinion.[1]

Like the pen or the knife, law is a versatile instrument that can be used equally well for the improvement or the degradation of humanity. In a healthily participative social democracy, law can be used to serve the general public interest.

That, of course, puts law in a very important position. In our rapidly developing world, all sorts of skills and knowledge are valuable. Those people, for example, with knowledge of computers, the Internet and communications technology are relied upon by the rest of us. There is now an IT expert or help desk in every school, every company, every hospital, and every local and central government office. Without their constantly applied expertise, many parts of commercial and social life today would seize up in minutes.

But legal knowledge is often just as important and as universally needed.

The American comedian, Jerry Seinfeld put it like this:

> To me a lawyer is basically the person who knows the rules of the country. We are all throwing the dice, playing the game, moving our pieces around the board, but if there is a problem the lawyer is the only person who has read the inside of the top of the box.[2]

Consider the extensive reach of modern law. Most people would agree that it is desirable to be governed by law and rules so that, in any department of life, we can understand in advance of any conduct, what is democratically permitted and how certain things must be done. Every time we examine a label on a food product, engage in work as an employee or employer, travel on the roads, go to school to learn or to teach, stay in a hotel, borrow a library book, create or dissolve a commercial company, play sports, or engage the services of someone for anything from plumbing a sink to planning a city, we are in the world of law. The extent and influence of law has never been greater. Law governs every aspect of what we do today. In the UK, about 35 new public Acts of Parliament are produced every year, thereby delivering thousands of new rules into our world. The legislative output of Parliament has more than doubled in recent times from 1,100 pages a year in the early 1970s to over 2,500 pages a year today. There are over 12,000 criminal offences under English law. Between 1997 and 2010, 4,289 separate offences were the subject of legislation. These include disturbing a pack of eggs when directed not to do so by an authorised officer, selling or offering for sale game birds that have been shot on a Sunday, and swimming in the wreck of the Titanic.

In a democracy, with so much complicated law, lawyers do a great deal not just to vindicate the rights of citizens and organisations but also, through legal arguments, some of which are adapted into law by judges, to help develop the law. Law courts, as we shall see, can and do grow new law and prune old law, but they do so having heard the arguments of lawyers. Consider this observation from the famous twentieth-century judge, Lord Denning, made in a case from 1954:

> What is the argument on the other side? Only this, that no case has been found in which it has been done before. That argument does not appeal to me in the least. If we never do anything which has not been

done before, we shall never get anywhere. The law will stand still whilst the rest of the world goes on: and that will be bad for both.[3]

However, despite their important role in developing the rules in a democracy, lawyers are not universally popular. Anti-lawyer jokes have a long history. The ancient Athenian philosopher Diogenes once went to look for an honest lawyer. 'How's it going?' someone asked him after a while. 'Not too bad,' answered Diogenes. 'I still have my lantern.'

The public image of lawyers has not changed much during the 2,400 years since Diogenes decided to close himself off from people by living in a large earthenware jar in Athens. In an episode of the television cartoon series *Futurama*, during a riot, one of the characters looks at a body on the ground and exclaims to another character: 'You killed my lawyer!', to which the instant reply is: 'You're welcome.'

When Malcolm Ford, the son of film actor Harrison Ford, was asked at his junior school what his father did for a living, he replied:

My daddy is a movie actor, and sometimes he plays the good guy, and sometimes he plays the lawyer.[4]

One of many anti-lawyer jokes concerns a little boy, Tim, who was in a class in an American infants' school. A teacher was asking all the children what jobs their parents had. One girl said her mother was a doctor, another said her father was a librarian. Then Tim was asked the question, and replied: 'My dad plays the banjo in a brothel.' The shocked teacher moved the conversation on, but later told Tim's mother when she collected her son. The mother said 'Oh, well, to tell you the truth, his dad is a lawyer, but you can't tell that to a four-year old.'

For balance, though, it is worth remembering that there have been, and are now, many heroic and revered lawyers. Any such parade of fame should include Marcus Tullius Cicero (106–43 BC), Sir Thomas More (1477–1535), Louis Dembitz Brandeis (1856–1941), Nelson Mandela (1918–), Clarence Darrow (1857–1938) and Mohandas Karamchand Gandhi (1869–1948) (see Chapter 10 for descriptions of their contributions).

Comments are sometimes made characterising lawyers as professionals whose concerns put reward above truth, or who make financial gain from misfortune. There are undoubtedly lawyers who would fit that bill, just as there are some scientists, expert medical witnesses, journalists, academic researchers, preachers, business gurus and others in that indictable category. But, in general, it is no fairer to say that lawyers are bad because they make a living from human problems than it is to make the same accusation in respect of ambulance drivers or IT technicians. A great many lawyers are involved in public law work, like that involving civil liberties, criminal defence work, welfare law, housing law and employment rights, which is not lavishly remunerated and whose quality relies on considerable professional dedication. Moreover, much legal work has nothing to do with conflict or misfortune, but concerns commerce, property conveyancing, document drafting and company work.

Another source of social disaffection for lawyers, and sometimes disaffection for the law, is a deficiency in public understanding of how law works, why it is cast as it is, and how it could be changed. Greater clarity and openness about these issues – through systematic education and legal public relations – would reduce many aspects of public disgruntlement with the law.

THE NATURE OF LAW

Throughout recorded history a great many statements have been made about the nature of law, and why we need it. There is an enormously varied and rich literature on this subject. Here we can really do no more than consider a few samples of these opinions. The writers who have addressed this theme come to it from a startling variety of viewpoints, and hold fundamentally different underlining assumptions about their subject.

The thirteenth-century Italian philosopher, and Dominican friar, St Thomas Aquinas, set law in the context of nature.

> There is in man a natural aptitude to virtuous action. . . . There are, indeed, some young men, readily inclined to a life of virtue . . . But there are others, of evil disposition and prone to vice, who are not easily moved by words. These it is necessary to restrain from wrongdoing by force and by fear. When they are thus prevented from doing evil, a quiet life is assured to the rest of the community . . .[5]

Another type of analysis of the nature and purpose of law, focusing on necessity, is one like this of the eminent twentieth-century lawyer and academic Denis Lloyd:

In any society, whether primitive or complex, it will be necessary to have rules which lay down the conditions under which men and women may mate and live together; rules governing family relationships; conditions under which economic and food-gathering or hunting activities are to be organised; and the exclusion of acts which are regarded as inimical to the welfare of the family, or of larger groups such as the tribe or the whole community. Moreover, in a complex, civilised community . . . there will have still to be a large apparatus of rules governing family, social, and economic life.[6]

Some writers have paid particular attention to what they regard as the moral purposes of law. This was the view of Sir Patrick Devlin, a judge who was later elevated to the highest level of the judiciary, the House of Lords. He said:

Societies disintegrate from within more frequently than they are broken up by external pressures. There is disintegration when no common morality is observed and history shows that the loosening of moral bonds is often the first state of disintegration, so that society is justified in taking the same steps to preserve its moral code as it does to preserve its government and other essential institutions. The suppression of vice is as much the law's business as the suppression of subversive activities; it is no more possible to define a sphere of private morality than it is to define one of private subversive activity . . .[7]

In science, in order to understand or appreciate the nature of something, or its function, it is sometimes useful to remove it from its surroundings to see what happens or ceases to happen when it is not there. A similar sort of experiment, although really a 'thought experiment', has been done in books that depict societies without law. Sir Thomas More, a distinguished lawyer, and later a famed Lord Chancellor, wrote in his story Utopia about a society without lawyers. The intriguing world he describes can provoke many thoughts about the role of law in our own society:

They have very few laws, because, with their social system, very few laws are required enough . . . For, according to the Utopians, it's quite unjust for anyone to be bound by a legal code which is too long for an ordinary person to read right through or, too difficult for him to understand. What's more, they have no barristers to be over-ingenious about individual cases and points of law. They think it is better for each man to plead his own cause, and tell the judge the same story as he'd otherwise tell his lawyer. Under such conditions, the point at issue is less likely to be obscured, and it's easier to get at the truth – for, if nobody's telling the sort of lies one learns from lawyers, the judge can apply all of his shrewdness to weighing the facts of the case, and protecting simple-minded characters against the unscrupulous attacks of clever ones.[8]

Some writers have used the structure of the political economy as being the main explanatory factor when exploring the nature of modern law. Friedrich Engels, the nineteenth-century writer, took this approach. He argued that:

Laws are necessary only because there are persons in existence who own nothing. . . . If a rich man is brought up, or rather summonsed, to appear before the court, the judge regrets that he is obliged to impose so much trouble, treats the matter as favourably as possible, and, if he is forced to condemn the accused, does so with extreme regret, etc., etc. and the end of it all is a miserable fine, which the bourgeois throws upon the table with contempt and then departs. But if a poor devil gets into such a position as involves appearing before the Justice of the Peace . . . he is regarded from the beginning as guilty; his defence is set aside with a contemptuous 'Oh! We know the excuse' and a fine imposed which he cannot pay and must work out with several months on the treadmill.[9]

One modern, and widely accepted, encapsulation of the nature of law is that of Professor A.W.B. Simpson. He says:

The principal functions of the law are, I should suggest, to be sought in the resolution of conflict, the regulation of human behaviour both to reduce conflict and to further social goals, the distribution of powers, the distribution of property and wealth, and the reconciliation of stability and change.[10]

The 'reconciliation of stability and change', Professor Simpson goes on to explain, is the balance that the law seeks to make between:

(a)   the need for the rules of a society to remain stable and predictable so that people can organise their affairs without the fear that they will constantly change, and

(b)   the need for rules to change and develop to reflect significant changes in social circumstances.

These various views on law, and analyses of it, are some illustrations drawn from a very diverse literature on the subject. People's basic assumptions – about morals, or science, or religion, or class, or human nature – will affect the way they regard any part of the law and its machinery.

THE RULE OF LAW

So it is clear that law is everywhere, and that opinions about its true nature are quite divergent.

It is now worth noting that in a democracy like the UK's, law is the highest power. The police or the military forces might have the most physical force at their command but only because they are invested with that power by law. In theory, and, generally in practice, the law is above everyone. Other forces, like morals, peer pressure and religion, exercise influence over people but, ultimately, the law is the set of rules that is most forcefully and systematically applied. It might be that the economy exercises a powerful influence over how things change, as with the end of apartheid in South Africa or the beginning of Sunday shop trading in the UK, but such changes are not established unless and until they are made in law.

The outcome of the 2001 American presidential election was only finally determined after a ruling by the Supreme Court of the United States. Similarly, just as the UK was about to go to war in Iraq in 2003, the legal opinion of senior law officers of the UK was sought to decide whether a war would be legal. Whatever one's opinion is about these matters, the fact that a legal opinion was seen as important is a telling fact.

Alongside the big questions such as these are hundreds of thousands of lesser ones about such things as whether manufacturers can camouflage the amount of salt they put in food by labelling it as sodium, or whether you can grow your leylandii three metres high.

Over the last thousand years in the UK, and in several other parts of the world, the law has been used progressively less as a tool for social repression, and more as a code utilised and relied upon by the majority of people in the conduct of everyday life.

The rule of law is now widely regarded as a desirable feature of social governance. Albert Venn Dicey, a Professor of Law at Oxford who died in 1922, noted that when we speak of 'the rule of law' as a characteristic of British life we mean:

> not only that with us no man is above the law, but (what is a different thing) that here every man, whatever be his rank or condition, is subject to the ordinary law of the realm and amenable to the jurisdiction of the ordinary tribunals . . .[11]

Few things can be more important to a modern democracy than the rule of law. This principle is the cornerstone of stable society because every person, group or social entity needs, at any time, to be able to determine what the social rules are on any given matter, and to act within them or to try to change them. The rule of law is the first rule of a democracy.

In an English High Court case in 1977, the late Lord Denning summed up the gist of the principle of the rule of law when he said:

> To every subject in this land, no matter how powerful, I would use Thomas Fuller's words over 300 years ago: 'Be you never so high, the law is above you.'[12]

The law, in other words, stands above the heads of even the most elevated people. In 2002, for example, Princess Anne was fined £500 for an offence under section 3(1) of the Dangerous Dogs Act 1991 after her English bull terrier bitch had bitten two boys in Windsor Great Park. Her case was listed at East Berkshire Magistrates' Court as 'LAURENCE, Anne Elizabeth Alice Louise, dob 15/08/50', she was asked in the normal way to stand up when the charge was addressed to her in court, and the case immediately following hers was of Stewart William Barber, a 19-year-old mechanic who had been charged with failing to provide the police with a second specimen of breath in a suspected 'drink driving' incident.[13]

It is worth noting that some early attempts to bring the mighty within the law failed. The scandal of Governor Edward Eyre was an early case in point. Eyre was appointed Governor of Jamaica in 1864. In 1865, in response to an alleged riot, 600 people were killed or summarily executed under his governorship and the same number savagely flogged. William Gordon, a black member of the legislature, was accused of being a ringleader, brought forcibly into an area of martial law and summarily executed. Eyre was dismissed, but for years afterwards the

Jamaica Committee (comprising members of the Victorian intelligentsia) attempted to get Eyre tried for his crimes. Among the committee members were the philosopher John Stuart Mill (who was chairman), the scientist and writer Herbert Spencer, Charles Darwin and Thomas Hughes, author of *Tom Brown's School Days*. Ultimately, Eyre escaped trial and was given a pension. The story is fully told in *Leading Cases in the Common Law* by A.W.B. Simpson.

In contrast to this, in recent times, there have been several instances of major public figures and national leaders being taken through the courts. Nowadays, the law is not just above the heads of powerful or wealthy people, it is above the heads of heads of states. They were never so high but the law was above them. The court appearances of General Augusto Pinochet of Chile, the former Chilean president, and the late Serbian leader Slobodan Milosevic are cases in point. At the end of 2003, four former government ministers of Rwanda were put on trial at a United Nations tribunal, indicted for their part in the 1994 genocide. That legal procedures are invoked against them is in itself indicative of a social stance that is less genuflexive towards political leadership than in the past. In 2004, Silvio Berlusconi, prime minister of Italy, and EU president, was indicted for serious criminal charges of corruption. A law was passed in Italy in 2003 which would have afforded to the prime minister immunity from prosecution, but in 2004 the Italian constitutional court annulled that law because it breached the principle that 'all must be equal before the law'. In 2005, Saddam Hussein was put on trial for war crimes in Iraq. Along with seven other defendants he was indicted over the deaths of 148 men and teenagers after a failed attempt on his life in Dujail in 1982. On 4 April 2005, the tribunal trying him, a panel of five judges, announced fresh criminal charges against Saddam Hussein and six others for alleged genocide and crimes against humanity in a campaign against the Kurds dating back to the late 1980s. In June 2012, the ousted Egyptian President, Hosni Mubarak, was subjected to a criminal trial and convicted of conspiring to kill protesters during the 2011 revolt that ended his rule. About 850 people were killed in the 2011 crackdown. He was sentenced to life imprisonment. However, following an appeal, a retrial was ordered in 2013.

Today, the attitude which prevails in many countries entails that governmental delinquency is more likely than it was in the past to be followed by a legal consequence. Government is being seen in many jurisdictions increasingly in terms of its being a service provided for the public and at its expense rather than a form of control by superiors from which the majority are fortunate to benefit. The rule of law is not a panacea for social ills. Some tyrannical regimes or totalitarian states can, in fact, show a fairly close adherence to several aspects of the rule of law.

Nazi Germany and apartheid South Africa were governed with close observance to the principles of the rules of law. It was the laws themselves that were iniquitous. The rule of law might also exist alongside endemic poverty and social insecurity for the majority of people. Nonetheless, it is not a doctrine to be easily dismissed as inconsequential. Noting that the rule of law was not in itself a provider of social justice, the writer E.P. Thompson went on to say:

> But the rule of law itself, the imposing of effective inhibitions upon power and the defence of the citizen from power's all intrusive claims, seems to me to be an unqualified human good. To deny or to belittle this good is, in this dangerous century when the resources and pretensions of power continue to enlarge, a desperate error of intellectual abstraction.[14]

That was written in 1975. The resources and pretensions of power have since multiplied, and this century has already fallen into distinctly dangerous times. If used effectively, though, the democratic process is an antidote to even the worst excesses of arbitrary power.

The value of the rule of law as a governing principle is that it is universal. It runs across status and class. Consider the words of Atticus Finch, the attorney in Harper Lee's *To Kill a Mockingbird*:

> We all know men are not created equal in the sense some people would have us believe – some people are smarter than others, some people have more opportunity because they're born with it . . . some people are born gifted beyond the normal scope of most men.

> But there is one way in this country in which all men are created equal – there is one human institution that makes a pauper the equal of a Rockefeller, the stupid man the equal of an Einstein and the ignorant man the equal of any college president. That institution, gentlemen, is a court.[15]

Some might want to add the proviso: 'as long as you can afford a good lawyer', a criticism that is part of a wider difficulty. A cartoon JB Handelsman featured in the *New Yorker* magazine in 1973 makes this point. An earnest lawyer, having read several documents spread over his desk in a plush office, says to his anxious client: 'You have a pretty good case, Mr Pitkin. How much justice can you afford?'

It is true that one of the dangers in extolling the merits of 'the rule of law' is that one can forget the uncomfortable reality that even where the same rules are applied equally to everyone, this does not of itself produce fairness if the people to whom the law applies have starkly contrasting circumstances. As the French writer Anatole France observed, we all have to live:

> [I]n the face of the majestic equality of the law, which forbids the rich as well as the poor to sleep under bridges, to beg in the streets, and to steal bread.[16]

None the less, even taking into account the ways in which the law applies unevenly across society, it is still a great force for social cohesion. And the more that a society is enriched by becoming more cosmopolitan and multicultural, the greater the need for all citizens to share respect for democratically passed and implemented law.

Today, law, lawyers, judges and legal systems are predominating forces across the world. If there is a social equivalent of the physical force of gravity then it is the force of law. The mass of law we have made, the rules to govern all aspects of what we do, is what keeps us together, more or less, in a 'social system'. The French social scientist Emile Durkheim wrote in 1893 about the way that the enforcement of the criminal law operates to 'maintain inviolate the cohesion of society' and to enhance social solidarity. The use of the law against offenders helps, in his phrase, to 'draw honest consciousnesses together, concentrating them'.[17] What is true of the punitive criminal law is also true, in a more subtle way, of the operation of the morass of civil law governing our lives as neighbours, educators, drivers, parents, children, travellers, scientists, employees, employers, engineers, artists and all of the other roles and statuses that we use. In a large, complex, multicultural, pluralistic society, law is the one single code of rules that binds everyone.

Our social rules have varied according to the social systems we have evolved – so slave society with its owners of people and slaves gave us one set of laws; feudal society with its serfs, lords of the manor and tithes gave us another set of laws; state capitalism with its five-year plans and government-run industry generated yet another rule book; and modern capitalism with its social media and online shopping, and where the ether is as much a platform of crime as is *terra firma*, has again re-written our legal code. Today, however, more than in the past, despite the sometimes potent regulatory forces of religion or public mores, it is the law that is the ultimate determinant of our social behaviour.

CLEAR AND ACCESSIBLE LAW

Law, then, is everywhere. It is divergently analysed, and it is above everyone. And more than ever, there is a growing public concern for law to be clear and accessible.

The introduction of The Freedom of Information Act 2000 has assisted the public to obtain non-personal information that was previously unavailable. This has forced government departments, local councils, schools, universities, etc. to be more open on matters of public policy, subject to certain exemptions such as national security.

Citizens of the twenty-first century want to order themselves by easily understood law made in plain and simple language. They don't want to come a-cropper of legal versions of Humpty Dumpty's dictum. In Lewis Carroll's 1871 book *Through The Looking-Glass – And What Alice Found There*, at one point in a dispute between Alice and Humpty Dumpty, Alice says 'I don't know what you mean by "glory".' The text continues:

> Humpty smiled contemptuously. 'Of course you don't, till I tell you. I meant – there's a nice knock-down argument for you.'
>
> 'But glory doesn't mean "a nice knock-down argument",' Alice objected.
>
> 'When *I* use a word,' Humpty said in a rather scornful tone, 'it means just what I choose it to mean – neither more nor less.'[18]

Too often, citizens are nonplussed upon discovering that the legal use of a word is different from its common meaning. Much of law has been complicated by an extravagant style of language. A nineteenth-century legal writer once noted that, whereas in ordinary life you might say 'I give you this orange', a property lawyer would insist that the orange is donated with the words:

> I give you all and singular, my estate and interest, right, title, claim and advantage of and in that orange, with all its rind, skin, juice, pulp and pips and all right and advantage therein, with full power to bite, cut, suck and otherwise eat the same orange, or give the same away as fully and effectually, as I the said AB am now entitled to bite, cut, suck, or otherwise eat the same orange, or give the same away, with or

without its rind, skin, juice, pulp, and pips, anything hereinbefore, or hereinafter, or in any other deed, or deeds instrument or instruments of what nature or kind soever, to the contrary in any wise, notwithstanding.[19]

Complaints about lawyers are not new. Cicero, one of the first great advocates, was berating lawyers for using outdated Latin in 38 BC. In his 'Pro L. Murena' he also attacks lawyers for thinking too much of themselves, and for their quibbling and verbosity. Medieval England saw much anti-lawyer feeling, especially complaints that lawyers stirred up unnecessary lawsuits, prolonged legal actions unnecessarily, that they concocted false bills and that there were too many of them. In 1596, for example, the judges ordered the Inns of Court to admit no more than four men to the Bar each year. The preamble to a 1601 Act in England to stop excessive legal bills noted that many fictitious fees had been charged to clients who 'growe to be overmuch burthened, and the practise of the juste and honest [lawyer] greatly slandered'.

It is true that lawyers are occasionally exposed for overcharging, sometimes in unusual ways. Most lawyers work hard, but some evidently find more time in the day than do others in which to work. In a case from Pennsylvania, America in 2003, the authorities investigating one lawyer found that, in the previous year, he had submitted bills for work including one 81-hour day and three 25-hour days. He defended himself by arguing that he had made 'innocent mistakes'.[20] Perhaps anyone in the sort of torpor likely to result from working 81-hour days will make innocent mistakes. In 1997, the English law firm James Beauchamp in Edgbaston, in the West Midlands, sent a £12,278 bill to the 80-year-old mother of one of its solicitors after he committed suicide. He had killed himself because of pressure at work. His firm's bill included £1,350 for calling at his home and arranging for police to break in, and £150 for visiting the mother to tell her that her son was dead.[21] As we have noted, though, at the beginning of this chapter, the extent of delinquency among lawyers is not significantly different from that among doctors or teachers, although the type of wrong that wayward lawyers commit against clients (property crime) is usually different from that committed by wayward doctors and teachers against their patients and pupils (corporal or sexual offending). It must be remembered, though, that such bad behaviour, in all professions, is extremely rare.

Some of the historical issues resonate in today's legal world. America now boasts over one million active lawyers in its population.[22] In the UK we have over 100,000 practising lawyers, over 35,000 judges and magistrates, and over

10,000 law graduates joining the social enterprise every year. At current rates of growth, there will be over a million lawyers in the UK in 2055. The income of solicitors in England and Wales is over £15 billion a year. Moreover, in addition to the practice of law by solicitors, barristers, and legal executives, there are now many thousands of law graduates who act in a primarily legal way in the course of their work. There are over 200,000 people in the UK working in the legal advice sector, including at Citizens' Advice Bureaux, law centres and legal advice clinics run at professional law schools. Law graduates also work in myriad branches of organisations like that of the Health and Safety Executive, consumer rights groups, and Amnesty International. In fact, today, about half of all law graduates in the UK do not proceed into conventional legal practice after they graduate. Although widely regarded as a new phenomenon, this is in fact not a new development. Delivering his inaugural lecture at Cambridge on 18 February 1955, Professor Charles Hamson noted the remarkable increase in law undergraduates who had no intention of making law their living. He thought their interest to be an academic one. He said that, 20 years after he had taught them law at Cambridge:

> [T]he number of my former pupils actually at the bar is small. . . . It may well be that the law school no more specifically provides for legal practitioners than the history school does for school masters . . .[23]

Objectively, however, although the enterprise of law is much in the public eye, and often contentious, the knowledge of law among citizens, and the use of law by citizens, are weak and at a low level. Citizens need a much more systematic education in law from school age. This theme has been addressed by Professor Michael Furmston. 'Most members of the public', Professor Furmston noted, 'are largely ignorant of the law [and] the key problem is that people do not realise or even imagine what the law might do for them.' He quoted Lord Windlesham in the House of Lords in 1974:

> A rough and ready understanding of the law, a feel for it if you like, is a mark of the democratic system itself. . . . There is not much point in having rights unless people are aware of what they are and know how to act on them.[24]

A great deal could be done to simplify the rules by which we live. In many areas legislative language could be much plainer and more comprehensible than it is. That is because much of the law that governs us today was written in previous ages, when there was no expectation that law was something that the general public had a right to see, read, understand and use for themselves. Law was something planned, devised, made, implemented and interpreted by a very narrow social élite. Sir Edward Coke, the seventeenth-century Chief Justice, once noted that the earliest lawyers in Britain wrote their law in Greek so that 'their discipline might not be made common among the vulgar'.[25] Today there is a very reasonable public expectation that law will be written in plain English. In a democracy, all law should be put in the simplest and clearest way that is compatible with what it is aiming to do.

THE GOLDEN METWAND

Law is now becoming a universal standard of behaviour, or, in a medieval phrase, law is a golden 'metwand', or measuring rod. Legality is the gold standard of all conduct.

Today our law is secular not religious. It is legitimate because it comes from Parliament or a law court identifies something as a principle of common law or equity. Before this, in the UK much law once presented itself through royal edicts that were seen to have divine authority: what the monarch declared was law because the monarch uttered the will of God. Historically the source of the law's authority metamorphosed from something God-given to something whose legitimacy came from a process: from being promulgated by Parliament, confirmed as law by judges.

Today, however, the entitlement of law to occupy the status of our supreme social code comes much more from the fact that it can be democratically made and controlled than from any notion that we should revere the law because it comes from our superiors.

The primacy of the law was firmly established by two cases. They confirmed that the law was a rule book beyond the power of the monarch to control, and that the judges alone had the job of interpreting the law.

During the early seventeenth century, there had been a growing unease between the king and the courts on the issue of who was the final determiner of the law. In *Bruce v Hamilton*, King James VI of Scotland was told in clear terms in 1599 by the Court of Session in Edinburgh that he had no power to command the court. According to Lord Birkenhead, Lord Chancellor from 1919 to 1922, this was one of the most courageous expressions of judicial independence ever made. Things came to a head in a case in 1607, again involving King James VI of Scotland, when, as James I of England, he clashed with judges in a case known as 'The Case of Prohibitions'.

A legal dispute had been judged personally by the king, acting, he thought, as the realm's fountain of justice. That decision was overruled by the ordinary courts. In his judgment, which was delivered in front of and with the support of all the common law judges, Sir Edward Coke, Chief Justice of the Common Pleas, was courageous in putting the king in his place. He noted that the king had tried to make a legal judgment by saying that he had as much power of rational reasoning as did the judges. Coke ruled that while the king did have 'excellent science' he was 'not learned in the laws of his realm of England'. Coke further noted that legal disputes about such matters as inheritance of goods:

> are not to be decided by natural reason but *by the artificial reason and judgment of law*, which law is an art which requires long study and experience, before that a man can attain to the cognisance of it: that the law was the golden metwand and measure to try the causes of the subjects; and which protected his majesty in safety and peace. . . .[26]

In other words, neither a king nor any judge can simply decide idiosyncratically what is 'fair'. He must instead apply the existing law. Such application is not without its problems. If it were very easy then there would be no legal disputes, lawyers or cases. Even so, it is generally better to be governed, in any setting, by rules than by the unpredictable whim of rulers.

When Coke made his ruling in 1607, the reason why the legal measuring rod glowed golden was that law came from a legislative and judicial aristocracy: people seen as socially and intellectually superior to the common multitudes over whom they presided. Today, the measuring rod against which all conduct is judged is golden for a different reason – because the law reflects democratic will.

In what does the merit of legal science – or the 'art of Law' as it was referred to by Sir Edward Coke – subsist? It subsists in the accumulated experience and expertise that enable its professionals to do many important things. These include the drafting of rules that accurately and unambiguously reflect social legislative intention, the reliable interpretation of rules already made, the proffering of advice to those who are affected by the rules, and the resolution of disputes. However we live socially, we shall always have a need for these social skills.

LAW AND SOCIAL CHANGE

Today people behave as they do socially for a variety of reasons. These reasons include what the law says, their religious ideas, their morals, and a desire to be socially accepted. Sometimes it is clear that the reason why people are behaving in a particular way, a way that is obedient to law, is not because of the law. For example, most people do not ride bicycles on a motorway or play their music exceptionally loudly at night, not because of the law, but because of safety concerns and neighbourliness, respectively.

It is also clear, however, that much social behaviour in the United Kingdom in the twenty-first century has been shaped to some extent by legislation passed in earlier times. For example during the 1960s and 1970s, laws against discrimination on the grounds of race and sex were passed. This was at a time when society was still largely sexist and racist. Television, comedy, newspapers and education all contained a significant output that is quite shockingly prejudiced by today's stand-ards. Law alone probably cannot change deeply-rooted social attitudes but it can help direct and shape social thinking. In calculating why the population in the UK has become less racist and sexist since the 1960s, one factor clearly of some relevance and weight is the fact that such discrimination was declared unlawful in many circumstances by Parliament. Of course, what the law says at any time might well itself be the cause of goading public opinion into wanting further changes in the same or another direction. This point was noted by A.V. Dicey, who noted in regard to reforming legislation on the status of women:

> Law and opinion are here so intermixed that it is difficult to say whether opinion has done most to produce legislation or laws to create a state of legislative opinion.[27]

In recent history, there are many instances of law-making designed to adjust legal rules to cope with changes in technology or changes in social attitudes or expecta-tions. For example with the spread of computers, the law has had to develop in many ways, including the formulation of rules about how contracts are made over the internet, and law concerning computer frauds. Changes in social attitudes to disability have led to more enlightened rules about the rights of people with disabilities.

Consider some further examples. These are mentioned here without judging the merits of the legal changes. They are given as illustrations of society using the law at an accelerating pace to reflect changes in our social, economic, moral, scientific and technological spheres.

From the world of science and the law – we have, in recent history, had to redesign our rules on precisely when independent human life begins (for the purposes of the law concerning abortion) and when human life ends (for the purposes of deciding when we may switch off life-support machines). Another example concerns DNA. In 2002, the Human Genetics Commission asked Ministers to discuss criminalising the theft of DNA material. A person's spittle can contain a lot of potentially embarrassing, and thus highly saleable, information. Particularly at risk are celebrities. Today, the DNA coding in minute particles of saliva left on cups could be taken without the consent of the salivator, and sent to a laboratory for analysis. The results could disclose information about parentage or a medical profile. It was reported that, while in a British pub in Oxford in 2002, Bill Clinton's guards removed his empty pint glass to prevent it being swiped by DNA hunters. This is an example of what, over the centuries, have been many movements for change to adapt legal rules to changing social phenomena.

The law has a vivid history of regulating property in line with social changes through the ages. The modern notion of theft, for example, was innovated by judges in a case in 1473 concerning a carrier who had run off with bales of wool that he was due to take to Southampton. His licence to possess the goods prevented his absconding being labelled 'theft', but this loophole was highly problematic in a society of rapidly expanding trade. Merchants relying on the movement of goods needed a greater legal deterrent than the threat of a civil action for breach of agreement against dishonest carriers, and so the conduct was duly criminalised. That greatly influenced what happened in tens of millions of criminal theft cases before the courts in the succeeding 500 years. And there is no reason to think that this was, historically, the final major legal change regarding property that will be made by society.

Turning from the world of science and property to the world of sexuality, sexual orientation and the family, there are also many legal developments. From the late twentieth century, the social fabrics and structures of British society have changed significantly and more quickly than during many earlier periods. We have seen a growth in single-parent families; openly gay and lesbian relationships; improved recognition of children as people with no less entitlement to legal rights and dignified legal status than adults; wider recognition of transsexuals; and a growing social inclination in the context of universal human rights that we should be open to people without prejudice.

Another illustration of this process can be found in the law concerning corporate manslaughter. There are various types of manslaughter (essentially an offence of killing a person but without the type of intention required for murder). One type of manslaughter is killing by gross negligence. Historically there was no specific law dealing with companies whose corporate recklessness killed people. The law of manslaughter, designed for individual alleged perpetrators, does not work well where the body accused of being grossly negligent is a corporate body. Globally, more people are killed worldwide by industrial accidents and diseases each year (2.2 million) than are killed in wars.[28] Each year in England and Wales about 300 people are killed at work or through commercially related disasters. This figure rises to several thousand if you include chronic deaths from conditions like asbestosis and mesothelioma, which people get while they are working but which take many years to kill them. These deaths are for the most part preventable and unnecessary. Most result from the direct and indirect impacts of commercial pressures on work practices. Culturally, however, they have been coded as unfortunate and almost inevitable corollaries of commerce and the profit system.

Glanville Evans, a 27-year-old welder, was killed when the bridge he was working on collapsed and he fell into the River Wye. The company that employed him had been reckless in instructing him to work in a perilous way, but an attempt to convict it for manslaughter failed.

Christopher Shute, a 30-year-old factory worker, was killed when he fell into a vat of hot paint and drowned while working in unsafe conditions at the Ford factory in Southampton. The company was fined for what the judge called an 'entirely unnecessary' death but it was not prosecuted for manslaughter.

The first case was in February 1965. The second was in August 2000. Between the two cases, over 36,000 people were killed at work or in commercially related disasters like train crashes. Management failures were responsible in most cases, yet only five companies were convicted of manslaughter during that time. The matter came to be seen as a serious crime not being taken seriously.

Deaths at work often involve horrific and ghastly facts as the victims are drowned, impaled, electrocuted, burnt alive, baked, frozen, poisoned or crushed. Such events, however, are almost always immediately reported in the news as 'accidents'. Such a label prejudges how the victim met his or her death. Downplaying a train disaster as an 'accident' is right in the sense that it was an unintended event. But people and companies can be inculpated in 'accidents'. Many people are in prison for having unintentionally (accidentally) killed someone – the crime of manslaughter. The fact that a killing was unintended does not stop it being treated as a serious crime if the killer acted in a grossly negligent way with someone else's life.

If a train company has been told that something about its operation is potentially very dangerous but, having examined the cost of reducing the risk, it decides against such rectification, then, if death and injury follow when the risk does materialise, the company cannot look dismayed and dismiss the incident as an 'accident'.

Since the early part of its history, the company lay outside of the criminal law. Lord Thurlow, the eighteenth-century Lord Chancellor, said it was in the nature of a company that 'It had no soul to damn, and no body to kick.' Certainly, the practice of excommunicating corporations had been pronounced contrary to Canon law by Pope Innocent IV at the Council of Lyons in 1245 (excommunication is the process of banishing a member of a church from the communion of believers and the privileges of the church). The company was brought within the jurisdiction of the criminal law for various purposes – concerning financial irregularity, for example – but not explicitly for the purposes of crimes of violence.

In 1990, in a great burst of publicity, the prosecution for corporate manslaughter of P & O Ferries (Dover) Ltd collapsed after Mr Justice Turner ruled that the evidence which the Crown intended to produce would be insufficient to prove the indictment. The prosecution had followed the capsising of *The Herald of Free Enterprise* on 7 March 1987 when 192 people died. The vessel had set sail with its bow doors open, and had been flooded. There was evidence that the company had been previously informed that there was serious danger of precisely such an incident occurring. Mr Justice Turner ruled that the Crown was not in a position to satisfy 'the doctrine of identification', that is, the principle by which the actions or omissions of someone at directorial level in the company are legally recognised as being those of the company itself. The court agreed that the offence of corporate manslaughter was one that existed in law, but only if all the necessary fault could be found to exist in at least one director or 'controlling mind' of the company. The partial knowledge of several directors – what is very common in corporate affairs – was not enough to convict the company.

As a result of factors like a Law Commission report on the subject in 1996 – and its recognition of a deepening public intolerance about commercially related death – it was announced in 1997 that there was to be new legislation specifically criminalising corporate killing. The Corporate Manslaughter and Corporate Homicide Act 2007, which followed ten years later, is designed specifically to criminalise 'corporate manslaughter', an offence broadly comparable to 'killing by gross negligence' on the part of an individual. Previously, manslaughter committed by a company was prosecuted under the old common law (judge-made law) of manslaughter that applied to individuals who killed. Under the 2007 Act, instead of having to identify a person who is tantamount to the 'controlling mind' of the company, and to prove that in him or her resided all the necessary fault, the new law says that the crime is committed when someone is killed as the result of a senior management failure involving a gross breach of the duty of care to others.

In such cases, juries will be invited to put the management of an activity into the context of the organisation's obligations under health and safety legislation, the extent to which the organisation was in breach of these, and the risk to life that is involved. The Act also provides for the jury to consider the wider context in which these health and safety breaches occurred, including cultural issues within the organisation such as attitudes or accepted practices that tolerated breaches.

Thus, the law is in the process of adjusting to meet the expectation that such delinquency will result in convictions if a company has been criminally negligent.

How far, though, a new law is effective is dependent on many factors, including socio-economic considerations, and political will. The process by which the law made companies responsible for culpable conduct causing death was a slow one. From the outset, the company as a distinct body was not liable for such a crime, and neither were the shareholders. In 1911, Ambrose Bierce defined a company in his *Devil's Dictionary* as 'an ingenious device for obtaining individual profit without individual responsibility'. Today we have a different attitude, and recognise that the small percentage of companies that commit crimes can and should be punished under the law.

The Corporate Manslaughter and Corporate Homicide Act 2007 was promulgated as a strong law. It made it easier for companies or organisations whose lethal gross negligence killed people to be prosecuted and convicted. That was an important development because the death rate at work and in commercially related disasters was high (over 50,000 people had been killed at work in the UK since 1967), the evidence from the Factory Inspectorate and later from the Health and Safety Executive (HSE) was clear that management was blameworthy in most cases, and yet there were only six convictions for manslaughter under the old common law prior to 6 April 2008 when the Act came into force.

In preparing the legislation, the government said in its Regulatory Impact Assessment that it estimated that the new offence would result in '10–13 additional prosecutions for corporate manslaughter each year'.[29] That would yield a figure of about 60 prosecutions to the end of 2012. In fact, however, there have been only three prosecutions. Over 150 people a year continue to be killed at work (Health and Safety Executive, *Fatal Injury Statistics*, 2007–8/2011–12).

In 2011, Cotswold Geotechnical Holdings became the first company to be convicted under the Corporate Manslaughter and Corporate Homicide Act 2007. It was fined £385,000 after Alexander Wright was buried in a 12-foot trench in which he should never have been asked to work. Mr Wright was taking soil samples for a housing development in Brimscombe Lane, near Stroud, in a pit unsupported by timbers when it caved in. In May 2011 the Court of Appeal upheld the conviction and the £385,000 fine imposed on the company.[30]

Later, in 2012, JMW Farms (Co Armagh) was convicted of manslaughter after Robert Wilson was killed in a fork lift truck incident. The company was fined a record £187,500, plus £13,000 costs, at Belfast's Laganside Crown Court for the manslaughter and health and safety offences.

Then, in July 2012, a third company was convicted of manslaughter. Lion Steel Ltd, of Hyde, Greater Manchester, a manufacturer of steel storage cabinets and racking, was fined £480,000 for corporate manslaughter. The company admitted the charge at Manchester Crown Court on 20 July in relation to the death of a 45-year-old employee, Steven Berry, who suffered fatal injuries when he fell through a fragile roof panel at the firm's Hyde factory in May 2008. The prosecution argued that Lion Steel and its directors failed to provide an adequate safe system for working on the roof. In particular, the court heard that Mr Berry had not been provided with adequate fall-arrest equipment or crawling boards and had not received any training on roof work. The prosecution also claimed that prior to April 2008, Lion Steel's insurers had warned the firm of the need to carry out adequate risk assessments, meaning its directors should have been aware there were inadequate procedures for accessing the roof at the Hyde site.[31] Judge Gilbart QC ordered the company to pay the £480,000 fine in four annual instalments by September 2015, and also ordered it to pay £84,000 towards the prosecution costs, this sum to be paid within two years.

So why have there been so few prosecutions when there is strong *prima facie* evidence that many cases of corporate manslaughter could be brought each year? In the House of Commons on 20 March 2012, Emily Thornberry (Islington South and Finsbury) (Lab) asked an important question (20 Mar 2012: Column 648):

> On 6 April it will be four years since the Corporate Manslaughter and Corporate Homicide Act 2007 came into force, but although between 250 and 300 people die at work each year – deaths which, according to the Health and Safety Executive, are usually avoidable – only two companies have ever been prosecuted under the Act. Does the Attorney-General know what is wrong, and if not, will he conduct urgent inquiries and make a statement to the House as soon as possible?[32]

The Attorney-General replied that he would seek the detailed views of the Director of Public Prosecutions, and write to Ms Thornberry, but that reply has not yet been published.

Why are so few cases being prosecuted? Following a national study of cases of possible corporate manslaughter 1995–99 (involving attendance at the relevant inquests, study of all the documentation, and interviewing HSE officers, coroners, lawyers, and scientists) I found that there was a strong *prima facie* case for prose-cuting about 40 cases of corporate manslaughter a year whereas, under the old common law, there were no cases being brought most years. The main obstacles to prosecution were a lack of resources and political will to prosecute, and a lack of training and legal understanding of how the law of manslaughter applied to corporate defendants.[33] Writing in *The Times* ('Call to get tough on corporate manslaughter', 5 April 2012), Richard Grimes, a health and safety expert and partner at Kingsley Napley LLP, gave a cogent analysis in which he arrived at similar conclusions regarding the limited application of the new legislation to those I drew from my empirical work about the limited application of the old common law.

He said:

> The problem is almost certainly not a shortage of bad enough cases. There have been hundreds of workplace deaths over the past four years, many of which will have resulted from a company's breach of its duty of care towards the deceased. It is right to remember that corpo-rate manslaughter prosecutions are intended to be reserved only for the worst cases – where, in the words of the act, the failing of the

company is 'gross' in that its behaviour fell 'far below the standard expected' of a company in those circumstances. But a significant proportion of these workplace deaths are likely to represent such a failing.

Concerning the question of resources, Grimes argues that:

> The reality then is that the lack of cases to date is not the result of the Act being overly complex, or a lack of suitable cases. It is more, I would argue, the result of those with responsibility to investigate and prosecute lacking the necessary resources, co-ordination and training.

He notes that under the protocol for liaison between the police and other agencies, it is the police who have primacy in the initial investigation that follows a fatal incident, and the police who are tasked, therefore, with investigating possible manslaughter. In the vast majority of cases, however, the officers investigating are detectives for whom such work represents a considerable departure from their normal responsibilities of investigating serious personal crime. Grimes observes that little seems to have been done to provide police officers investigating fatal accident cases with the training required to enable a proper evaluation of corporate culpability under the Act. Moreover, negligence, which lies at the heart of the offence, is wholly different from the mental elements in most other criminal offending. The corporate manslaughter offence poses unique challenges and complications that surely, Grimes notes, require a specialist investigation team equipped with the appropriate resources and training.

In 1883, Mr Justice Byron ruled that a company that simply tried to compensate workers whom it had made redundant was acting unlawfully, because the sole purpose for which a company could act was to make a profit.[34] There was no room for corporate social responsibility in 1883. We have come a long way since then, but the decades of campaigning by legal and social reformers that resulted in the Corporate Manslaughter and Corporate Homicide Act 2007 will have been wasted if the legislation is neither an effective deterrent nor an implemented law.

THE LAW AND DEMOCRACY

Finally, consider the relationship between law and democracy. For the greater part of English legal history, justice was something parcelled out to the majority of the population by its social, economic and educational superiors. The only experience 95 per cent of the population had of law was feeling the threat of being taken before the criminal courts, or occasionally standing, cowed and head bowed, in the witness box as they were addressed by a judge.

In recent times, however, we have witnessed a growing inclination of citizens to gain and then to *vindicate* (successfully to enforce) their legal rights in all walks of life. The relationship between voting and law is very important. The more people are involved in democratic decisions, the stronger the laws and regulations that are made. A democratic society has ownership of the laws it makes. Individual laws, and 'the law' in general, then enjoy greater respect and support. The percentage of those voting in general elections has fallen since the Second World War from 84 per cent in 1950 to 65 per cent in 2010. There has, however, been a growth in other forms of public democracy. People in great numbers vote in radio polls, internet surveys and on television shows. They vote by phone call, by text message, by email and on websites. It is worthy of note that in the UK, 90 per cent of the adult population now has a mobile phone, and 47 million people (out of a total population of 62 million) are now internet users. Figures from the Office for National Statistics show that 33 million adults accessed the internet daily in 2012, up from 16 million in 2006.[35] So, sufficient equipment to enable the electorate to vote easily and more frequently than once every five years exists already.

Whatever system of politics we have, a globally industrialised community universally connected to electronic systems of communication, and one that wishes to behave in an ordered and democratic way, will have to have many clear rules. Imagine trying to operate international travel, or national education, or traffic, without rules. The proliferation of rules, and their importance, means that we also need rules about how we make rules, and rules about how we change rules, and rules about how we interpret rules, and rules about how we adjudicate rules, and rules about how we enforce rules. Rules are the software of the social system. They are the essence of democracy. Their importance is constant, ubiquitous and immense.

If there are solutions, or even partial solutions, to the endemic problems of crime, disorder, war and poverty they will have to come from democratic changes. That means an even more important role for all aspects of law.

FURTHER READING

Sir Carleton Kemp Allen, *Law in the Making*, Oxford: The Clarendon Press, 1964.

Lord Denning, *The Discipline of Law*, London: Butterworths, 1979.

A.V. Dicey, *Lectures on the Relation Between Law and Public Opinion in England During the Nineteenth Century*, Honolulu: University Press of the Pacific, 1905 (2001 edition).

Michael Furmston, 'Ignorance of the Law', *Legal Studies*, Vol. 1, 1981, 36–55.

Sir Thomas More, *Utopia*, 1516 (1961 translation by Paul Turner).

Judges

2

Judges are at the heart of the law. The earliest judges used to rely on divine wisdom to settle cases. The judicial function was largely one of supervising events – like trial by ordeal – designed to reveal a divine truth. Later, judges came to have the function of applying what today we would call 'rules of procedure' to decide cases. Before there was any significant written law, judges were reliant on what communities said was the custom by which ownership of something was determined, or rights of way were established, or what was right and what wrong behaviour. So judges simply evaluated the arguments on either side according to general principles. It was from such a system, as we shall see in more detail in Chapter 4, that the doctrine of precedent developed. Judges eventually came to be officially appointed as part of 'the King's Court', a body that included all sorts of officials. The law 'court' system today originates in the forum that served the monarch – the royal court.

Today, until judges apply the law in cases, it can often be difficult to imagine or guess what exactly is meant by the law as it appears on the pages of parliamentary legislation or previous judgments. And not only do judges shed light on the meaning of laws, they have actually created many of them.

In a case in 1875 Lord Justice Mellish said that:

> The whole of the rules of equity and nine-tenths of the common law have in fact been made by judges.[1]

The same was true a century later. In 1972, Lord Reid said:

> Those with a taste for fairy tales seem to have thought that in some Aladdin's cave there is hidden the Common Law in all its splendour and that on a judge's appointment there descends on him knowledge of the magic words Open Sesame. Bad decisions are given when the judge has muddled the password and the wrong door opens. But we do not believe in fairy tales anymore.[2]

Even the law that judges do not make – parliamentary legislation – gets much of its meaning from what the judges rule that it means. The distinguished jurist A.V. Dicey noted this. He said:

> Statutes themselves, though manifestly the work of Parliament, often receive more than half their meaning from judicial decisions.[3]

In fact, the origin of the legislature is the law court. In the United Kingdom, the main legislature still retains its early official title: The High Court of Parliament. It evolved historically from a simple adjudicative body, clarifying what was the relevant law and how it should be applied, to a body that declared the law in a more innovative way.

Judicial law-making is more openly required since the Human Rights Act 1998, because under its provisions judges must now often decide an issue by evaluating what is 'necessary in a democratic society in the interests of public safety' or for 'health and morals' or 'national security' or 'the economic well-being of the country'. The Human Rights Act 1998 also allows judges to declare that parliament-made legislation is incompatible with human rights.

Judges, tribunal judiciary and magistrates determine a range of disputes – for instance between individuals, between individuals and corporations or public bodies, and between corporate bodies. They resolve disputes relating to children and other family issues. They preside over criminal trials where the guilt or not of the accused is to be determined by a jury. They sentence those found guilty of crimes, and decide the sum of compensation to be paid in civil cases, or the appropriate court order. The court system has developed over centuries, and includes various types of courts and tribunals, dealing with different sorts of cases. In line with that system, judges of differing judicial status, in both salaried (full-time and part-time) and fee-paid posts, sit in different courts and tribunals.

PROFILE OF THE JUDICIARY

There are 3575 judges in England and Wales (including all ranks and all deputies). Of these 22 per cent are women and 4 per cent are from ethnic minorities.[4]

Judges are appointed from the ranks of experienced and able lawyers – both barristers and solicitors. They swear a judicial oath 'to do right to all manner of people after the laws and usages of this realm, without fear or favour, affection or illwill'. They carry out that oath every day of the working week, and, in extraordinary cases, outside those hours, and not always in the hundreds of courtrooms up and down the country. Judges have presided in all sorts of locations – 'the court' technically refers to the place where the judge presides over a case as opposed to a courtroom or courthouse. In 2000, the judge presided by the bedside of Anthony Tobias, a quadriplegic man. The defendant, who had been charged with fraud, could not leave his house so Luton Crown Court went to his bedroom in Steve-nage, Hertfordshire.[5]

Under the Supreme Court Act 1981, it is possible for the Lord Chancellor to authorise the High Court or the Crown Court to sit anywhere in England and Wales. In one case in 1973, for example, Mr Justice Megarry was permitted to take the Chancery Division to Iken in Suffolk in order to take the evidence of an 84-year-old witness who was in poor health.[6] Apart from establishing the court in unusual places, English law allows for the phenomenon of the judicial view or visit. These can be conducted at a place where something key to a case is alleged to have happened (a *locus in quo*) or the location of an object that it is inconvenient or impossible to bring to court.

In one report from 1696, a judge went to inspect some land to decide on a tricky point of alleged trespass.[7] In 1998, a district judge, in order to assist his decision in a customer-against-tour-company dispute, went to inspect the facilities offered in a very cheap package holiday in Malta.[8] For the modern judiciary, the beer-fuelled conga, squeaking bed-springs and unhygienic beach toilets can apparently become part of workaday judicial duties. Judicial functions have also been exer-cised from such unlikely locations as a creek in the River Thames near Barn Elms (where the nineteenth-century judge Vice-Chancellor Shadwell was bathing), a box in the Royal Opera House, and on Brighton Pier.

The image of the typical judge as very old is outdated. There are currently 81 judges under 40 years of age, and 614 under 50. Fifty years ago, someone who was 60 was regarded as old. Today, of course, there are many members of rock groups who go on national and even international tours in their sixties.

The youngest age at which a judge has been appointed in England and Wales is 31, in the case of Sir Francis Buller who was appointed Second Judge in the County Palatine of Chester on 27 November 1777, and made a judge of the High Court one year later, aged 32 years and one month.

Today, all judges appointed after 1993 are subject to a retirement age of 70. Histor-ically, though, some continued to sit and deliver judgments long after they could have travelled to court on a free bus pass. Sir William Francis Kyffin Taylor was still on the bench at Liverpool when aged 93 years and nine months. He retired in 1948. Lord Denning retired in 1982, when he was 83. While most judges are very alert, some have exhibited various forms of inattention. When, in 1823, Lord Eldon was pressed for a decision in *Collis v Nott*, which he had heard in 1817, he admitted that he 'had entirely forgotten it'.[9] Lord Thankerton, who died in 1948, would sometimes knit while presiding. In a civil case in 1953, in which a Gray's Inn law student sued two police officers, Mr Justice Finnemore left the court early on Friday afternoon, while the jury was still out, leaving someone else to take the verdict. Other judges have been chronicled doing things in trials which, while uplifting in some circumstances, do not look good if done from the bench. These include writing letters, drinking port, and even turning over pages of *The Times*.

There are all sorts of shocking, funny and disturbing stories about various eccentric members of the judiciary. That, though, is equally true of consultant doctors, head teachers and cabinet members. Generally, judges are balanced, erudite and judicious people whom society trusts with regularly making extraordinarily challenging decisions.

TYPES OF JUDGE

There are several categories of senior judge. Table 2.1 plots the different types.

The highest court today is the Supreme Court. The Supreme Court is the final court of appeal in the UK for civil cases. It hears appeals in criminal cases from England, Wales and Northern Ireland. It hears cases of the greatest public or constitutional importance affecting the whole population.

The Supreme Court was established in 2009 (having been authorised by the Constitutional Reform Act 2005) to achieve a complete separation between the United Kingdom's senior judges (who had sat in the House of Lords) and Parliament, emphasising the independence of the new Supreme Court Justices and increasing the distinction between Parliament and the courts.

In August 2009 the Justices moved out of the House of Lords (where they sat as the Appellate Committee of the House of Lords) into their own building on the opposite side of Parliament Square in London. The impact of Supreme Court decisions extends far beyond the parties involved in any given case, shaping our society,

Table 2.1 **Categories of Judge**

			In Post
Justices of The Supreme Court (formerly Lords of Appeal in Ordinary)			**12**
Heads of Division	Lord Chief Justice		**5**
	Master of the Rolls		
	President of the Queen's Bench Division		
	President of Family Division		
	The Chancellor of the High Court		
Lords Justices of Appeal			**38**
High Court Judges	Chancery Division	17	**110**
	Queen's Bench Division	19	
	Family Division	74	
Judge Advocates			**8**
Deputy Judge Advocates			**5**
Masters, Registrars, Costs Judges and DJs Principal Registry of the Family Division (PRFD)			**46**
Deputy Masters, Deputy Registrars, Deputy Costs Judges and Deputy District Judges (PRFD)			**67**

Source: Judicial Database 2012

and directly affecting our everyday lives. For instance, in their previous role as the Appellate Committee of the House of Lords, the Justices gave landmark rulings creating the crime of marital rape and defining the defence of provocation to murder.

This court has 12 judges: a President, a Deputy President, and ten Justices of the Supreme Court. They are appointed by the monarch and referred to as, for example, 'Justice Williams'. At present all of the Supreme Court Justices are white, and only one of them is a woman.

The Court also has the jurisdiction to decide devolution issues that were exercised by the Judicial Committee of the Privy Council. The Judicial Committee of the Privy Council is still the final court of appeal for 19 commonwealth jurisdictions.

Below the Supreme Court Justices in the hierarchy are five 'Divisional Heads'.

The Lord Chief Justice of England and Wales is head of the judiciary of England and Wales and President of the Courts of England and Wales. He or she is referred to by abbreviation in law reports as 'Lord Carr C.J.' or 'Sir Hugh Jones L.C.J.'

The Master of the Rolls heads the civil branch of the Court of Appeal and is referred to in law reports as 'Lord Jones M.R.'

The President of the Queen's Bench Division and Judge in Charge of the Administrative Court is referred to as 'Jones P.' in abbreviation.

The President of the Family Division is the head of that branch of the High Court and is referred as 'Jones P.F.D.' in abbreviation.

The Chancellor of the High Court is the Head of the Chancery Division of the High Court, which deals with cases involving large sums of money and nationally important legal financial issues.

Together with the Lord Chief Justice and the Master of the Rolls, the Lords Justices are Judges of the Court of Appeal. There are currently 37 such judges in office. They are referred to as Lord or Lady Justice White or, in the reports, as 'Green L.J.' or in plural 'White and Green L.JJ.'

There are currently 110 High Court Judges. Seventeen are assigned to the Chancery Division, 19 to the Queen's Bench Division and 74 to the Family Division. They are known as Mr Justice Smith or Mrs Justice Smith or Ms Justice Smith, abbreviated to 'Smith J.' or in plural 'Smith and Jones JJ.'

Below the senior judiciary, a Circuit Judge is a judge who normally sits in the county court or Crown Court. Formerly known as county court registrars, District Judges sit in the county courts or district registries in a specific region. They have the power to try actions in a county court below a specified financial limit, which is reviewed from time to time. Cases above that limit are generally heard by a Circuit Judge. The numbers of Circuit and District Judges and part-time judges (called Recorders) is as follows: 665 Circuit Judges, 1155 Recorders and 447 District Judges. These judges deal with both civil and criminal matters. They are referred to as, for example, Judge Smith.

JUDICIAL APPOINTMENTS

The system for judicial appointment used to be a notoriously secretive and contro-versial business in which the Lord Chancellor would privately 'take soundings' among judges about the suitability of certain lawyers to become judges. Positions were not subject to open competition. Today the process is more open. The Lord Chancellor, known for all general purposes as the Minister for Justice, continues to appoint judicial office holders (or recommends them for appointment by the Queen), but their recruitment and selection is carried out by the independent Judi-cial Appointments Commission or JAC (see Chapter 4). The Commission works to ensure that, after open competition, the best possible candidates are recom-mended to the Lord Chancellor. The qualifications required for the different levels of judicial office are as follows.

Justices of the Supreme Court

The procedure for appointing a Justice of the Supreme Court of the United Kingdom is governed by the Constitutional Reform Act 2005, as amended by the Tribunals and Enforcement Act 2007. Applicants must have held high judicial office for at least two years or have been a practitioner for at least 15 years. The Lord Chancellor convenes a selection commission. The President of the Court chairs the selection commission. The legislation does not prescribe a process that a selection commission has to follow, although the commission must have regard to any guidance given by the Lord Chancellor as to matters to be taken into account in making a selection. The Act does prescribe a set of people who must be consulted by the selection commission, including the senior judges (the Heads of Division).

The Heads of Division

The Heads of Division (the Lord Chief Justice, the Master of the Rolls, the President of the Family Division and the Chancellor) are also appointed by the Queen on the recommendation of the Prime Minister, who receives advice from the Lord Chancellor. Before giving advice, the Lord Chancellor customarily consults senior members of the judiciary. The statutory qualification is to be qualified for appointment as a Lord Justice of Appeal (see below) or to be a judge of the Court of Appeal. In practice, Heads of Division are generally appointed from among the Lords of Appeal in Ordinary or Lords Justices of Appeal.

Lord Justices of Appeal

Lords Justices of Appeal are appointed by the Queen on the recommendation of the Prime Minister, who receives advice from the Lord Chancellor. Before giving advice, the Lord Chancellor customarily consults senior members of the judiciary. The statutory qualification is a ten-year High Court qualification or to be a judge of the High Court. Appointment is usually on promotion from the ranks of experienced High Court Judges.

High Court Judges

Qualification for Appointment

High Court Judges are appointed by the Queen on the recommendation of the Lord Chancellor. Before making recommendations, the Lord Chancellor customarily consults senior members of the judiciary about these appointments. The statutory qualification is a ten-year High Court qualification or to have been a Circuit Judge for at least two years. High Court Judges are assigned on appointment to one of the three Divisions of the High Court: the Chancery Division, the Queen's Bench Division or the Family Division.

Additional Qualifications and Experience

Appointments to the High Court, if not on promotion from another salaried office (usually the Circuit Bench), are in practice generally made from senior and leading members of the legal profession who have been in practice for between 20 and 30 years. The Courts and Legal Services Act 1990 (as amended by the Access to Justice Act 1999) made it possible for solicitors to be appointed to the High Court Bench and in October 2000 the first solicitor to be directly appointed as a High Court Judge took office. Practitioners who are appointed to the High Court Bench will normally have had a substantial and successful practice, often having developed areas of specialisation, and be held in high regard by the profession. They will normally have sat previously as Deputy High Court Judges and/or Recorders.

Appointments Process

Appointments are made to fill particular vacancies as they arise. Applications for appointment to the High Court are invited from suitably qualified practitioners and Circuit Judges on a regular basis by advertisement in the press. All Supreme Court Judges are consulted on those who have applied.

Part-time Judges

There are now two main kinds of 'part-time' judge. First, there are fee-paid judges (as opposed to full-time salaried judges). These are usually practising lawyers or holders of some full-time judicial offices who sit as part-time judges for a number of days per year (on average about 20). Following a review of the terms of service of fee-paid judicial office holders in England and Wales, fee-paid appointments have generally been for a period of not less than five years, subject to the relevant upper age limit. Where appropriate, appointments are automatically renewed, except on limited and specified grounds. Removal from office is only on limited and specified grounds. The grounds include misbehaviour, incapacity, and persistent failures to sit as a judge or to comply with training requirements.

In the courts the main categories of fee-paid judge are Deputy High Court Judges, Recorders, Deputy District Judges (Civil) and Deputy District Judges (Magistrates' Courts), and Deputy Masters and Registrars of the Supreme Court. Many tribunal appointments are also made on a fee-paid basis.

Second, in 2001 the Secretary of State and the Lord Chancellor approved the introduction of a salaried part-time working facility for new appointments to some traditionally 'full-time' judicial offices. In 2005, this arrangement was extended and is now available for most salaried posts.

JUDICIAL ANIMATION OF THE LAW

Laws state many things. To be convicted of murder, a defendant must be shown to have had an intention to kill or cause serious injury. For an agreement to be enforceable – and thus a contract – it must have been completed by an offer from one party being accepted by another party. For a will to be valid it must have been made by a testator of sound mind. These rules, though, could be interpreted in different ways, so their judicial application to real human dramas is a very important part of the legal process. Knowing what a rule says does not help much unless you know how it will be applied. Hence the dry observation of the writer Roy M. Cohn: 'I don't want to know what the law is, I want to know who the judge is.'[10]

Until it unfolds in a courtroom, the law is a dull and dusty set of rules. Ancient laws governing when members of the royal family can appear in court are utterly irrelevant to us until they are animated in a court case like the trial in London, in 2002, of Paul Burrell.

Mr Burrell was the butler to Princess Diana. He was indicted for theft from members of the royal family. The thefts included items such as crockery and photos. The trial was discontinued when the Queen sent evidence to the court that she had recalled a conversation with Mr Burrell during which he had mentioned that, following the death of the princess, he was keeping some things that had belonged to the Princess of Wales. That exonerated him.[11]

Turning to another area of law, the 'doctrine of necessity' (that unlawful things can be done without punishment when there is some compelling reason why they should be done) might seem a rather inert part of the law until a court has to decide whether conjoined twins can be surgically split in circumstances where, in consequence, one will inevitably die. Those were the facts of the case of Gracie and Rosie Attard, from the Maltese island of Gozo, who were separated at a hospital in Manchester in 2000 after the Court of Appeal gave doctors permission to operate. The twins' parents strictly observed the Roman Catholic faith and had objected to the separation as it would entail the death of one of the children.[12]

The words in law books are suddenly given colour, depth and texture when they are applied by judges in courts dealing with real cases.

Judges then, are immensely important people, especially in a society in which laws affect our lives as much as sunshine and rain. In many countries today, judges are not independent – they are appointed (USA) or sacked (Zimbabwe) by governments for reasons that include political considerations. In the UK, that sort of direct control over justice by politics is seen to be wrong.

BATTLE OF THE LAW-MAKERS

In modern Britain it is the democratically elected body of Parliament that has the function of making law. How then does such work co-exist with the creative law interpretation of judges in the higher courts? In a debate in the House of Commons in 1996, Tony Marlow MP asked this question:

> Do the judiciary now have a democratic mandate to decide which laws are acceptable, or does this House and Parliament, on the balance of views in the country, continue to decide what the laws should be, while the judiciary apply them without being informed by their personal prejudices?

The honourable members were discussing the government's proposals to use legislation to overturn a Court of Appeal decision that withdrawing welfare bene-fits from most asylum seekers was unlawful. Following the court ruling, Peter Lilley, Social Services Secretary, announced that the court ruling would be effec-tively nullified by new clauses to be put into the Asylum and Immigration Bill then before Parliament.

In some ways, since the Human Rights Act 1998, the question posed by Tony Marlow MP in 1996 must be answered differently now than it would have been then. Today, although judges cannot strike down as invalid democratically passed legislation, they can, under section 4 of the Act, make a declaration that it is incon-sistent with the human rights principles protected by the Act. The courts have issued several important declarations using this section of the Act. For example, in the case of Elizabeth Ann Bellinger in 2003, the question was whether someone who was by gender reassignment a woman could marry a man. The House of Lords declared that in so far as section 11(c) of the Matrimonial Causes Act made no provision for the recognition of gender reassignment, it was incompatible with Articles 8 (right to respect for private and family life) and 12 (right to marry) of the European Convention on Human Rights and Freedoms. Since the Human Rights Act came into force on 2 October 2000, there have been 27 declarations of incompatibility.

Moreover, not only can the courts nowadays declare legislation incompatible with human rights law (and thus prompt MPs to engage in an accelerated change of the law) but also, under section 3 of the Act, judges must interpret primary and subor-dinate legislation passed in the UK in a way which makes it compatible with the

European Convention on Human Rights and Freedoms. The judiciary is placed under an obligation to ensure such compatibility 'so far as it is possible to do so'. The obligation for judges to render British legislation compatible with the human rights protected under the Act extends so far as to even stretch the natural meaning of the statutory words in order to achieve compatibility. For example, in the case of *Ghaidan v Godin-Mendoza,* the Supreme Court interpreted the phrase 'husband and wife' in the Rent Act 1977, to include cohabiting same-sex couples so as to ensure that they had the same succession rights as married heterosexual couples. This interpretation brought the Rent Act 1977 in line with Article 8 (the right to respect for private and family life) of the European Convention on Human Rights.

In recent history, from even before the Human Rights Act, the constitutional clash between the judiciary and Parliament has manifested itself in several battles between the senior judiciary and government ministers. Various Home Secretaries, for example, have been at odds with the judiciary over issues including the legality and desirability of Parliament acting to curb the sentencing discretion of trial judges, the imprisonment without charge or trial of suspected terrorists, the retention of data by the police and the interpretation of Article 8 of the European Convention on Human Rights (the right to respect for private and family life) in the context of immigration.

These disputes revolve around the constitutional role of the judges. Even in fairly recent history, it was still widely accepted that judges did not make law but simply interpreted it: they construed difficult phrases in legislation, and they applied old common law principles to novel situations, but they never substantially changed the law. Today the naivety of that view is surprising and most commentators think that judges do play a creative part in fleshing out and shaping the law. The key questions now are in what circumstances judges should become legally inventive, and how far should they go?

The political configurations around this issue are rather peculiar. Historically, when Parliament has become involved in any spat with the judiciary, it has been liberal and radical thinkers who have sided with Parliament while conservative thinkers have generally favoured the judiciary. In today's confrontation, the opposite is true. Progressive personalities are feteing the senior judiciary as guarantors of freedom while conservatives are championing parliamentary democracy in support of a succession of recent Home Secretaries, including Michael Howard, Jack Straw, David Blunkett, Charles Clarke, John Reid and Theresa May, who have clashed with the judiciary.

Worry about law-making judges can be partially allayed by reference to the relatively tolerant political dispositions of many of those on today's benches. But should the principle of parliamentary sovereignty (part of the constitution since the Bill of Rights in 1689) be abrogated as a result of such an ephemeral and trivial battle between what some see as 'bad politicians' and 'good judges'? The constitutional difficulties that need to be addressed in public debate now stem from the fact that the judiciary is an unelected and largely unaccountable body whose members carry no public mandate. In any case, there is no clear or commonly accepted code identifying the circumstances in which they can be permitted, like Judge Dredd, to make up new law.

In cases which go to the Supreme Court, for example, there is no reliable way of predicting whether the court will keep the old law and say that any change must come from Parliament, or whether it will act boldly to alter the law itself. As you will see later (in Chapter 4), the Supreme Court is, in some circumstances, permitted to overrule a precedent set by itself. If the judiciary is a law-giver of unpredictable and volatile propensities, then on what basis should it be endowed with the constitutional right to protect public interests? Senior judges sometimes make controversial decisions but, in general, the way they develop the law is in line with widely held principles and policy.

Consider the institutional capriciousness of law-making in the House of Lords. In 1992,[13] the House of Lords saw fit to abolish the then 256-year-old rule against a charge of marital rape. Lord Keith noted that:

> The common law is . . . capable of evolving in the light of changing social, economic and cultural developments.[14]

It followed, he said, that the old rule that forbade a charge of marital rape reflected the state of affairs at the time it was enunciated in 1736, and should be abolished as 'the status of women, and particularly of married women, has changed out of all recognition in various ways'. In creating a new crime, the Lords did not shrink back from such law-making because this was a matter of public policy or because Parliament had legislated on this area in modern times without changing the rule against marital rape.

Conversely, in a case in 1995, the House of Lords shied away from changing the *doli incapax* (incapacity to commit crimes) rule concerning the criminal liability of children.[15] The case involved a 12-year-old boy from Liverpool caught using a crowbar to interfere with a motorbike. He was convicted of attempted theft. His defence argued that the required 'mischievous discretion' had not been proven, but, on appeal to the Divisional Court, it was ruled that the antiquated rule (under which defendants aged 10–14 years must be shown to know that their actions were seriously wrong before they can be convicted of a crime) was no longer part of English law. The House of Lords could have agreed and changed the law but it declined to do so. Quite contrary to the view in the marital rape case, where the Lords made new law, Lord Lowry in this case stated that judicial law-making should be avoided where disputed matters of social policy are concerned. But was changing the rule about whether a husband can rape his wife not based precisely on such a change of social policy? Lord Lowry stated that:

> The distinction between the treatment and punishment of child 'offenders' has popular and political overtones, a fact which shows that we have been discussing not so much a legal as a social problem, with a dash of politics thrown in, and emphasises that it should be within the exclusive remit of Parliament.[16]

In the event, the rule was eventually changed by Parliament. In 1998, section 34 of the Crime and Disorder Act abolished the rebuttable presumption that a child aged 10 to 14 is incapable of committing a criminal offence. So, for example, prosecuting a 12-year-old for a crime will require the prosecution simply to prove whatever type of mental state – such as intention or recklessness – is relevant. The prosecution will not first have to show the child knew its actions were seriously wrong.

Yet in another case, in 1993, the Lords' Appellate Committee was in a law-making mood and decided to sweep away a 223-year-old constitutional rule that had prevented Hansard (the transcribed record of everything said in Parliament) being consulted by law courts as a way of helping them to understand what the members of Parliament and the Lords had intended when they passed the legislation. The specially convened enlarged Appellate Committee of seven could have ruled that changing the law was not something they were able to do, particularly as the case involved a controversial constitutional principle (Article 9 of the Bill of Rights, which prohibits the questioning in any court of freedom of speech and debates in Parliament). But the Committee decided that it would change the law, because 'the time had come'. Lord Griffiths, for example, said that:

> I have long thought that the time had come to change the self-imposed judicial rule that forbade any reference to the legislative history of an enactment as an aid to its interpretation.[17]

Again, conversely, in the case of a soldier, Private Lee Clegg, in 1995 the Lords declined to make any changes to the law of self-defence, seeing that as something suitable only for Parliament. Lord Lloyd of Berwick approved the words of Lord Simon in an earlier case:

> I can hardly conceive of circumstances less suitable than the instant for five members of an appellate committee of your Lordship's House to arrogate to ourselves so momentous a law-making initiative.[18]

Historically, there is a reasonable body of evidence to illustrate the unpredictability of the Lords as a law-making agency – that is, in respect of it acting in its judicial capacity, not its legislative one. The Houses of Parliament include the House of Commons and the House of Lords. For the purposes of judicial decisions, 'The House of Lords', as we have seen, included panels of only five senior judges who, historically, 'advised' the whole House on the preferred judgment in case. In its legislative capacity, the House of Lords includes the work of the whole House – 818 members if they all sit, although annual average attendance is under 400. There are 701 life peers, 92 hereditary peers, and 25 bishops.

In Parliament, by contrast with the House of Lords' judicial work, the capricious-ness of law-making is quite forgivable, even desirable, because it is a democratic agency and its activity should reflect the will of a demotic electorate. Parliament has an excellent website through which all its mysteries are explained: www.parliament.uk.

THE JUDICIARY AND THE ADMINISTRATION OF THE COURTS

For the purposes of judicial administration, England and Wales are divided into six regions or 'circuits'. The term originates from the twelfth century, when judges of the English superior courts were sent regularly 'on circuit' to every county to try civil actions and criminal cases. The circuits are: South Eastern, Western, Midland and Oxford, Wales and Chester, Northern, and North Eastern. Each circuit has two Presiding Judges, except for the South Eastern circuit which has three, who are serving High Court Judges appointed by the Lord Chief Justice with the agreement of the Lord Chancellor. The Presiding Judges have general responsibility for the judicial administration of the circuits. They deploy High Court and Circuit Judges throughout their circuit and also ensure that staff of Her Majesty's Court Service

Table 2.2 Judges in England and Wales

		South Eastern & RCJ	Midland	North Eastern	Western	Northern	Wales	Total in post
Circuit Judges	**Total**	**270**	**91**	**79**	**61**	**107**	**32**	**640**
Recorder	Barristers	466	204	122	141	156	58	1147
	Solicitors	47	8	9	16	4	4	88
	Total	**513**	**212**	**131**	**157**	**160**	**62**	**1235**
District Judges	**Total**	**161**	**68**	**65**	**49**	**77**	**24**	**444**
Deputy District Judges	**Total**	**230**	**115**	**92**	**77**	**114**	**40**	**668**
District Judges (Magistrates' Court)								134
Deputy District Judges (Magistrates' Court)								166

Source: Judicial Database April 2009

allocate cases for hearing efficiently. They take action to prevent delays in hearings, see to the well-being of the judges on their circuit, and provide a judicial and administrative link with the senior judiciary, in particular the Lord Chief Justice.

JUDGES AND COMMUNICATING WITH THE PUBLIC

In recent times several senior judges have given radio and television interviews, including the head of the Supreme Court, Lord Neuberger. Such openness affords a refreshing contrast with the past. A letter written by Lord Chancellor Kilmuir on 12 December 1955 to the Director-General of the BBC stated that a judge should be 'insulated from the controversies of the day' and, to avoid criticism, should not participate in broadcasts. The statements in the letter became known as the 'Kilmuir Rules' and kept judges out of any public debate until the rules were abrogated by Lord Chancellor Mackay in November 1987.

These days, society is more open than it was when the Kilmuir Rules applied. Senior judges can, without any lessening of the esteem in which they are generally held, contribute to public discussion.

Lord Kilmuir had been especially against judges doing 'anything which could fairly be interpreted as entertainment' – a proposition transgressed, in the years following his 1967 death, by events like Lord Denning's incontestably entertaining BBC radio appearance on Desert Island Discs while he was Master of the Rolls.

THE TRAINING OF JUDGES

The Judicial Studies Board (JSB), which was established in 1979, is responsible for judicial training and for advising on the training of lay magistrates. It is chaired and directed by senior judges but includes lay magistrates, lawyers, administrators and academics. One of the main activities of the JSB is to run induction courses to enable newly appointed part-time judges to develop the skills required. No newly appointed Recorder, Deputy District Judge or Deputy District Judge (Magistrates' Courts) can sit as a judge without first having attended an induction course run by the JSB. The courses are residential and last for four or five days They are very intensive and concentrate on the practical aspects of sitting as a judge and running a court. Emphasis is placed on practical exercises such as, if appropriate, sentencing, directions to the jury and summing up. The newly appointed judges must also sit-in for at least a week with an experienced judge and, if they are to hear criminal cases, they must also visit local prisons and the Probation Service.

The JSB also organises 'refresher' seminars, to which both salaried and fee-paid judges are invited. The subjects covered include changes in the law, and topics of current importance. In addition to the standard induction and refresher courses the JSB also arranges training on subjects of special interest and it issues books and other guidance for use by judges. Tribunals have their own local arrangements for training, but again an induction course has to be attended and satisfactorily completed before any member can undertake sittings.

The in-service training of judges from other jurisdictions has not always been conventional. According to the eighteenth-century barrister James Boswell, 'a judge may grow unfit for his office in many ways'. In the case of Judge Nestor Narizano, who was dismissed from office in Argentina in 2005, it was shown that he was studying on a psychology course when he should have been in court. He declaimed: 'I was fired because I read two hours of Freud each day.' Tales from the couch should not take precedence over work from the bench. In fact, the study of the mind has not always been judicially popular. In a child custody case in October 1966, Lord Justice Harman, rejecting psychiatric evidence, and speaking of his own childhood, said 'psychiatrists had not been invented in those days and no one was any the worse for it'.

The training and ongoing education of judges in the UK today is undertaken in an inspiringly systematic and assiduous way. In its strategy document it notes:

> The JSB's purpose is to ensure that high-quality training is delivered to enable those who discharge judicial functions to carry out their duties effectively, in a way which preserves judicial independence and supports public confidence in the justice system.[19]

All serving judges must attend 'gatekeeper courses' in order to exercise new areas of jurisdiction. Gatekeeper courses support the system of judicial authorisation (known as 'ticketing'). Attendance on some courses is a prerequisite for exercising the relevant jurisdiction – for example, no judge can hear cases involving a charge of rape without first having attended the Serious Sexual Offences Seminar. Other gatekeeper courses include the Serious Fraud Seminars, the Housing and Family Law Seminar for District Judges, the Public Law Induction Course, and the Private Family Law Induction Course.

JUDICIAL INDEPENDENCE

In the UK, judicial independence is a key principle of the constitution. It requires that judges decide cases according to the law and their own judgement, free from outside influence. In particular, the interests of justice require that in their work, judges remain independent of, and not subject to, the views or control of the government. In the UK, no judge can be a director of a commercial company, nor must they be influenced by pressure from individuals or groups with an interest in the outcome of a case. In each case a judge must administer justice in accordance with the law and according to the circumstances of the case, whether his or her decision is popular or not.

Judicial independence does not, however, just mean independence from outside influence but also the independence of one judge from another. Judges can seek advice from fellow judges and will take account of views expressed by other judges in other cases, and they must take note of judgments given by higher courts, which are binding. But no judge, however eminent, is entitled to tell another judge how to exercise his or her judgement in any individual cases.

At the core of the principle of an independent judiciary is the idea that we are governed by law and due process, not political whim or autocracy. Circumstances in Britain saw judges standing up to monarchs and politicians from early times. William Gascoigne (1350–1419) was supposed, as Chief Justice, to have jailed Prince Hal after being hit by him – a sentence which, in fact, showed some restraint as the usual punishment for such a judicial assault was an on-the-spot, non-elective amputation. Ever since The *Case of Prohibitions* (1607), when Chief Justice Coke clashed with James I and ruled that the king could not act as a judge, it has been clear that the judicial branch of government is neither an instrument nor an agency of the executive. In fact, the challenge from the Bench to political pretensions occurred in Scotland before it did so in England. In *Bruce v Hamilton*, the King, as James VI of Scotland, had already been told in clear terms in 1599 by the Court of Session in Edinburgh that he had no power to command the court (see Chapter 1).

Developments in various parts of the world in recent times have sharpened the focus in the UK on the desirability of an independent judiciary. In 2001, the Supreme Court of Zimbabwe was expanded from five judges to eight in an apparent attempt to ensure that the court, which had often ruled against the government, became more compliant to the will of the executive branch of government. In the same year, in Indonesia, gunmen shot dead a judge who sentenced Tommy Suharto (the youngest son of the former dictator President Suharto) to 18 months' jail. In San Salvador in 2001, the Guatemalan chief public prosecutor who secured the conviction of three military officers for the murder of a prominent Roman Catholic bishop was forced by repeated death threats to flee the country.

JUDICIAL IMPARTIALITY

How neutral or disinterested in the matter before the court can we require a judge to be? There are clear rules which oblige a judge to stand down from presiding in a case if he or she has a financial interest in the matter to be tried or if any party or witness is an acquaintance or relative. Today, following some especially colourful cases in recent times, there is a keen social and judicial awareness that a civil or criminal trial might be open to appeal if the judge is found to have an association with or social interest in something indirectly connected with an issue before the court.

In August 1999, a judge disqualified himself from presiding in a case because he was involved in pheasant shooting. When he found himself about to hear an appeal from an animal rights campaigner at Winchester Crown Court, Judge Patrick Hooton stood down. The case was an appeal against conviction for aggravated trespass on land where a pheasant shoot was taking place, and Judge Hooton admitted to the court: 'I am a member of the Countryside Alliance. I support shooting. I have taken part in shooting and beating.'[20]

All judges, of course, have active and varied social interests. Many aspects of their lives and the lives of their families will inevitably overlap with matters related directly or indirectly to cases in which they are asked to preside. The old understanding of judicial duties involved a principle that, having been appointed as a person of balanced and independent thinking, a judge would be able to bring unbiased analysis to a case irrespective of any strong opinion he or she might encounter at the breakfast table or in a club at the weekend. The demands on judges raise important questions – both philosophical (just how neutral can a person be?) and logistical (have we enough judges in each region to step in every time another judge has to decline a case through declared interests?).

For centuries, the English legal system has operated a rule that no one may be a judge in his or her own cause. This means that judges cannot judge a case in which they have an interest. This is sometimes known by the phrase *nemo judex in causa sua* (from the Latin 'nobody (should) be a judge in his own case'). In *Dimes v Grand Junction Canal* (1852), the then Lord Chancellor, Lord Cottenham, owned a substantial shareholding in the defendant canal company. In this case the Lord Chancellor sat as a judge on an appeal from another court where the judges had decided in favour of that company. In the appeal, the Lord Chancellor endorsed that decision of the lower court, which was good news for the company. There was then a further appeal to the House of Lords on the grounds that the Lord Chancellor should have been disqualified from hearing the first appeal because he had a financial interest in one of the parties. In the final appeal Lord Campbell said:

> No one can suppose that Lord Cottenham could be, in the remotest degree, influenced by the interest he had in this concern; but, my Lords, it is of the last importance that the maxim that no man is to be a judge in his own cause should be held sacred. And that is not to be confined to a cause *in which he is a party*, but applies to a cause in which he has an interest.[21] (Emphasis added)

Even if a judge is unaffected by his or her interest in coming to a decision, it would still be wrong to preside in such a case because it might look like the judge was improperly swayed, even if in fact there was no such sway. Thus, in the famous dictum of Lord Hewart in a case from 1924, *R v Sussex Justices ex parte McCarthy*, it is of fundamental importance that 'justice must not only be done but should manifestly and undoubtedly be seen to be done'.

This rule was given another dimension in the extraordinary case in 1999 of *In Re Pinochet Ugarte*. General Pinochet, the former Chilean head of state, was over in England on a visit when he was arrested for crimes of torture and mass killing allegedly orchestrated by him in Chile during the 1970s. His extradition had been requested by Spain. The legal question for the English courts was whether General Pinochet enjoyed diplomatic immunity.

His case was eventually rejected by the House of Lords (by a 3:2 majority) in November 1998. Pinochet's lawyers then alleged that the Lords' decision was invalid as one of the majority Law Lords, Lord Hoffmann, could not be seen to be impartial as he had a connection with the organisation Amnesty International, which had been granted leave to intervene in the proceedings and had made representations to the Lords through counsel. Lord Hoffmann at this time was an unpaid director of the Amnesty International Charitable Trust.

Amnesty International was in favour of General Pinochet being brought to trial. So, if Lord Hoffmann was connected to Amnesty, as he was, it would look like his judgment might be biased when he was deciding a case concerned with whether Pinochet should be extradited to Spain for trial. In January 1999, on an appeal brought by Pinochet, another panel of Law Lords set aside the decision of the earlier hearing on the basis that no one should be a judge in his own cause. The House of Lords stated that if the absolute impartiality of the judiciary was to be maintained, there had to be a rule which automatically disqualified a judge who was involved, whether personally or as a director of a company, in promoting the same causes in the same organisation as was a party to the suit.[22]

Lord Browne-Wilkinson stated that, although previous cases had all dealt with automatic disqualification of judges from hearing particular cases on the ground of pecuniary interest, there was no good reason in principle for limiting automatic disqualification to such financial interests. The rationale of the whole rule was that a person could not be a judge in his own cause. Lord Hutton said:

> I have already stated that there was no allegation made against Lord Hoffmann that he was actually guilty of bias in coming to his decision, and I wish to make it clear that I am making no finding of actual bias against him. But I consider that the links . . . between Lord Hoffmann and Amnesty International, which had campaigned strongly against General Pinochet and which intervened in the earlier hearing to support the case that he should be extradited to face trial for his alleged crimes, were so strong that public confidence in the integrity of the administration of justice would be shaken if his decision were allowed to stand.[23]

Leaving aside any opinion about the neutrality of the current judiciary, there is considerable evidence to support the proposition that, historically, judges have often been biased towards certain causes and social classes. In his excellent book *Politics of the Judiciary*, for example, Professor J.A.G. Griffith provides a plethora of concrete examples of judges who have shown a certain bias to one side of the debate in cases involving industrial disputes, trade unions, civil liberties, Northern Ireland, police powers, religion and other matters.

It is ironic that, while for centuries judges have been permitted to preside in cases where their highly contentious political views have quite evidently affected their decisions (sexist, racist and unsympathetic to the working class), the first senior judge to be successfully acted against for apparent bias was someone whose external connection concerned nothing more than opposition to torture and governmental killings.

Some city law firms have compiled files on judges with a view to applying to have a judge removed from a case if that is in their client's interest. In 2000, in *Locabail (UK) Ltd v Bayfield Properties Ltd*, the Court of Appeal heard together five cases in which it had been alleged that the judge could be regarded as having a reason to be biased (note that this is a different allegation than one that says the judge was biased).

The court then explained the general principles that would govern such disputes. A judge who allowed his judicial decision to be influenced by partiality or prejudice deprived a litigant of the right to a fair trial by an impartial tribunal and violated a most fundamental principle on which the administration of justice rested.

The court held that the most effective protection of this right was, in practice, afforded by disqualification and setting aside a decision where real danger of bias was established. Every such case depended on its particular facts, real doubt being resolved in favour of disqualification of the judge from sitting in that case. It would, however, be as wrong for a judge to step down following a weak objection as it would be for him to ignore a strong objection.

The court ruled that, in determination of their rights and liabilities, civil or criminal, everyone was entitled to a fair hearing by an impartial tribunal. That right, guaranteed by Article 6 of the European Convention on Human Rights, was properly described as fundamental. The reason, the Court of Appeal suggested, was obvious. The Court ruled that all legal arbiters were bound to apply the law as they understood it to the facts of individual cases as they found them without fear or favour, affection or ill-will: that is, without partiality or prejudice.

Solicitors often sit as part-time judges. So what happens if they act as a judge in a case with connections to their firm or former firm? In *Locabail*, the court stated that such lawyers might not be aware of the connection if their firm is large and the connection relates to a case on file from several years before. The court decided that the position of solicitors was somewhat different from that of other judges, for a solicitor who was a partner in a firm of solicitors was legally responsible for the professional acts of his partners and did, as a partner, owe a duty to clients of the firm for whom he personally might never had acted and of whose affairs he personally might know nothing.

The court decided that, while it was vital to safeguard the integrity of court proceedings, it was also important to ensure that the rules were not applied in such a way as to inhibit solicitors from sitting as judges. Problems are more likely to arise where a solicitor sits as a judge in a part-time capacity (because the rest of their time will be in practice and being involved in a law firm that might have a wide range of clients), and in civil rather than criminal cases. In *Locabail*, the Court of Appeal held that problems of 'apparent bias' could usually be overcome if, before embarking on the trial of any civil case, the solicitor conducted a careful 'conflict search' within his or her firm. To check, in other words, that the names of the parties and witnesses in the case he or she was about to judge did not crop up as clients of his or her law firm.

The Court of Appeal ruled that it would be 'dangerous and futile' to attempt to define or list the factors which may or may not give rise to a real danger of bias. Everything will depend on the facts of any given situation, which may include the nature of the issue to be decided. The court did say, though, that:

> We cannot, however, conceive of circumstances in which an objection could be soundly based on the religion, ethnic or national origin, gender, age, class, means or sexual orientation of the judge. Nor, at any rate ordinarily, could an objection be soundly based on the judge's social or educational or service or employment background or history, nor that of any member of the judge's family; or previous political associations; or membership of social or sporting or charitable bodies; or Masonic associations; or previous judicial decisions; or extra-curricular utterances (whether in textbooks, lectures, speeches, articles, interviews, reports or responses to consultation papers); or previous receipt of instructions to act for or against any party, solicitor or advocate engaged in a case before him; or membership of the same Inn, circuit, local Law Society or chambers.[24]

In a case in 2006, the legal issue was whether a High Court judge should have 'recused' (an old form of refused) himself from presiding because he knew someone in a case he was about to try. The Court of Appeal ruled that he should have recused himself. It stated that, if there was evidence of an apparent bias, then inconvenience, costs and delay in finding a substitute judge were not acceptable reasons for the original judge proceeding to preside. In this company case, the judge had said he had known a witness for the claimants for 30 years.

The judge, Mr Justice Evans-Lombe, said in his judgment[25] that he had a connection with the company AWG (a party to the case) and with a witness, Mr Jewson. He said that AWG was a company whose primary business is supplying water to industry and the public in East Anglia and in particular in Norfolk. He said his family were farmers and landowners in Norfolk, and explained that:

> I have had dealings with AWG, not always harmonious, over the years on such subjects as access for the purpose of sinking boreholes and running pipelines.

> Mr Jewson lives in the next village to the village where I and my family live, being approximately 1 mile distant. Our families have known each other for at least 30 years. Our children are friends and we have dined with each other on a number of occasions. Mr Jewson and I in the past were tennis players. Mr Jewson has recently been appointed Lord Lieutenant of Norfolk. I would have the greatest difficulty in dealing with a case in which Mr Jewson was a witness where a challenge was to be made as to the truthfulness of his evidence . . .

The judge took the view that there would be no need for him to stand down if Mr Jewson was replaced by another witness. On appeal, Lord Justice Mummery stated that, while the very experienced and well-intentioned judge was never suspected of actual bias, the safest course of action was for the judge to stand down to avoid any possible perception of bias. Even without the witness appearing, the case had still involved him.

A decision of Bath justices in 1939 that William Cottle had deserted his wife was quashed by the High Court because his wife's mother was a friend of the chairman of the bench. His wife had hoped that the chairman would 'put him through it'.[26] In *Kirk v Colwyn* (1958), Lord Evershed once recused himself from a case involving his anaesthetist, saying 'I have slid into unconsciousness under his care.'

REMOVAL OF JUDGES FROM OFFICE

Not all judges are perfect. They are no more or less universally impeccable than surgeons or government ministers.

There are several cases of judges behaving badly. In the sixteenth century, Bishop Hugh Latimer wrote of judges that 'They all love bribes. Bribery is a princely kind of thieving.' In the following century, Francis Bacon, who became Lord Chancellor in 1618, faced 28 charges of bribery and corruption, to which he wrote a confession in 1620. He had accepted substantial bribes from a variety of litigants for him to rule in their favour. He was fined £40,000 and sent to the Tower. Then Lord Macclesfield, who became Lord Chancellor in 1718, was found guilty of corruption, fined £30,000 and thrown out of office for 'selling offices' by demanding an honorarium whenever he appointed a Master in Chancery. He asked for so much money that the only way the new judges could afford the sums was to pass on the cost, so to speak, to the parties to the actions in their courts.

Before 1688 judges held office during the 'King's pleasure'. The practice began to change after the English Revolution of that year, when William of Orange landed in England and King James fled abroad. Before 1688, when judges displeased the king they were likely to be summarily dismissed. One way in which the independence of the judiciary is protected is through judges' security of tenure. So today judges hold office 'during good behaviour', meaning that, in effect, unless they commit a serious crime or are publicly disgraced they have secure tenure.

In 1701, the Act of Settlement placed the judicial commissions on a statutory basis, saying they were to be made *quamdiu se bene gesserint* (for as long as they shall have behaved well). Since then, the Heads of Division, Law Lords (now Justices of the Supreme Court), Lords Justices of Appeal and High Court Judges can only be removed by the Queen after an address from both Houses of Parliament. That has never happened in the case of an English judge. Only one judge has ever been removed since 1701 on an address from both houses – Sir Jonah Barrington, an Irish judge, in 1830. He was found to have misappropriated money belonging to litigants and to have ceased to perform his judicial duties many years previously. In 1975 an English High Court judge was found to have driven with more than the permitted degree of alcohol in his blood, but was permitted to remain in office.

The position of Circuit Judges and other judicial officers is different as they can be removed by the Lord Chancellor if necessary for incapacity or misbehaviour. The only occasion on which that power has been used against a salaried judicial office-holder was in 1983, when Judge Bruce Campbell, a Circuit Judge, was removed from office after he had pleaded guilty to several charges of smuggling cigarettes and whisky.

If it were reasonably easy to dismiss judges from office, then they might be wary about delivering judgments which, although correct according to the law, might offend powerful people. In such a setting, powerful people might be able to have the judge dismissed. The current arrangements were designed to give proper security of tenure to judges without making it too difficult to dismiss judges who, for whatever reason, become wholly unsuitable to remain in office.

MAGISTRATES

There are over 29,000 lay magistrates in England and Wales, just over half of whom are women. They are also known as Justices of the Peace (JPs). There are also 141 legally qualified full-time magistrates with the title 'District Judge (Magistrates' Courts)'.

The magistracy helps to foster a great deal of public confidence in the criminal justice system. Allowing such an important part of life – who gets convicted of crimes – to be settled largely by members of the public as opposed to judges is widely seen as socially beneficial.

Magistrates usually sit as part of a 'Bench' of three magistrates, including one who has been trained to take the chair and helps guide the bench through its business, and speaks for it. There is always a legally qualified court clerk to advise on law and procedure. Magistrates come from a wide range of backgrounds and occupations.[27] The selection process aims to appoint people with common sense and personal integrity, with a good knowledge of people and their local community, the ability to listen to all sides of an argument and to contribute to fair and reasonable decisions.

Academic qualifications are not required. No knowledge of the law is required because each bench sits with a court clerk who is legally qualified. The clerk is there to advise magistrates on relevant aspects of the law and sentencing guidelines are also provided. All magistrates are given a programme of practical training which prepares them to sit in court. This is compulsory and involves talks and discussions and practical exercises, observing in court, and visits to prison establishments.

Magistrates are required to sit for a minimum of 26 half-days each year and to be available for full-day sittings. Most magistrates sit for about 35 half-days and they are not allowed to sit more than 70 times in a year. Of course, not all sittings can command the highest levels of attentiveness from all magistrates. They are, after all, only human. Peter Park, a defendant at Trowbridge magistrates' court in June, 2000, may have a view on this. During his cross-examination in a case of causing affray, snoring was heard to come from the bench. Michael Pearce, who had been a magistrate for 30 years, later woke with a snort. The Chairwoman, Janet Wilson-Ward, adjourned the court for a 'coffee-break' and then returned to order a re-trial.[28]

It would be wrong, though, to assume that the salaried judiciary is immune from such lapses. 'It is a reasonable assumption', said Lord Justice Bowen in a case in 1883, 'that a man who sleeps upon his rights has not got much right.'[29] We should also be mindful of the judge who sleeps on his cases. A Court of Appeal decision from 1997 on this issue provides ammunition to cynical observers of the English legal system. In *R v Thomas Guy Moringiello*, a case in which a former United States attorney had been charged in England with deception offences, and had largely conducted his own defence, the court held that 'it does not follow because a judge has been asleep that prejudice has been caused at all'.[30] In an authoritative judgment on the point, an animatedly awake Court of Appeal dismissed the defendant's appeal against his conviction. It ruled that such allegations of judicial slumbering must be made at the time they are alleged to have occurred so that it could be established which parts of the evidence had been missed. It was conceivable that a judge could have dozed momentarily during a part of the proceedings that were of no great consequence but, in any event, the judge should be given an opportunity to respond to the allegation at the time of the alleged inattention.

Today, magistrates carry out their duties locally and deal with 95 per cent of criminal cases in England and Wales. They consider the evidence in each case and reach a verdict. If a defendant is found guilty, or pleads guilty, they decide on the most appropriate sentence – these range from an unconditional discharge (in effect no punishment at all, when the technical commission of an offence is regarded as not serious in any way) to a maximum 12-month term of custody or a fine of up to £20,000 for some offences. They also have the power to commit a convicted defendant to the Crown Court to be sentenced there if their powers are insufficient in view of aspects of the crime that have become evident during the case. Magistrates deal with the less serious criminal cases, such as minor theft, criminal damage, public disorder and motoring offences. When sitting in the Family Proceedings Court, magistrates deal with a range of issues affecting families and children. Local authorities are now responsible for giving or refusing licences to people who want to sell alcohol to the public. But an applicant may appeal to local magistrates against a local authority decision.

Apart from lay magistrates, there are 141 salaried, full-time professional judges, drawn from senior lawyers, called 'District Judges (Magistrates' Courts)'. They used to be known as stipendiary magistrates. The bracketed designation is to distinguish these judges from the District Judges in the County Courts. In the magistrates' courts, a District Judge has the same powers as a bench of two or more magistrates. He or she may sit alone, except in the Family Court. They generally sit in London and larger cities and occasionally assist local benches.

MAGISTRATES AND POPULAR JUSTICE

Decisions of who is convicted of crime, and who is sentenced to prison or receives other punishment by the state, are, understandably, of great concern in any society. It is widely accepted that the more such decisions are in the hands of ordinary responsible members of the community (as opposed to an elite judiciary) the greater is the public trust in the legal system.

For the greater part of English legal history, justice was something delivered to the population by people who were regarded by both themselves and by most people in the general population as coming from a social elite. The lay magistracy affords an element of democracy to the justice system. However, even magistrates – as representatives of the people – were, for most of the history of the office, drawn from a rather privileged section of society.

The move to a more representative magistracy has been slow. The role of lay magistrates in the judicial system can be traced back to the year 1195. In that year Richard I commissioned certain knights to preserve the peace in unruly areas. They were responsible to the king for ensuring that the law was upheld; they preserved the 'King's Peace' and were known as Keepers of the Peace.

An Act in 1327 had referred to 'good and lawful' men to be appointed in every county to 'guard the peace'. That role developed into the lay magistracy. The title Justices of the Peace (another term for lay magistrates) derives from 1361, in the reign of Edward III. Justices of the Peace still retain the power to bind over unruly persons to be of good behaviour. The bind-over is not a punishment but a preventive measure, intended to ensure that people thought likely to offend will not do so.

Before 1835, justices in towns were appointed in accordance with rights granted by charter. The Municipal Corporations Act 1835 provided for them to be nominated for the boroughs by the Lord Chancellor in consultation with local advisers, while, for the county benches, he continued to confirm the preferences of local officials called Lord Lieutenants, who had their own opaque methods for finding suitable candidates. The appointment of both town and county magistrates was vested in the Crown, acting on the Lord Chancellor's advice.

For centuries, the recruitment strategy excluded 50 per cent of the population (females), and regarding the remaining 50 per cent, only focused upon those men who were from about the top 20 per cent of the economic ladder. In 1919 the Sex Disqualification (Removal) Act permitted women to sit as magistrates. Thus, taking the English legal system as having begun in 1066, when William the Conqueror invaded from Normandy, and representing the last 945 years as one 24-hour day, females were excluded from the judicial process until just before 10 o'clock at night.

It was not until The Sex Disqualification (Removal) Act 1919 came into force on 23 December 1919 that women became magistrates. The first woman magistrate, Mrs Ada Summers, Mayor of Stalybridge, outside Manchester, sitting *ex officio* (Latin for 'from one's office', i.e. by virtue of her job as mayor) was sworn in on 31 December 1919. At that time mayors of boroughs were justices by right of mayoral office. Mrs Summers was therefore probably the first woman also to adjudicate in court. In the first five years after the Act was passed, 1,200 women were appointed to commissions and, during the next decade, about a hundred were appointed each year. By 1929 all county benches included at least one woman magistrate, although 55 borough benches were all-male.

Many changes have been made in recent history. During the last 20 years there has been a great effort from government to appoint to the magistrates' benches from a wider social base. This change can be seen as having been made, in some respects, as a response to substantial social changes such as the growing diversification of racial and cultural components of UK society, and changes in family patterns. When it is noted that there are over 1.5 million criminal cases prosecuted every year, and that 95 per cent of them are dealt with in the magistrates' courts, it can be appreciated why, in order for the government to ensure that people have confidence in the legal system, the social composition of the bench should be seen to reflect the sociological profile of the people whom it judges.

In October 2003, Lord Falconer of Thoroton, the Lord Chancellor, made this observation:

> Magistrates are recruited from members of the local community . . . no qualifications are required, but applicants are expected to demonstrate common sense, integrity, intelligence and the capacity to act fairly . . . I consider it particularly important that the magistracy is seen to be representative of all sections of our society and that no one group of people should feel that they are under-represented on the magistrates' bench.[31]

One point not to overlook in these debates about the representativeness of the bench is that members of our various social categories (minorities, like Asians; and majorities, like females) are on the bench not to act as champions of people from their group but to ensure that the bench has a good range of social experiences that can be applied to decision-making. This was well summed up by a black magistrate from London who was quoted in a very stimulating book on the magistracy. He said:

> When a young black defendant sees me on the bench you can see him do a double-take. That's good in one way, but in another it gives him false hope. You can almost hear him saying, 'Root for me.' He doesn't understand that justice isn't about the way you look or the colour of your skin. Justice is blind. The magistrates aren't there for the good of the defendant. They're there for the greater good, because they are concerned members of the community.[32]

In April 2012, about 8.1 per cent of the 25,170 magistrates came from minority ethnic communities that make up 8 per cent of the general population. Thus, the bench's ethnic mix is pretty much that of the population in respect of ethnicity. The same is true of the gender balance: just over half of magistrates are women, reflecting the general population. A very significant part of the magistracy, however, seems to come from the same socio-economic echelon: the comfortable middle class (from all ethnic groups). Members of the working class who work in call centres, factories, quarries, steelworks, on the railways and in office cleaning do not feature in any great numbers on the bench. Similarly, only 4.5 per cent of magistrates are disabled, compared with 15 per cent of the adult working age population in England and Wales.

FURTHER READING

Tom Bingham, *The Business of Judging*, Oxford: Oxford University Press, 2000.
Lord Denning, *Landmarks in the Law*, London: Butterworths, 1984.
Trevor Grove, *The Magistrate's Tale*, London: Bloomsbury, 2002.
David Pannick, *Judges*, Oxford: Oxford University Press, 1987.
Shimon Shetreet, *Judges on Trial: A Study of the Appointment and Accountability of the English Judiciary*, Amsterdam: North-Holland, 1976.

3

Lawyers

The contribution of lawyers to society is enormous and very important. They do not, however, enjoy a universally good reputation. Naturally, stories like the one concerning Cyrus Inches QC, a renowned Canadian lawyer, do not help. As he lay on his side in bed after an operation in 1955, he turned, contrary to instructions, to rest on his other side. He was rebuked by the nurse but replied, 'My dear young lady, I'm a lawyer, and I'm used to lying on both sides.'

To help their public image, Canadian lawyers considered establishing a 'truth and reconciliation' panel in 2005 to discover why they do not enjoy greater respect.[1] Among possible public misgivings is the alleged propensity of some lawyers to argue something perverse in order to benefit their clients, particularly in protecting civil and criminal defendants. Such criticism, however undeserved, has long roots. The first treatise on adoxography – skilfully praising worthless objects – was published in England in 1593 by Anthony Munday. It contained essays celebrating poverty, drunkenness and stupidity, and its preface claimed it would be especially useful to lawyers.[2]

In modern, complex, developed democracies, there are many thousands of rules that affect people directly in their lives, and people require the expertise of specialists in order to follow and understand those rules in certain situations. You might need a lawyer not just because you have been arrested for a crime you are alleged to have committed, but also because you have been sued or wish to sue, because you want to set up a company, make a will, get advice about a mentally ill family member, sell a property, avoid an eviction, protect your rights to an invention you have made, or get a divorce.

Lawyers therefore enable people to protect or vindicate their rights. Culturally, although commonly the subject of some barbed jokes and comments, lawyers are widely respected as good leaders and as knowledgeable and sometimes witty people. Of all the Prime Ministers since 1730, 12 have been lawyers – more than double as many in the same profession as the next nearest grouping, the military, from whose offices five people became Prime Minister.

The following exchanges illustrate the sharpness with which some lawyers have responded spontaneously in court. The remarks are attributed to Andrew Clark, Joseph Choate, F.E. Smith, and an unknown lawyer in a story recounted by Sir John Mortimer QC.

JUDGE: I'm a little tired of your jewels of Chancery learning.

COUNSEL: If your Lordship will bear with me, I am about to cast my last pearl.

. . .

JUDGE: If you say that again, I shall commit you for contempt.

COUNSEL: I have said it once. To repeat it is therefore unnecessary.

. . .

JUDGE: I have listened with care to your arguments and I am none the wiser.

COUNSEL: Possibly not, m'lud, but far better informed.

. . .

JUDGE: Has your client not heard of the precept *res ipsa loquitur*?

COUNSEL: M'lud, the people of Barnsley talk of little else.

In addition to these virtues, lawyers also help to develop the law. Historically, law courts provided the forum for settling disputes. In the earliest periods of legal history, the court's main function was to provide the process and principles of evidence by which disputes were resolved, rather than applying a detailed set of rules about whatever was in dispute. As there was no great body of recorded decisions and legislation, the early courts were prone simply to reflect customary social rules about right and wrong, how property was owned and transferred, and who was liable for what. From merely implementing social codes, the courts – through the arguments of lawyers – came to define, refine, and then redefine what became the common law. This was characterised by the distinguished legal academic A.W.B. Simpson in this way. He noted that, instead of the courts simply saying what was to happen to murderers, the experts who dealt with murders began to develop their own ideas as to what was to count as murder. They began to sharpen up customary or conventional or ethical standards; they began to develop their own definitions of murder. In the common law system that process began when jury trial began to supersede divine and therefore infallible modes of trial, for jurymen could obviously make mistakes and needed to be corrected by official experts.

The experts become nervous about leaving to the layman the whole business of adjudication, for example not only the decision as to what the accused had done, but also whether it ought to count as murder. So they began to take over the job of adjudication, at least in part. Thus what is to count as murder becomes a matter for the experts to settle, what we call a question of law.[3]

Today, the country's 135,406 lawyers are engaged in a massive social enterprise. Apart from vindicating rights, protecting the interests of individual and organisational clients, and helping to develop the law, they are a significant part of the economy. The law firms of England and Wales generated income of £19.3 billion in 2009[4] and the top 100 law firms made profits in excess of £4 billion. If the rate of growth in the profession continues at the rate at which it has been expanding since the 1970s then by 2055 we shall have one million lawyers. Whether such a development is an index of a healthy rights-conscious society or an unhealthy, disputatious society is an interesting question. The global lawyer–citizen ratio is 1:2,370, whereas in England and Wales it is 1:433. There has certainly been a significant increase in the proportion of lawyers in the general population. In 1968 there were 54 million people in the UK, of whom 23,000 were solicitors in England and Wales, whereas in 2013 we have a population of 63.2 million (17 per cent growth) and 120,202 solicitors in England and Wales (422 per cent growth).

THE LEGAL PROFESSION

Speaking about *the* legal profession can be seen as something of a misnomer, because strictly speaking there are several different and distinct components carrying out legal work for money. The main three groupings are barristers, solicitors and legal executives. In England and Wales, there are 15,204 practising barristers, 128,000 practising solicitors, and 7,907 practising legal executives.

Broadly speaking, the work of the barrister is that of a court advocate and writer of detailed professional legal opinions for the client – although this advice is furnished through a solicitor with whom the client deals directly. The work of solicitors varies greatly. Some work as sole practitioners in small high-street practices, whereas others work in large international firms with thousands of staff. Solicitors usually deal directly with clients – individual and corporate clients – giving advice, preparing documents, briefing barristers (often referred to as 'counsel'), and sometimes working in court advocacy. Legal executives tend to specialise in particular areas of law such as aspects of family law, criminal law, or civil law.

For many centuries, different types of organised work in law evolved very gradually in relation to the particular tasks required by the social and economic goings-on of the day. Barristers have the longest traceable professional history, but it is worth noting that at the outset of what became the noble and revered professional Bar, advocacy was regarded as simply work that was required to be done in what was, at the time, an innovative way. As courts of various kinds began to develop, so people being judged by them began with growing regularity to get others to speak on their behalf. In Britain, a man was entitled to have an advocate – called a *forespeca* in Saxon times. During the reign of Alfred the Great (871–900), for example, a man was accused of stealing a belt, and one of his accusers tried to claim his land. One writer of the time recorded that the defendant 'sought me and prayed me to be his intercessor. Then I spoke on his behalf and interceded for him with King Alfred'.[5] Such beginnings can be compared with the emergence of information technology (IT) today. Twenty years ago there began to appear little departments or units – or sometimes simply one expert – dedicated to installing, maintaining, and problem-solving information technology in companies, hospitals, colleges, and schools. Computers were becoming a common feature of organisational work. Since then, all sorts of specialist work (such as software engineers, security experts and webmasters) have developed. The original barristers were called 'story-tellers' (from the Latin narrators), and they were engaged simply to tell the story of a client in court. At that time there were no requirements for doing the job, and those doing it were not organised in any particular way.

The title 'solicitor' is derived from the Latin *sollicito*, meaning 'I bother or worry'. The people originally doing the work that would evolve into today's profession were engaged, on behalf of their clients in the late thirteenth century, in bothering or 'chasing up' court officials to expedite the resolution of cases. The role, in more modern language, was that of a 'fixer'. They were associated with the Court of Chancery, where their main function was to expedite the conduct of cases on behalf of their clients, which very often got caught up in the chaotic administrative systems of the clerks who administered the court's list. This work was called 'soliciting causes'. The modern solicitor arose from a mixture of this role with that of attorneys, who performed a similar role in the common law courts. The work of legal executives was organised professionally under the auspices of the Institute of Legal Executives (ILEX) in the 1980s, and is currently in an early stage of evolution as part of the legal professions.

There has been much snobbery in all quarters of the legal community at all stages of the development of the legal professions, as one authoritative text records of the early nineteenth century:

> It was possible for solicitors to become wealthy men; and some of them 'got in the landed gentry as quickly as they could'. It was true that these were the exceptions rather than the rule. The ordinary solicitor was still not 'acceptable', and was regarded as a tradesman. In litigation, his were the menial tasks. But he was developing areas of interest where the supervision and advice of the Bar was less needed; and for the very few this meant a position of considerable importance.[6]

Even by the 1960s things had not changed significantly. Solicitors continued to be irritated by the attitude of barristers, who occasionally referred to them in such phrases as 'the junior half' of the profession and described their role as being one 'to prepare cases for the Barrister to take over in court'.[7] In a memorandum of the British Legal Association in 1964, a grouping of solicitors stated, under the heading 'Relationship between Barristers and Solicitors', that:

> Solicitors and Barristers should be on a footing of complete professional equality. If a solicitor writes to a barrister (or other solicitor) the envelope should be addressed 'Mr A Watson' or to 'A Watson Esq', and the letter should start 'Dear Watson' and should finish 'Yours sincerely' or other suitable ending. It should be not addressed to a clerk. The notion that barristers are too superior to receive letters personally is mistaken. The examinations for barristers are less stringent than those for solicitors, and the present idea that barristers are superior should be discouraged.[8]

The definition of a 'profession' is still a contentious issue. Whether a branch of work is a profession is not something that can be settled by reference to a single, official definition. So the point at which certain types of work like management, computer science, or that of legal executives becomes indisputably professional is not settled. The Royal Commission on Legal Services (1969) emphasised five main features of a profession: (a) central organisation: a governing body with powers of control and discipline; (b) the primary function of giving advice or service in a specialised field of knowledge; (c) the restriction of admission to those with the required standard of education and training; (d) a measure of self-regulation by the profession; and (e) the importance of the duty owed to the client, subject only to the responsibility to the court.

LAWYERS AND FEES

Many other issues concerning the legal professions are given a better perspective when looked at historically. For example, it is sometimes wrongly supposed that the extravagant fee claims of some lawyers are a relatively new phenomenon, influenced by American practice or the imperatives of modern business. Occasional overcharging, however, has a long history. Medieval England saw much anti-lawyer feeling, especially complaints that lawyers stirred up unnecessary lawsuits, prolonged legal actions, and concocted false bills. The preamble to a 1601 Act in England to stop excessive legal bills noted that many fictitious fees had been charged to clients who 'growe to be overmuch burthened, and the practise of the juste and honest [lawyer] greatly slandered'.[9] Most lawyers are, however, perfectly honourable about the fees they charge.

The determination with which some lawyers seek fees in questionable circumstances has also come into question. Britain has had chronic problems with 'ambulance-chasing' lawyers. A letter to *The Times* on 27 December 1912 referred to lawyers' touts who obtained cases by 'haunting the side doors of our metropolitan hospitals and buttonholing the distressed relatives of those who have met with accidents'. Clients were acquired by 'a ghoulish alertness in studying the newspapers for announcements of accidents'. The phenomenon was later decried in a 1928 Law Society paper entitled 'Ambulance Chasing'. The practice was widespread in the 1950s, and was condemned in a 1964 parliamentary debate.

It is clear that most legal work is very challenging, requires considerable education and training, and should be well remunerated. However, although legal practice can demand professional knowledge and skill of the highest order, public disquiet sometimes follows exposure of lawyers' earnings. In 1999, for example, the first published advert for a £1m salaried lawyer (to join an American firm in London) raised some eyebrows. The case of the German lawyer, Dr Juergen Graefe, in 2004, though, was novel even by the standards of high legal pay. He charged £308,000 for writing a single letter. He acted for an elderly pensioner client from St Augustin, near Bonn, who was sent a tax demand for €287m (£187m). The client's income was actually only €17,000. The lawyer wrote one standard letter to the authorities to get the demand rectified. Under German law, however, he is entitled to calculate his fee based on the amount of the reduction that he obtained for his client. A court later confirmed his fee for the letter at €440,234 (£308,000). It was met by the state. He might have been pushing his luck to write a thank-you letter.

It should be remembered that while there is periodic news of both solicitor partners and QCs (senior barristers) who have been rewarded with very high annual incomes – these days over £1m a year – such cases represent a very small fraction of legal practitioners as a whole and of those lawyers who have publicly funded practices, only a handful earn over £500,000 per year.

A FUSION OF THE PROFESSIONS

Another example of a modern debate best set in its longer history is the idea that the two main branches of professional legal practice (barristers and solicitors) should be fused. The case for an amalgamation of the two branches of the profession is not new. It was argued for in an article in *The Times* entitled 'The Monopoly of the Bar' on 5 January 1884. It regarded fusion as a way of cheapening the cost of litigation for the clients; in many cases it would cost the client more to bring the case than he would win in a verdict. The figures supported that analysis. For example, a Law Society report showed that many actions cost clients (who had to pay for several lawyers) more than they won in damages. Out of 714 successful common law cases tried in London in the legal year 1881–82, only 160 resulted in a verdict of more than £200. However, as a report of the Law Society had noted in 1881:

> In an action for damages in which something under £200 is recovered, the costs of the trial alone must, under the present system, generally exceed the amount of the verdict . . . It is almost a mockery to see the huge framework of our legal procedure – at least two, sometimes three, counsel drawing heavy fees, besides the solicitor who had charge of the case – creaking and groaning under the prodigious task of determining whether a man is entitled to £50 or £100 for the injury he has suffered from some breach of contract or wrongful deed.[10]

It is arguable now that fusion has effectively been organised covertly and gradually. Solicitors' monopolies over conveyancing and the right to conduct litigation have been technically removed (by the Courts and Legal Services Act 1990 and the Access to Justice Act 1999, respectively), and the Bar's monopoly over rights of audience, even in the higher courts, has also been removed (by the same legislation). What a lawyer chooses to specialise in is thus not entirely a choice limited by which branch of the profession he or she has joined. We began the new century with specialist criminal law solicitor-advocates operating from dedicated offices in some cities (a sort of solicitors' 'chambers'), and barristers who are effectively working as in-house lawyers in companies, carrying out work that seems very like that traditionally done by solicitors.

SOLICITORS

The solicitor can be characterised as a legal general practitioner: a lawyer who deals with clients directly and, when a particular specialism or litigation is required, will engage the services of counsel, that is, a barrister. Looking at the solicitor as a legal GP and the barrister as a specialist, however, can be misleading. Most solicitors, especially those in large practices, are experts in particular areas of law. They may restrict their regular work to litigation or commercial conveyancing (transferring rights in land and property) or revenue work. Many barristers on the other hand might have a fairly wide range of work, including criminal, family matters, and a variety of common law areas such as tort (civil wrongs, such as negligence) and contract cases.

As mentioned previously, one group of people practising in the Court of Chancery came to be known as 'solicitors'. Originally, they performed a variety of miscellaneous clerical tasks for employers such as landowners and attorneys. Their name was derived from their function of 'soliciting' or 'prosecuting' (expediting) actions in courts where they were not officially recognised as fully fledged advocates. Eventually, various occupational groups who were performing legal work but who had not been admitted to the Inns of Court (where barristers worked) merged and organised themselves as a distinct profession.

It was not, however, until 1831 that 'The Society of Attorneys, Solicitors, Proctors and Others, not being Barristers, Practising in the Courts of Law and Equity in the UK' was given its royal charter. This body emerged as the governing body of solicitors, the term 'attorney' falling from general use.

Figures published in 2013 show that there are 164,998 solicitors 'on the Roll', that is, people qualified to work as solicitors, of whom 128,169 have a current practising certificate. During the last ten years there has been a significant increase in the size of the profession as a whole and in the proportion of women and minority ethnic group solicitors. According to a survey undertaken by the Law Society in 2011, of the total number of solicitors with current practising certificates, 56,720 were women, 14,600 were from an ethnic minority background and 30,010 were employed outside of private practice (e.g. being employed by organisations like the Crown Prosecution Service). The number of women with practising certificates has increased by 79.7 per cent since 2000, and as half of the entrants into the profession are now women, this number looks set to grow. The number of practising solicitors from an ethnic minority background now stands at 11.1 per cent of the profession. The geographical distribution of solicitors across the country is not even: over one-quarter (27.3 per cent) of the 10,362 firms in England and Wales were located in London and these employed 43.9 per cent of the 85,128 solicitors in private practice, as at 31 July 2009. Approaching one-half of all solicitors firms (41.9 per cent) are based in the South East (including London). Although the profession has grown over time, 2013 saw the first fall in the number of solicitors in private practice since records began. Some have speculated that this is a result of the new ways of delivering legal services that are outlined below.

One very significant area of concern for solicitors at the beginning of the twenty-first century is the extent to which their monopolies of certain sorts of practice have been eroded. They have already lost their monopoly on conveyancing (although only a solicitor is authorised to give final endorsement to such work if carried out by a licensed conveyancer). In 1999, the Access to Justice Act introduced the provision that the Lord Chancellor would in future be able to authorise bodies other than the Law Society to approve of their members carrying out litigation. This, however, should be seen in the wider context of the policy to break down the historical monopolies of both branches of the legal profession. Since the Courts and Legal Services Act 1990 (CLSA), we can note the growth of solicitors' rights of audience in court, and a corresponding anxiety at the Bar when these rights were granted. Another big change for the legal profession has been the introduction of alternative business structures (known as ABS), which allow anyone who is 'fit and proper' to provide legal services, regardless of whether or not they have a legal qualification. This includes insurance companies and supermarkets, and has been given the nickname, 'Tesco law'.

The 1999 Act entitles every barrister and every solicitor to a 'right of audience' before every court in relation to all proceedings. The right, however, is not unconditional. In order to exercise it, solicitors and barristers must obey the rules of conduct of the professional bodies and must have met the prescribed training requirements, such as the requirement to have completed pupillage in the case of the Bar, or to have obtained a higher courts advocacy qualification in the case of solicitors who wish to appear in the higher courts.

Solicitors' Training

The standard route to qualification is a law degree followed by a one-year Legal Practice Course (LPC) and then a term as a trainee solicitor, which, like the barrister's pupillage, is essentially an apprenticeship. Non-law graduates can complete the Graduate Diploma in Law in one year and then proceed as a law graduate. All newly admitted solicitors must now undergo regular continuing education, which means attendance at non-examined legal courses designed to update knowledge and improve expertise. After completion of the LPC and traineeship, a trainee solicitor may apply to the Law Society to be 'admitted' to the profession. The Master of the Rolls will add the names of the newly qualified to the roll of officers of the Supreme Court. To practise, a solicitor will also require a practising certificate issued by the Solicitors Regulation Authority. The fee paid to the SRA runs from about £900 for a single regulated solicitor. Firms also have to pay a separate fee to help fund the cost of the SRA's regulatory work. The reason is that between 60 per cent and 80 per cent of regulatory activity is focused on firms rather than individuals. The annual fee payable by a firm varies according to its size and can be a few thousand pounds for a small firm to £347,000 for a firm with a turnover of £150,000,000. Additionally, solicitors have to pay an annual premium for indemnity insurance.

Solicitors' Rights of Audience

A 'right of audience' is an old term for the right of a lawyer to be heard by a law court, a right to be an advocate before the bench. Traditionally, this right was restricted to barristers. Today however, following a change in the law made in 1990, 5,000 solicitors, known as solicitor-advocates, have qualified to act as advocates in particular courts after qualifying as solicitors, gaining appropriate case experience, and sitting further examinations.[11]

Some solicitors (those who are also barristers or part-time judges) are granted exemption from the new tests of qualification for advocacy. Others need to apply for the grant of higher courts qualifications, in civil proceedings, criminal proceedings, or both. A holder of the higher courts (criminal proceedings) qualification has rights of audience in the Crown court in all proceedings (including its civil jurisdiction) and in other courts in all criminal proceedings. A holder of the higher courts (civil proceedings) qualification may appear in the High Court in all proceedings and in other courts in all civil proceedings. Applicants for these qualifications must have practised as a solicitor for at least three years.

The qualifying scheme is designed only for solicitors who are already lower court advocates – something for which ordinary qualification as a solicitor will suffice. An applicant must be able to demonstrate the following three elements: two years' experience of advocacy in the lower courts and experience of the procedures of the relevant higher court; competency in a written test on evidence and procedure; and satisfactory completion of an advocacy training course. The jurisdiction of the different courts (in the sense of what types of cases are within their scope, rather than their geographic scope) is examined in the next chapter.

Large City firms of solicitors already have litigation lawyers trained to qualify for advocacy in the High Court. One problem for these large firms is, however, that they have found it very difficult for their applicants (for audience rights) to meet the Law Society's requirement for county court advocacy experience. Although the expansion of this court's jurisdiction under the CLSA 1990 (in particular commercial litigation involving sums up to £50,000) has given more county court work to large firms, they generally do very little of this. Large firms have had to take on perhaps hundreds of county court cases just to get the ones that will go to trial, and, even then, these would only be a means to an end, namely the qualification to appear in the High Court.

Some barristers are concerned about the threat to their traditional work. A potentially significant development is BarDIRECT, a scheme set up in 1999 that enables certain professions and organisations to have direct access to barristers without referral through a solicitor. While this initiative could be one of the keys to the continuing success of the Bar, it is argued that it makes barristers no different from solicitors and could even encroach on the solicitors' market.

NEW FORMS OF ORGANISATION FOR LAWYERS

A business organisation called the limited liability partnership (LLP) was introduced by the Limited Liability Partnership Act 2000. This new business form seeks to amalgamate the advantages of the company's corporate form with the flexibility of the partnership form. Although called a 'partnership', the new form is a distinct legal entity that enjoys an existence apart from that of its members. The LLP can enter into agreements in its own name, it can own property, and it can sue and be sued. Traditional partnerships, by contrast, entail liability for the partners as individuals. Although the LLP enjoys corporate status, it is not taxed as a separate entity from its members. Solicitors do not seem to have been keen to adopt these as their preferred form of firm, however. Of those formed by July 2009 – 2,175 from 16,812 firms – most were formed because of international constraints on mergers; that is, the foreign firm could not merge with the British one unless the British one became an LLP. One perceived risk that seems to be important to many lawyers is that an LLP can be sued itself, whereas in a partnership proceedings might be launched against only one or two partners.

Another feature of change is the evidently widening gap between the work and income of the top few hundred commercial firms and the 8,000 smaller high-street firms. A series of mergers has created a few relatively huge law firms, and the merger of an English firm with an American one produced the world's first billion-dollar practice. In 1999, partners at Clifford Chance voted to merge with the USA's Rogers & Wells, and Punders in Germany, to form a firm that now employs 7,000 people in 29 offices worldwide. It specialises in corporate finance, commercial property, anti-trust law and litigation. Keith Clark, senior partner at Clifford Chance, explained that the aim of the merger was to create a truly international firm capable of offering an integrated legal service to an increasingly global business community. He has said, 'Clients don't want all the time delays and inefficiencies of dealing with half a dozen legal firms around the world. What they want is one firm that has the capacity to be a one-stop shop for all their corporate needs.'[12] By 2010, the firm employed 3,600 lawyers and had 600 partners. The firm, one of the largest in the world, billed £1.26 billion in legal fees in 2009.[13]

During the 1980s, law firms, by doing all the legal work on mergers for commercial companies (for example telecommunications, energy and manufacturing) helped to create a new environment of transnationals operating on a world basis. Now, that new material environment has affected the very law firms that helped to create it. These law firms are now themselves changing into global firms in order to do the ordinary legal work for the new commercial giants. By contrast, law firms that gave a public funding service to underprivileged groups are progressively reducing such activity. As Paula Rohan has noted, 'After almost sixty years of giving the most disadvantaged members of society access to legal advice, the system is on its last legs – at least according to a major *Gazette* survey.'[14] As a consequence of very low rates of remuneration, and political attacks on publicly funded lawyers, 78 per cent of the 291 firms who responded to the survey were considering cutting down on their public funded work, and 91 per cent stated they were dissatisfied with the current system.

THE INSTITUTE OF LEGAL EXECUTIVES

The Institute of Legal Executives (ILEX) represents over 20,000 legal executives employed in solicitors' offices. Legal executives are legally trained (the institute runs its own examinations) and carry out much of the routine legal work that is a feature of most practices. The institute was established in 1963 with the support of the Law Society. The Managing Clerks' Association, from which ILEX developed, recognised that many non-solicitor staff employed in fee-earning work, and in the management of firms, needed and wanted a training route that would improve standards and award recognition for knowledge and skills. The education and training facilities ILEX offers have developed in number and diversity so that ILEX is able to provide a route to a career in law that is open to all.

Legal executives are, in the phrase of the ILEX website (http://www.ilex.org.uk), qualified lawyers specialising in a particular area of law. They will have passed the ILEX Professional Qualification in Law in an area of legal practice to the same level as that required of solicitors. They will have at least five years' experience of working under the supervision of a solicitor in legal practice, or the legal department of a private company, or local or national government. Fellows are issued with an annual practising certificate, and only Fellows of ILEX may describe themselves as 'legal executives'. They specialise in a particular area of law, and their day-to-day work is similar to that of a solicitor.

Legal executives might handle the legal aspects of a property transfer; assist in the formation of a company; be involved in actions in the High Court or county courts; draft wills; advise clients accused of serious or petty crime, or families with matrimonial problems; and many other matters affecting people in their domestic and business affairs. Legal executives are fee-earners – in private practice their work is charged directly to clients – making a direct contribution to the income of a law firm. This is an important difference between legal executives and other types of legal support staff who tend to handle work of a more routine nature.

In 2000, six legal executives qualified to become the first legal executive advocates. The advocates now have extended rights of audience in civil and matrimonial proceedings in the county courts and magistrates' courts. In some circumstances, fellows of ILEX can instruct barristers directly.

BARRISTERS

One thing for which lawyers are known is their loquacity. According to a standard definition, an opening speech from counsel in a criminal or civil case is one 'briefly outlining the case'. In 2004, the opening speech for the claimants in *Liquidators of BCCI v Bank of England* ran for seventy-nine days. In 2005, counsel for the bank passed the 80-day mark in his opening speech for the defendant. Sometimes, what lawyers have to address is so factually and regulatorily complicated that judges' judgments are also very long. In a complicated land case in 1976, about Ocean Island in the West Pacific, phosphate, and the Banaban people, Vice-Chancellor Sir Robert Megarry read an exquisitely comprehensive 131,000-word judgment that now occupies two hundred pages in the law reports. It took him three days to read the judgment in court.[15]

The English legal system has a history from ancient Celtic times of forensic orality. It was the illiteracy of these times, and the Anglo-Saxon era, that generated the oral legal tradition. Repetition and tautology also became important because the ear cannot backtrack to check, as can the eye on the page. From the sixteenth century, the advent of law reporting enhanced the role of the advocate. A profusion of reported precedents can beget weeks of advocacy. Some litigation like the BCCI case is so factually fraught that unusually long speeches are justified.

The barrister is often thought of primarily as a court advocate, although many spend more time on drafting pleadings (now called statements of case) and writing advices for solicitors. Professional barristers are technically competent to perform all advocacy for the prosecution or defence in criminal cases, and for a claimant or defendant in a civil claim. More generally, however, established barristers tend to specialise in particular areas of work. Over 60 per cent of practising barristers work in London, although in 2009, for the first time, the number of sets of chambers (the name given to the office where a barrister works) outside of London exceeded the number of sets of chambers in London.

Barristers often assist in getting to the truth of a matter by virtue of very conscientious study of voluminous files, and expert questioning of witnesses. All sorts of clever tactics have been used, and some have become renowned. For example, the advocate Sir Patrick Hastings (1880–1952) was once cross-examining a witness in a major trial. At a key moment in his questioning, he paused and then searched anxiously through all his papers. Eventually, and with visible relief, he found the page he was looking for. He held the paper before him, and continued questioning his witness. The witness became rattled, and from then on all his answers became favourable to Sir Patrick's client. Eventually, the advocate finished his cross-examination and put down the mysterious piece of paper without having formally introduced it into the case. The paper was then seen by those near him to be blank.

Then there is the story of the redoubtable early twentieth-century barrister F.E. Smith, who later became Lord Chancellor (1919–22). Smith once appeared for an insurance company at London County Court. An injured man was claiming that an accident had crippled his right arm. 'How high could you raise your arm *before* the accident?' Mr Smith asked in a casual and apparently innocuous way. The claimant obligingly demonstrated, and, in doing so invalidated his claim.

In 2010, there were 12,241 barristers in independent practice in England and Wales, of whom 8,381 were men and 3,860 were women. Of the 12,241 barristers, 9,275 are self-classified as 'white British'. Queen's Counsel (QCs) are senior and distinguished barristers of at least ten years' standing who, as a result of outstanding merit, have received a patent as 'one of her Majesty's counsel learned in the law'. In 2010, there were 1,318 Queen's Counsel, of whom 1,179 were men and 139 were women.[16]

The Bar had been organised as an association of the members of the Inns of Court by the fourteenth century. Today, there are four Inns of Court (Inner and Middle Temples, Lincoln's Inn and Gray's Inn), although there were originally more, including Inns of Chancery and Serjeants' Inns, the latter being an association of the king's most senior lawyers. Until 1990, the barrister had a virtual monopoly on advocacy in all the superior courts (in some cases solicitors could act as advocates in the Crown Court). That was abolished by the Courts and Legal Services Act (CLSA) 1990.

Barristers' Training and Organisation

Entry to the Bar is now restricted to graduates and mature students. An aspirant barrister must register with one of the four Inns of Court in London. Commonly, a barrister will have a law degree and then undertake professional training (the Bar Professional Training Course) for one year leading to the Bar Examinations. Alternatively, a non-law graduate can study for the Graduate Diploma in Law for one year and, if successful in the examinations, must undertake the Bar Professional Training Course (BPTC) before proceeding to the Bar Examinations. The successful student is then called to the Bar by his or her Inn of Court. It is also a requirement of being called to the Bar that, during study for the vocational course, the student attends his or her Inn to become familiar with the customs of the Bar. The student then undertakes a pupillage to a junior counsel. Note that all barristers, however senior in years and experience, are still 'junior counsel' unless they have 'taken silk' (so-called because of the silk gown worn by a QC) and become a QC. Barristers who do not intend to practise do not have to complete the pupillage. The Bar receives considerable criticism for being elitist and not very representative of the general population. Of the 14,890 practising barristers in 2010, only 5,344 were women, 1,564 were from an ethnic minority background and 62.6 per cent of pupil barristers had attended Oxford, Cambridge or a Russell Group university.

The Inns of Court are administered by their senior members, who are called benchers. To be called to the Bar, students must complete twelve 'qualifying sessions' (traditionally called 'dining' from when eating a prescribed number of dinners at the Inn was a significant part of the process of becoming a member of it). The sessions can now be completed in a number of ways, including residential weekends, education days, and dinners organised by the Inns. In medieval England, the court lawyers in London came to share accommodation in what today would be a form of fraternity house. An Inn of Court was originally, therefore, a hostel for court lawyers. It was in these institutions that there developed a variety of professional protocols and systems of ranking that exist today. Today's four Inns of Court are those remaining from over a dozen that, for various historical reasons, fell into disuse.

Since the reign of Edward I, discipline over the Bar has been the responsibility of the judges, in practice carried out by the benchers of the Inns but subject to the visitorial jurisdiction of the judges. The General Council of the Bar (Bar Council) was formed in 1894 to deal with matters of professional etiquette. In 1974, the Bar Council and the governing body of the Inns, the Senate, combined to form the Senate of the Inns of Court and the Bar. However, in 1987, in line with the recommendations of a report on the constitution of the Senate by Lord Rawlinson PC QC, a council of the Inns of Court was re-established separately and the Courts and Legal Services Act 1990 designated the Bar Council as the authorised body for the profession.

The Bar Standards Board was established in January 2006 as a result of the Bar Council separating its regulatory and representative functions. As the independent regulatory board of the Bar Council, it is responsible for regulating barristers called to the Bar in England and Wales. It takes decisions independently and in the public interest and is not prejudiced by the Bar Council's function of representing the interests of its members.

In the film *Catch Me If You Can* (2002), which is based on a true story, Leonardo DiCaprio plays a conman who impersonates a range of professionals, including an airline pilot and a doctor. He also assumes the identity of a lawyer, and, in one of the film's twists, eventually does become legally qualified. The case of Paolo Bonaccorsi in 2003 presents a bizarre contrast. Mr Bonaccorsi was appointed as a senior governmental lawyer in Calabria, Italy, in 2001. It gradually became evident, however, that he did not seem to know any law. Checks then revealed that he was not registered as a lawyer and his legal qualifications were fakes. Since formalised examinations in England and Wales were established for solicitors (1838) and barristers (1872), there has been a reliable way of determining whether a person is a qualified lawyer. Under the Solicitors Act 1974, it is an offence for unqualified people to act as solicitors, and pretending to be a barrister was criminalised in 2007. In 2002, Emma Cross, a solicitor from Newcastle, exposed her opponent in a case as someone who was impersonating a barrister. The impostor escaped legally unscathed, however: he was not technically 'exercising rights of audience', as he was acting in a tribunal case, not a law court.

Queen's Counsel

Queen's Counsel (QCs) are senior barristers of distinguished merit. They are given this status by the Queen on the advice of the Lord Chancellor. There were, until the suspension of the system in 2003, annual invitations from the Lord Chancellor for barristers to apply for this title. Applicants needed to show at least ten years of successful practice at the Bar. However, under arrangements announced in 2005, a new independent selection procedure has replaced the widely criticised former system, which relied on secret soundings among senior legal figures. Candidates are now chosen by the Lord Chancellor on the recommendation of an independent panel set up by the Law Society and the Bar Council. If appointed, the QC becomes known as a 'Leader' and he or she often appears in cases with a junior. The old 'Two Counsel Rule', under which a QC always had to appear with a junior counsel, whether one was really required or not, was abolished in 1977. He or she is restricted to high-level work (of which there is less available in some types of practice), so appointment can be financially difficult, but in most cases it has desirable consequences for the QC as he or she is able to increase fee levels considerably. In 2013, the Queen approved 84 new QCs from 183 applications.[17] Of the 183 applicants, 155 were men (of whom 70 were successful) and 26 were women (of whom 14 were successful). There were 21 minority ethnic applicants, of whom three were successful.

Law arises from and reflects life. So, the greater the extent to which the body of legal practitioners reflects the people it serves, the better. Historically, 50 per cent of the British adult population was excluded from practising law. Indeed, the eminent seventeenth-century judge and jurist Lord Coke famously stated that women could not be attorneys. Even once concessions were made at the entrance gates to legal academe during the nineteenth century, women experienced endemic chauvinism in their career progression. In a case in 1914, arising from an attempt of a woman to become a solicitor, even her lawyers dutifully accepted the proposition that women had no public functions, and that 'in the camp, at the council board, on the bench, in the jury box there is no place for them'.

By 1964, there was still formal opposition to female barristers being admitted to some circuit meetings and dinners because they would 'inhibit the atmosphere' and 'completely alter the character and nature' of the events. It was also feared that some women might attend the meetings because they felt that 'in so doing they are in some way advancing their professional chances' – something, it seems to have been assumed, that men would never want to do. While female entry to most law schools has been balanced in the UK for over 25 years, entry to the Bar has been less even with only 30 per cent of the profession being female. Professional advancement at the Bar has been even less equal: only 10 per cent of QCs are female.

Barristers' Chambers

Barristers work in sets of offices called chambers. Most chambers are run by barristers' clerks, who act as business managers, allocating work to the various barristers and negotiating their fees. Imagine the situation where a solicitor wishes to engage a particular barrister for a case on a certain date and that barrister is already booked to be in another court three days before that date. The clerk cannot be sure whether the first case will have ended in time for the barrister to be free to appear in the second case. The first case might be adjourned after a day or, through unexpected evidential arguments in the early stages in the trial, it might last for four days. If the barrister is detained, then his brief for the second case will have to be passed to another barrister in his chambers very close to the actual trial. This is known as a late brief. Who will be asked to take the brief, and at what point, is a matter for the clerk. The role of the barrister's clerk is thus a most influential one.

Since 2003, lay clients have been able to enjoy direct access to barristers; see <http://www. barcouncil.org.uk>. It is now possible for barristers to accept instructions from some licensed organisations (as opposed to the normal practice of being briefed by solicitors) and from ordinary people in some situations.

OTHER HELP IN THE COURTROOM

Anyone is at liberty to represent himself or herself in legal proceedings as a 'litigant in person'. A person may also be accompanied in court by a person who assists by way of note-taking, quiet prompting and the offering of advice, a right first recognised in a case in 1831. The name 'McKenzie friend' to describe such an assistant was coined after a case in 1970 involving a couple from Camberwell Grove in London and a complicated divorce petition. In this case, the Court of Appeal ruled that Ian Hanger, a young Australian barrister who was in court to assist Mr McKenzie *pro bono* (short for *pro bono publico*, Latin for 'the public good', i.e. without charge), should not have been silenced simply because he was not formally representing a litigant.[18] The McKenzie friend is not an absolute right – such an assistant can be sent away by a court if it takes the view that the help being offered to the litigant is confused, time-wasting, or otherwise harmful to the administration of justice. In one case a magistrates' court that refused to allow some respondents to be represented by an anti-poll tax organisation was held to be in the wrong when the decision was judicially reviewed. The magistrates had refused the intended McKenzie friend without any evidence that he was a time-waster or disrupter.[19] It was, however, later held by the Court of Appeal that in public proceedings a litigant in person should be allowed the assistance of a McKenzie friend unless the judge was satisfied that fairness and the interests of justice did not require the litigant to have such assistance. If the judge refused to hear the McKenzie friend it was preferable for the judge to explain why at the time of the refusal, but absence of an explanation would not automatically invalidate any subsequent hearing. The acceptability of an absence of an explanation would depend on the circumstances of the case.[20]

LEGAL CLAIMS AGAINST LAWYERS

Lawyers are, for the general public, the most central and prominent part of the law. They are, arguably, to the legal system what doctors are to the health system.

However, until relatively recently in legal history, barristers could not be sued by their clients for negligent performance in court or for work that was preparatory to court work.[21] A patient injured by the negligence of a surgeon in the operating theatre could sue for damages, but a litigant whose case was lost because of the negligence of his advocate was not able to. It all seemed very unfair. Even the most glaringly obvious courtroom negligence was protected against legal action by a special advocates' immunity. The claim that this protection was made up by lawyers (and judges who had been lawyers) for lawyers was difficult to refute. It was not until the year 2000 that this immunity was abolished, instigated by a major court case.

The major case consisted of three individual cases in which a claimant had raised a claim of negligence against a firm of solicitors. In each case, the firms relied on the immunity attaching to barristers and other advocates from claims of negligence. At first instance, all the claims were struck out. Then, on appeal, the Court of Appeal said that the claims could have proceeded. The solicitors appealed to the Lords and two key questions were raised: should the old immunity rule be maintained, and, in a criminal case, what was the proper scope of the principle against 'collateral attack'? A 'collateral attack' is when someone convicted in a criminal court tries to invalidate that conviction outside the criminal appeals process by suing his trial defence lawyer in a civil court. The purpose of such a 'collateral attack' is to win in the civil case, proving negligence against the criminal trial lawyer, and thus by implication showing that the conviction in the criminal case was unfair.

The House of Lords held (Lords Hope, Hutton and Hobhouse dissenting in part) that, in the light of modern conditions, it was now clear that it was no longer in the public interest in the administration of justice that advocates should have immunity from suit for negligence for acts concerned with the conduct of either civil or criminal litigation.

Lord Hoffmann said that over thirty years had passed since the House had last considered the rationale for the immunity of the advocate from suit. Public policy was not immutable and there had been great changes in the law of negligence, the functioning of the legal profession, the administration of justice and public perceptions. It was once again time to re-examine the whole matter. Interestingly, Lord Hoffmann chose to formulate his opinion in a creative mode to reflect public policy, rather than in the tradition of what can be seen as slavish obedience to the details of precedent:

> I hope that I will not be thought ungrateful if I do not encumber this speech with citations. The question of what the public interest now

requires depends upon the strength of the arguments rather than the weight of authority.[22]

The point of departure was that, in general, English law provided a remedy in damages for a person who had suffered injury as a result of professional negligence. It followed that any exception that denied such a remedy required a sound justification. The arguments relied on by the court in the earlier decision to retain lawyers' immunity from prosecution (*Rondel v Worsley*) were also considered, and, one by one, they were rejected.

The propriety of maintaining such immunity depended upon the balance between, on the one hand, the normal right of an individual to be compensated for a legal wrong done to him, and, on the other, the advantages that accrued to the public interest from such immunity. These advantages included a finality of litigation: if the loser of a case could sue his or her lawyer for having lost the case, then the same action would, in essence, be rerun in another expensive and time-consuming case. It would amount to a litigant saying, 'My case was strong but was lost only because of my weak lawyer.' Another public interest in preventing lawyers being sued was that vulnerability of lawyers to legal action would impair the courage of their advocacy – they would become too cautious and timid. However, the court held there was no longer sufficient public benefit to justify the maintenance of an advocate's immunity in civil proceedings. The Lords also ruled that the immunity should be abolished in relation to all proceedings, and not merely in relation to the conduct of civil proceedings.

On the matter of 'collateral attack' the Lords made these observations. Not all re-litigation of the same issue would be manifestly unfair to a party or bring the administration of justice into disrepute. Sometimes there were valid reasons for re-hearing a dispute. It was therefore unnecessary to try to stop any re-litigation by forbidding anyone from suing their lawyer. As they stated, it was 'burning down the house to roast the pig; using a broad-spectrum remedy without side effects could handle the problem equally well'.[23] The scope for re-examination of issues in criminal proceedings was much wider than in civil cases. Fresh evidence was more readily admitted. A conviction could be set aside as unsafe and unsatisfactory when the accused appeared to have been prejudiced by 'flagrantly incompetent advocacy'.[24] After conviction, the case could be referred to the Court of Appeal if the conviction was on indictment (i.e. from a Crown Court trial), or to the Criminal Cases Review Commission if the trial was summary (i.e. in the magistrates' court).

It followed that it would ordinarily be an abuse of process for a civil court to be asked to decide that a subsisting conviction was wrong. That applied to a conviction on a plea of guilty as well as after a trial. The resulting conflict of judgments was likely to bring the administration of justice into disrepute. The proper procedure was to appeal or, if the right of appeal had been exhausted, to apply to the Criminal Cases Review Commission. The word 'ordinarily' was used because there were bound to be exceptional cases in which the issue could be tried without a risk that the conflict of judgments would bring the administration of justice into disrepute.

Lord Steyn made this dramatic observation:

> public confidence in the legal system is not enhanced by the existence of the immunity. The appearance is created that the law singles out its own for protection no matter how flagrant the breach of the barrister. The world has changed since 1967. The practice of law has become more commercialised: barristers may now advertise. They may now enter into contracts for legal services with their professional clients. They are now obliged to carry insurance. On the other hand, today we live in a consumerist society in which people have a much greater awareness of their rights. If they have suffered a wrong as the result of the provision of negligent professional services, they expect to have the right to claim redress. It tends to erode confidence in the legal system if advocates, alone among professional men, are immune from liability for negligence.[25]

The case of *Moy v Pettmann Smith (a firm)* (2005), however, gives some comfort to advocates regarding advice provided to clients at the door of the court, in other words when, at the last moment before a case begins, an offer to settle the case is made by the other side and a lawyer has to advise his or her client under some pressure of time whether to accept it. The House of Lords decided that advice given by lawyers in such circumstances does not have to be absolutely perfect in order to avoid an action for negligence by a dissatisfied client.

THE PROLIFERATION OF LAWYERS

In an episode of *The Simpsons*, the amiable delinquent Bart expresses an ambition to become a lawyer. 'That's good, son,' says Lionel Hutz, Springfield's attorney-at-law. 'If there's one thing America needs now, it's more lawyers.' Then, after Mr Hutz cautions us to imagine what the world would be like without lawyers, the scene washes into dream imagery of a joyful community in which people of all ages and races dance in a circle to the song 'I'd Like to Teach the World to Sing (In Perfect Harmony)'.

In truth, however, the malice behind most lawyer-hate is a misdirected lay resentment of the laws that are being enforced, or the social order from which they spring. This was recognised by John Stuart Mill, who observed in 1869 that 'the laws of most countries are far worse than the people who execute them'.[26]

As the book has observed, the extent and influence of law has never been greater. The legislative output of Parliament is now running at over two thousand pages of new law a year.

However, although one might have argued that the 'no win, no fee' arrangements, new civil procedure rules and accident claim firms introduced in the 1990s would breed an infectious and baleful compensation culture, no such explosion of litigation has taken place. In fact, the number of legal cases has fallen. We are not obsessively suing one another into oblivion. According to *Judicial Statistics*, published by the Ministry of Justice, 153,624 writs and originating summonses were issued in 1995 in the Queen's Bench Division of the High Court. By 2002 the number had fallen to just 18,624. By 2011, the figure was 13,928. This is the court that deals with all substantial claims in personal injury, breach of contract, negligence actions and other civil matters.

The number of claims issued in the county courts (which deal with less substantial civil disputes in the law of contract, negligence and debt) has also fallen significantly in recent times. In 1998, the number of claims issued nationally was 2,245,324 but by 2011 the number of annual claims had fallen to 1,553,983. This can be contrasted with judicial review claims in the Administrative Court, which increased by 12 per cent from 2010 to 2011.

The general drop in cases going through court probably means that more cases are being settled out of court. There has not been any precipitous fall in client–solicitor consultations, nor has there been a fall in consultations at the Citizens' Advice Service, so people are evidently taking legal advice as before but then litigating many fewer cases all the way to the courts. That is generally a good thing, because rights are legally vindicated in a relatively efficient way. However, on 1 April 2013 the Legal Aid, Sentencing and Punishment of Offenders Act 2012 will come into force and drastically reduce the availability of public funding for civil cases. It remains to be seen whether this will have an impact on the number of claims going through the courts.

FURTHER READING

Brian Abel-Smith and Robert Stevens, *Lawyers and the Courts*, London: Heinemann, 1967.

J.A. Brundage, *The Medieval Origins of the Legal Profession: Canonists, Civilians, and Courts*, Chicago: Chicago University Press, 2008.

Charles Hamson, *The Law: Its Study and Comparison, An Inaugural Lecture*, Cambridge: Cambridge University Press, 1955.

David Pannick, *I Have to Move My Car: Tales of Unpersuasive Advocates and Injudicious Judges*, Oxford: Hart, 2008.

Richard Susskind, *The End of Lawyers?: Rethinking the Nature of Legal Services*, Oxford: Oxford University Press, 2008.

Cases and the Courts

4

The UK legal system generates a good deal of judicial law-making. Such creativity, though, has not always been recognised. In 1892, Lord Esher said in *Willis v Baddeley* that there was 'no such thing as judge-made law, for the judges do not make the law'.[1]

Today, most observers are more likely to accept the statement of Lord Simon of Glaisdale, who said in *Lynch v Director of Public Prosecutions for Northern Ireland* (1975), 'I am all for recognising frankly that judges do make law.'[2] Lord Scarman was just as explicit when he noted in a House of Lords case, *Duport Steel v Sirs* (1980), that 'In our society, the judges have in some aspects of their work a discretionary power to do justice so wide that they may be regarded as lawmakers.'[3]

Today, to reflect a healthily expanding public concern with 'justice through the law', a great deal of public, social, medical, political, sporting and educational life has become justiciable. Our law, though, must be allowed to develop in a socially organic way where possible, so that our senior judges can avoid the ossification of established rules.

Desirably, therefore, in cases that go to the Supreme Court (and that went to the House of Lords before October 2009) it is always an open question whether the court will retain established precepts or whether it will act boldly to alter the law itself. For change, compelling arguments must be advanced by counsel.

CASES THAT CHANGED THE LAW

In some legal systems, like many of those in continental Europe, the law is codified. It is set out in encyclopaedic form in many volumes, much of it being designed as a single system of rules. The law in England and Wales evolved incrementally, developing from case to case. Many hundreds of cases have made major changes in the law. The following cases are good illustrations of this practice.

The Case of Prohibitions (*Prohibitions Del Roy*) (1607)

During the early seventeenth century, there had been a growing unease between King James VI of Scotland (who was also James I of England) and the courts on the issue of who was the final determiner of the law. Things came to a head when a legal dispute that had been judged personally by the king was overruled by the ordinary courts. In his judgment, Sir Edward Coke, Chief Justice of the Common Pleas, ruled that disputes were to be tried by legal experts according to law, not the best efforts of an untrained monarch. The law was the 'golden metwand' (measuring rod) against which to judge the claims of citizens.

Bushel's Case (1670)

This case established the freedom of the jury to return a verdict that is not the one the judge or the authorities want. A jury had acquitted the Quakers William Penn and William Mead, who had been improperly indicted for unlawful assembly in Gracechurch Street near Tower Bridge in London. Penn was a member of Lincoln's Inn, and later founded Pennsylvania. The jury was told by the judge, 'You shall not be dismissed till we have a verdict that the court will accept.' The jurors were locked up without food or drink and fined for their defiance, but refused to be browbeaten by the bench. One juror, Edward Bushel, brought this related action that established the autonomy of the jury.

Milroy v Lord (1862)

A trust is an arrangement in which a person (a settlor) transfers property to trustees to hold for the benefit of one or more people (beneficiaries) who are entitled to enforce the trust in the courts. Millions of people are affected by trusts, and billions of pounds are bound up in them. In this case, Thomas Medley purported to assign shares in a Louisiana bank to Samuel Lord upon trust for the benefit of Eleanor Rainey Dudgeon (who later became Mrs Milroy), but the transfer was not properly made so the trust was held to be invalid. Lord Justice Turner set out ground rules for the constitution of a trust and ruled that a voluntary settlement could be made in either of two ways: by proper transfer of the property to trustees, or by the settlor declaring himself a trustee of the property. He said, '[I]f the settlement is intended to be effectuated by one of the modes to which I have referred, the Court will not give effect to it by applying another of those modes.'

Salomon v Salomon (1897)

Once a company has been incorporated it forms a separate legal entity from the individuals who compose it. In this leading case, Mr Salomon, a boot manufacturer, set up a company in which he held nearly all the shares and in which he was managing director. The company borrowed money from him in his private capacity and issued debentures to him. He was therefore entitled to first charge on the company's assets. The company became insolvent and went into liquidation. Mr Salomon sought to be treated as a 'secured' creditor and to have his claim satisfied before that of other creditors, and the House of Lords upheld his claim.

Carlill v Carbolic Smoke Ball Company (1893)

During a flu epidemic, Mrs Louisa Elizabeth Carlill, a writer and wife of a lawyer, bought one of the defendant's products, the 'Carbolic Smoke Ball'. The company advertised in a newspaper, the *Pall Mall Gazette*, praising the Smoke Ball and promising to pay £100 to anyone who used the ball but caught the flu. Mrs Carlill used the ball and got the flu, and she won her lawsuit for various reasons. The case established many modern contract principles, including that offers must be sufficiently clear to allow the courts to enforce agreements that follow from them, and that an offer may be made to the world at large. Mrs Carlill died 50 years later, aged 96, from old age and, her records show, from influenza.

Donoghue v Stevenson (1932)

On 26 August 1928, Mrs May Donoghue sat in the Wellmeadow Café in Paisley and drank ginger beer bought for her by her friend. The bottle contained the decomposed remains of a snail which were not, and could not be, detected until the greater part of the contents of the bottle had been consumed. Mrs Donoghue suffered from shock and severe gastroenteritis. In his judgment, Lord Atkin stated that 'You must take reasonable care to avoid acts or omissions which you can reasonably foresee would be likely to injure your neighbour.' The case established that a manufacturer owes a duty of care to the ultimate user of his product, but the underlying reasoning of the decision supported the development of other types of negligence claim. Seventy years on, a mountain of cases has been brought by citizens under this principle. They have been brought against accountants, shops, drivers, nurses, surveyors, engineers, sports referees, teachers, the police, media companies, and even lawyers.

Woolmington v Director of Public Prosecutions (1935)

This was the case in which Viscount Sankey, the Lord Chancellor, proclaimed that 'Throughout the web of English Criminal Law one golden thread is always to be seen, that is, the duty of the prosecution to prove the prisoner's guilt.' It was held that if the jury are left in any reasonable doubt of the accused's guilt, he or she is entitled to be acquitted. Reginald Woolmington, a farm labourer from Castleton near Sherborne, had been convicted at Bristol Assizes of killing his wife Violet by shooting her through the heart. He admitted firing the gun that killed her, but said it went off accidentally when he was showing her how he would commit suicide if she did not return to live with him. His conviction was quashed on appeal because the trial judge had given to the jury an explanation of the law which the appeal court ruled was incorrect. The trial judge had said that for a murder conviction it was necessary for the jury to be sure that the accused had intended to kill his victim. So far, so good. But the judge then said that the jury could presume the accused had an intention (the actual word the judge used was 'malice', which at that time connoted 'intention') from the circumstances of the drama, unless they thought he had managed to show that he did not have such an intention. The appeal court said that in criminal cases where it is necessary for the prosecution to prove intention, they must always do just that. Intention can never be presumed, subject to being disproved by the person accused. Hence the phrase that everyone is 'innocent unless proven guilty'.

Central London Property Trust v High Trees Ltd (1947)

The landlord of a block of flats on Nightingale Lane, near Clapham South tube station in London, agreed to reduce the £2,500 p.a. rent by half during the war. After the war the landlord company sought to go back on its promise and recover back payments of the sums it had agreed to forgo. It lost. This case shows that novel principles of equity can still be formulated in modern times. It holds that a person who has made a promise by which he intentionally modifies his contractual rights against another person will not be allowed to resile from such a promise. The case swings on Mr Justice Denning's doctrine of 'promissory estoppel'. For the promise to be upheld, it must have been acted upon by the person to whom it was made.

Associated Provincial Picture Houses Ltd v Wednesbury Corporation (1948)

This case is a foundational precedent for modern cases of judicial review. It concerned a local authority that had, under the Sunday Entertainments Act 1932, granted a licence to the claimants so that they could open their cinema on Sundays. The Act allowed for a licence to be granted with 'such conditions as the authority thinks fit'. The authority imposed the condition that children under 15 were not to be allowed into cinemas on Sundays. The company argued that the provision was 'unreasonable' and therefore *ultra vires*, that is, 'beyond the powers' of the corporation. It argued that the court should be the arbiter of whether a condition was reasonable. The Court of Appeal dismissed the appeal, and the reasoning of Lord Greene, the Master of the Rolls, soon crystallised into a hallowed and frequently cited legal proposition. He ruled that where Parliament had entrusted discretionary powers to another body, such as a local authority, the courts could declare that some decisions were 'unreasonable', and thus beyond what the authority was authorised to do. The courts could not simply substitute their own opinion for that of the other body. To be unreasonable, the decision would have to be one where an authority had 'taken into account matters which it ought not to take into account, or, conversely, has refused to take into account or neglected to take into account matters which it ought to take into account'. Even if the decision-making process passes that test, the decision could still be challenged in the courts if it was one which 'no reasonable body could have come to'. In an earlier case, in 1926, a judge cited the instance of a red-haired teacher who had been dismissed because of the colour of her hair, as an example of a patently unreasonable decision. Lord Greene, in this 1948 case, adopted that example, saying, 'That is unreasonable in one sense. In another sense it is taking into consideration extraneous matters. It is so unreasonable that it might almost be described as being done in bad faith; and, in fact, all these things run into one another.' These principles have since become the touchstone of the courts when deciding judicial review cases, and the legal phrase 'Wednesbury unreasonable' is shorthand for a decision of a public body or official that violates the criterion established in this case.

Van Duyn v Home Office (1974)

Yvonne van Duyn, a Dutch woman, wanted to enter the UK to take up employment with the Church of Scientology. She was refused entry, and challenged the decision under a European directive guaranteeing the freedom of movement for workers. This right is subject to exceptions based on public policy. Under the European Communities Act 1972, the UK had entered the European Community. The High Court made a preliminary reference to the European Court of Justice (ECJ). The question arose whether the rights conferred under the Article of the EEC Treaty were directly applicable and enforceable by the individual in the courts of a member state. The ECJ ruled that the rights were enforceable by individuals in the courts of the member states. Directives were held to impose on member states a precise obligation that does not require the adoption of any further measure or national law.

HL v United Kingdom (2004)

This case, commonly referred to as the 'Bournewood' case, resulted in the UK government providing greater safeguards for people who do not have mental capacity and who are deprived of their liberty in care homes. Mr HL was a man with severe autism and challenging behaviour who lacked the mental capacity to decide where he should live. Mr HL attended a day centre until one day, when his behaviour became too challenging for the carers to deal with, he was admitted to a psychiatric hospital. While in the hospital Mr HL had no contact with his family and the doctors intended for him to stay in the hospital indefinitely. Because Mr HL lacked capacity to decide where to live, he was neither able to consent nor object to his placement in the hospital, and English law had no mechanism for allowing him to access a court in order to challenge the placement. Mr HL's lawyers brought a challenge against the placement on the basis that it infringed his right to liberty under Article 5 of the European Convention on Human Rights. They argued that in order for the placement to be lawful, Mr HL had to be able to access a court in order to challenge it before a judge. The case went all the way to the European Court of Human Rights in Strasbourg, where the judges held that Mr HL's Article 5 rights had been breached. As a result, the UK government enacted legislation to enable people without capacity to access the courts to challenge deprivations of liberty in care homes, in the form of the Mental Capacity Act 2007.

THE COMMON LAW SYSTEM

The English legal system is a 'common law' legal system. Before medieval times the law in what we now call Great Britain was largely regional. Different regional kingdoms had different laws. Over time, the same system of law was applied by judges across the single kingdom established after 1066 and so became common to all parts of the country. This was known as 'the common law'.

This means that many of our primary legal principles have been made and developed by judges from case to case in what is called a system of precedent. The common law (or judge-made law) is at least as important to us as the law made by the other main source of law: Parliament. For instance, there is no Act of Parliament telling us that murder is a crime. Murder is a common law crime which has been refined over the centuries by judges. The definition of murder – adapted from a version first crystallised in a legal treatise by Sir Edward Coke in 1641 – is a crime committed when 'A person of sound mind and discretion kills any reasonable creature in being and under the Queen's peace with intent to kill or causes grievous bodily harm.'[4] This rather archaic formula is given modern interpretation in the courts. All the words and phrases in it have been heatedly contested by lawyers at one time or another, and some of what it means is not clear at first sight. The phrase 'any reasonable creature in being', for example, does not mean that it is not murder if you assassinate your unreasonable neighbour. It refers to what were identified in the Court of Appeal as 'the most extreme cases' of physically abnormal birth, certainly more abnormal than conjoined twins. In the year 2000, it was held in *Re A (children) (conjoined twins: surgical separation)* that each twin was certainly a 'reasonable creature in being'.[5]

How the Common Law Developed

Prior to the Norman Conquest of England in 1066, there was no unified, national legal system. Before then, the English legal system involved a mass of oral customary rules, which varied according to region. The law of the Jutes in the south of England, for example, was different from that of the Mercians in the middle of the country. Each county had its own local court dispensing its own justice in accordance with local customs that varied from community to community, and which were enforced in an arbitrary fashion. For example, courts generally consisted of informal public assemblies that weighed conflicting claims in a case and, if unable to reach a decision, might require an accused to test guilt or innocence by carrying a red-hot iron or snatching a stone from a cauldron of boiling water or some other 'test' of veracity. If the defendant's wound healed within a prescribed period, he was set free as innocent. If not, execution usually followed.

Unlike continental civil law, the English system does not originate from any particular set of texts but from what has been called 'tradition expressed in action'. This means that, from early times, rules fashioned from amalgams of what was proper in a situation, and anything that could be gleaned from ancient practice, were applied and then handed over by each generation to the next. The word 'tradition' comes from the Latin verb *tradere*, which means 'to hand over', or 'to give across'. The common law began as customary law used in the king's court to settle disputes and conflicts which affected the monarch directly. To begin with, these only included the graver crimes, which became 'Pleas of the Crown'. After the Norman invasion in 1066, there were still many different types of court apart from the royal court: the stannary (tin mining) courts of Devon and Cornwall; the courts of the royal hunting forests; and principally, in potential rivalry with the royal court, the feudal and manorial courts. It was during Henry II's reign (1154–89) that the clerics in his court began specialising in legal business and acting in a judicial capacity.

In 1154, Henry II institutionalised common law by creating a unified court system 'common' to the country through incorporating and elevating local custom to the national level, ending local control, eliminating arbitrary remedies, and reinstating a jury system of citizens sworn on oath to investigate criminal accusations and civil claims. Judges of the realm went on regular journeys throughout the country bringing the king's justice to every citizen. Their aim was that there should be a common system of law throughout the land. These travelling judges, who had no local roots, became a corpus with national jurisdiction. They were thus much less susceptible to the corruption that had spoilt a similar attempt earlier in the twelfth century in which the royal judges had actually been based in the local communities. It was under Henry II that judges were for the first time sent on 'circuits', hearing pleas in the major places they visited and taking over the work of the local courts. In time, the decisions of the judges were written down. As the decisions of these courts came to be recorded and published, so the practice developed where past decisions would be cited in argument before the courts and would be regarded as being of persuasive authority.

These practices developed into the common law of England and Wales, the law which was available throughout the realm. In the words of the legal writer A.W.B. Simpson, 'It was common as a prostitute is common: available to all.'[6] On this point, it is perhaps the most convincing of the reasons why Henry II should be regarded as the 'father of the common law' – that he was largely responsible for the regional and itinerant royal justice through which (by sending his judges up and down the country) the law truly became common.

In the expansion of the king's legal powers, an important role was played by the clerics (clergymen). They had a history of legal involvement because much of the earliest law was church law. From the twelfth century, they developed a range of claim forms, called 'writs', and established procedures that enhanced their own importance as experts, so providing themselves with a generous income. Another important development was the expansion of the 'king's peace'. This was the monarch's, as opposed to a local lord's, right to deal with any local disorder or crime.

In this way, the royal courts obtained a lot of business and thereby power. Assisting in that process was the interpretation given to the Statute of Gloucester (1278) by the royal judges. By a deft interpretation of a rule, the course of legal history was changed substantially. The statute provided that no cases involving an amount of less than 40 shillings should be brought before the royal courts, but should go instead before local tribunals. The judges interpreted this to mean that no personal actions to recover a sum greater than 40 shillings could be commenced in the local courts, thus reserving all important legislation for themselves. It is relevant here that the judges were anxious to attract litigants because their fees varied with the amount of business done.

As mentioned earlier, the basis of the common law is precedent. The doctrine of binding precedent is known as the doctrine of *stare decisis*, which is Latin for 'to let the decision stand'. In other words, once a principle is decided it should be followed in future cases. Within the hierarchical structure of the English courts, a decision of a higher court will be binding on a lower court. In general terms, this means that when judges try cases, they will be informed by lawyers of similar situations that have come before a court previously, and the outcomes of those cases. If the precedent was set by a court of equal or higher status to the court deciding the new case, then the judge in the present case should follow the rule of law established in the earlier case. If the precedent is from a lower court in the hierarchy, the judge in the new case might not follow that rule of law but will certainly consider it.

There are three elements to the system of precedent: a hierarchy of courts, binding decisions, and a system of reliable law reporting. The remainder of this chapter looks at how the hierarchy of the courts works. The next chapter will examine which parts of a case decision bind future courts to decide the same way, and how these decisions are reported.

THE HIERARCHY OF THE COURTS

Broadly speaking, the court hierarchy reflects two things. First, different sorts of courts are needed for different sorts of cases: relatively trivial disputes or minor prosecutions at one end of the spectrum and major cases at the other. A dispute over an allegedly defective dishwasher is a different matter from an action on behalf of 80,000 creditors of a failed private bank in an action against the Bank of England. Second, judges and courts can be wrong, so a second opinion (and sometimes a third) is occasionally needed as a failsafe protection. The hierarchy allows for cases to be taken to an appeal, and sometimes more than one appeal, up the levels of jurisdiction.

There are other interpretations of the hierarchy. Lord Asquith (1890–1954), who sat as a judge at all levels of the legal system, once said, 'A trial judge should be quick, courteous and wrong. That is not to say that the Court of Appeal should be slow, rude and right, for that would be usurping the function of the House of Lords.'[7]

A court hierarchy establishes which decisions are binding on which courts. In general, the higher up a court is in the hierarchy, the more authoritative its decisions. Authoritative means having a status that requires decisions to be followed in future by courts lower down in the hierarchy.

Consider this example. There used to be an assumption that calling children as witnesses in family law cases should only be done 'in an exceptional case'. The rule was changed by the Supreme Court in a case *Re W (Children)* in 2010. The court ruled that there should be no such assumption and that a family court should use its discretion, guided by a set of principles, on a case-by-case basis. It can in several situations be very important to call children as witnesses. The hierarchy of the courts means that this decision cannot be ignored or contradicted by any other court in the UK as the Supreme Court is the highest court.

Similarly, before it was ended as the highest court in 2009, if the House of Lords ruled, as it did in *R v R* (1991), that non-consensual sex between a man and woman is rape even if they are married to each other, then the Court of Appeal, which is lower in the hierarchy, cannot subsequently deny that such is the law. However, if the High Court gives various views about a principle in different cases, the Court of Appeal will need to decide which ruling really represents the law. In the 1970s, it was not clear whether a successful claimant in a car accident case should have his or her compensation reduced for 'contributory negligence' if their injuries would not have occurred, or would not have been so bad, had they worn seat belts. Reviewing the decisions in the Court of Appeal, Lord Denning, Master of the Rolls, said, 'Half the judges think that, if a person does not wear a seat belt, he is guilty of contributory negligence and his damages ought to be reduced. The other half thinks that it is not contributory negligence and they ought not to be reduced.'[8] Denning thought the damages should be reduced, and, with the agreement of his two fellow judges in the case, cut the injured driver's £450 damages by £100.

It can be helpful to examine a diagram of the court structure for England and Wales. There are about 600 magistrates' courts in England and Wales and 29,000 magistrates dealing with a great many cases every day. The cases are numerous (over one million a year) and do not usually involve any dispute over what the relevant law means, so these cases do not have to be followed by other magistrates' courts in the system of precedent. By contrast, the Supreme Court deals with only about 60 cases a year and its decisions bind all other courts.

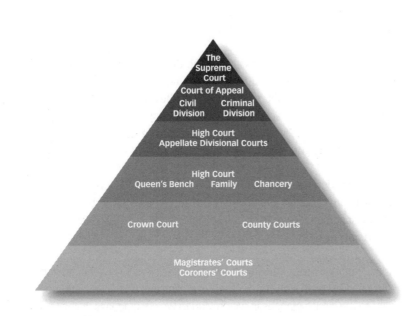

Figure 4.1 The court structure

The Supreme Court of the United Kingdom

Supreme Court decisions are binding on all other courts in the legal system, except on the Supreme Court itself.

Until 1966, the House of Lords used to be bound by its own previous decisions. Before 1966, if the House of Lords decided on something – say, the method that should be used to compensate a company if it was taken over by a public body (as the Lords did in 1894) – then such a ruling was binding in other cases unless Parliament stepped in to change the law The rationale for that practice was that decisions of the highest court in the land should be final so that there would be certainty in the law and finality in litigation. However, the current practice enables the highest court to adapt English law to meet changing social conditions and enables the Lords to pay attention to the decisions of superior courts in the Commonwealth. In 1966, Lord Gardiner, the Lord Chancellor, said when announcing the current practice:

> Their lordships regard the use of precedent as an indispensable foundation upon which to decide what is the law and its application to individual cases. It provides at least some degree of certainty upon which individuals can rely in the conduct of their affairs, as well as a basis for orderly development of legal rules.

> . . . Their lordships nevertheless recognise that too rigid adherence to precedent may lead to injustice in a particular case and also unduly restrict the proper development of the law. They propose therefore to modify their present practice and, while treating former decisions of this House as normally binding, to depart from a previous decision when it appears right to do so.

> In this connexion they will bear in mind the danger of disturbing retrospectively the basis on which contracts, settlements of property and fiscal arrangements have been entered into and also the especial need for certainty as to the criminal law.[9]

The possibility of the Lords changing its previous decisions was a recognition that law whether expressed in statutes or cases, is a living and changing institution that must adapt to the circumstances in which, and to which, it applies, if it is to retain practical relevance. The House of Lords 1966 Practice Statement on departure from its own previous decisions applies equally to the Supreme Court.[10]

The Court of Appeal

The Court of Appeal is always bound by previous decisions of the Supreme Court, and by House of Lords decisions delivered before October 2009 when the Supreme Court was established. The Court of Appeal is also generally bound by its own previous decisions. There are, however, three exceptions to this general rule. In 1944, Lord Greene, Master of the Rolls, listed these exceptions in *Young v Bristol Aeroplane Co Ltd*.

First, the Court of Appeal can go against one of its earlier decisions (indeed, logically, it must) if there is a conflict between two previous decisions of the Court of Appeal. In this situation the latest court (the third one in succession) must decide which of the two earlier case decisions to follow and which to overrule. How can there be two earlier but contradictory Court of Appeal decisions that apparently say different things about the same law? Why did the second decision not follow the first? The answer is that it can happen if a judge is unaware of a decision made in a previous similar case. The Court dealing with the third case is therefore able to choose the better of the earlier two.

Second, the Court of Appeal can go against its own previous decision if the earlier one has since been overruled, either expressly or by implication, by the House of Lords. An express overruling would obviously occur if the House of Lords has actually considered the earlier Court of Appeal precedent and has openly overruled it, but it is equally possible that a precedent from the Court of Appeal could be implicitly overruled without the actual case being cited and considered. In that situation, the Court of Appeal, in line with the normal rules of precedent, is required to follow the decision of the House of Lords. For example, in 1964, a House of Lords decision on a misstatement made by a bank about one of its customers invalidated various earlier Court of Appeal decisions. Not all of these were explicitly overruled. One such 'survivor', though, from 1939, was rightly brushed aside by the High Court when it came up for consideration in 1979 in a case about an allegedly negligent solicitor.[11]

The previous decision was given *per incuriam* (Latin for 'through an error'); in other words, that previous decision was taken in ignorance of some authority, either statutory or case law, which would have led to a different conclusion. In this situation, the later court can ignore the previous decision in question. The missing authority must be an important one that would have led to a different conclusion; the mere possibility is not enough. There are so many case authorities that it is simply not possible to cite all of them in any given case. However, it is the absence of any consideration of the essential authorities that renders a decision *per incuriam*.

The instances of decisions being ignored on the basis of a ruling of *per incuriam* are very rare. For example, in *R v Lambeth London Borough Council, ex parte W*, the issue was whether social services had a duty to provide assistance to a family that was intentionally homeless or not entitled to help from the local housing authority. The Court of Appeal said social services had a power to help but not a duty. In making this ruling, the Court said that an apparent earlier authority from the Court of Appeal in 2001 need not be followed because it had been made *per incuriam* – the earlier court had not had its attention drawn to a piece of relevant and applicable legislation, section 122 of the Immigration and Asylum Act 1999. This decision was later approved by the House of Lords.[12]

The European Communities Act 1972 gives the Court of Appeal grounds for ignoring any of its previous decisions that conflict with subsequent decisions of the European Court of Justice. This effectively fits the European Court of Justice into the traditional hierarchical structure of precedence as the court of last resort in relation to Community law matters.

Section 2 of the Human Rights Act 1998 requires all courts and tribunals to take into account any judgment, decision, declaration or advisory opinion of the European Court of Human Rights. The Human Rights Act 1998 renders decisions of the European Court of Human Rights directly binding on the UK. When there is a conflict between the European Court of Human Rights and the Supreme Court, the Supreme Court decision binds the lower courts in the UK, but Parliament is expected to change the law. This is what happened with the now infamous prisoner voting case, where the European Court of Human Rights held that the blanket ban on prisoners being able to vote in the UK was a violation of the European Convention on Human Rights. However, Parliament does not want to change the law to bring the UK into line with the European Court's decision. As a result, for the time being the domestic courts must apply the law as it stands, regardless of the position taken by the Human Rights Court..

Divisional Courts

The legal terminology for these courts is not very straightforward. The High Court is divided into three 'Divisions', each one dealing with different sorts of cases: the Family Division (dealing with cases involving divorce, children, and so forth), the

Chancery Division (dealing with property, trusts and finance cases), and the Queen's Bench Division (dealing with cases involving things such as contracts and negligence cases).

Each of these divisions, however, also has a capacity to act as a court to hear appeals from lower courts, and when the judges sit in that capacity the court is called a 'Divisional Court of the High Court'. The Divisional Courts hear appeals from courts and tribunals below them in the hierarchy. They are bound by the doctrine of *stare decisis* in the normal way and must follow decisions made by the House of Lords and the Court of Appeal. In turn, their decisions bind the courts below them in the hierarchy, including the ordinary High Court cases. A Divisional Court is also normally bound by its own previous decisions, although in civil cases it may make use of the exceptions open to the Court of Appeal (e.g. in *Young v Bristol Aeroplane Co Ltd* (1944)) and, in criminal appeal cases, the Queen's Bench Divisional Court may refuse to follow its own earlier decisions if it feels the earlier decision was made wrongly.

The High Court

The High Court is bound by the decisions of superior courts. Decisions by individual High Court judges are binding on courts inferior in the hierarchy, but such decisions are not binding on other High Court judges, although they are of strong persuasive authority and tend to be followed in practice. It is possible, however, for High Court judges to disagree and for them to reach different conclusions in a particular area of the law. But how does a later High Court judge select which precedent to follow? It is usually accepted, although it is not a rule of law, that if a judge has actually considered a previous decision and has given a reason for not following it, then this later judgment is the one that other High Court judges should follow.

Conflicting decisions at the level of the High Court can, of course, be authoritatively decided by reference upwards to the Court of Appeal and then, if necessary, to the House of Lords, but when the cost of such appeals is borne in mind, it is apparent why, even on economic grounds alone, it is important for High Court judges not to treat their discretion as licence to destabilise the law in a given area. In relation to conflicting judgments at the level of the Court of Appeal, the High Court judge is required to follow the later decision. Additionally, there are some specialist courts that exist as part of the High Court and follow the same rules of precedent as those by which it operates. Those specialist courts are as follows:

The Technology and Construction Court

The UK's technological activity is extensive and worth hundreds of millions of pounds each year. The same is true of the construction industry, which employs 2.2 million people and provides one-tenth of the country's gross domestic product (i.e. the worth of all the country's work). It is a social activity worth £7 billion per year. It is perhaps not surprising that these areas deserve a specialist court to deal with all the legal disputes they generate. Known until 1998 as the Official Referees' Court, the Technology and Construction Court is one of the specialist courts of the Queen's Bench Division. It is the specialist court of the construction industry, with civil engineering disputes forming a significant part of its work. It is also the specialist court of the High Court, dealing with complicated and technical civil disputes that are not within the province of any other tribunal.

The Administrative Court

The main work of this court is the procedure of judicial review – the procedure by which the courts check that decisions made by public bodies and officials are made according to the proper processes and mindful only of appropriate considerations. This is a wide and still growing field. Examples of the types of decisions that may fall within the range of judicial review include decisions of local authorities in the exercise of their duties to provide various welfare benefits, and special education for children in need of such education; some decisions of the immigration authorities; applications for *habeas corpus* (Latin for 'you [must] have [i.e. produce] the body', meaning that an imprisoning authority has to bring the person to court and justify the detention); and applications for an order preventing a vexatious litigant from instituting or continuing proceedings without the leave of a judge.

The Patents Court

This court forms part of the Chancery Division of the Supreme Court. It deals with disputes about rights to exploit inventions.

The Companies Court

This is the collective name given to judges of the Chancery Division of the High Court who deal with matters arising from the Companies Acts, such as disputes over the formation and winding up of limited liability companies. Winding-up, also known as liquidation, is the formal process by which a company is dissolved. A liquidator assumes control of a company from its directors, collects the assets, pays debts, and distributes any surplus to members according to their rights.

The Court of Protection

The Court of Protection is a specialist court established by the Mental Capacity Act 2005. It is a supreme court of record with the same rights, privileges and authority as the High Court. The Court of Protection makes decisions, and appoints others to make decisions (called deputies) on behalf of people who lack mental capacity under the Mental Capacity Act 2005. These decisions relate to incapacitous people's financial affairs, property, health and welfare. The Court sits at the Royal Courts of Justice in London as well as in a number of regional courts, including Newcastle, Bristol, Manchester and Cardiff. The Court is served by five High Court judges, 33 district judges and 40 circuit judges.

Below the High Court in the court hierarchy are the Crown Court, county courts and magistrates' courts. None of these courts can create binding precedent. Their decisions can never amount to more than persuasive authority.

The Crown Courts

These courts try serious criminal cases, as well as hearing appeals from the magistrates' courts. Officially there is just one Crown Court, which sits in over 90 permanent centres throughout England and Wales. Each centre is designated as first, second, or third tier reflecting the seriousness of the offences tried. County and district boundaries have no statutory significance in determining where a case should be heard. Most Crown Court cases are heard at the centre most convenient to the magistrates' court that committed the case for trial.

The County Courts

These courts primarily deal with civil law. Despite their name, the county courts do not fit within county boundaries in England and Wales; in fact, the 230 county courts are scattered around the towns and cities that require their services.

Disputes arising from certain provisions under the Law of Property Act 1925, where the capital value or the interest in land does not exceed £30,000, together with personal injury claims for less than £50,000, and bankruptcy matters, are heard by the District Judge at the county court. Circuit Judges hear more complex cases, including family cases. The county courts must follow precedent but do not create it.

The Magistrates' Courts

These courts deal with about 96 per cent of criminal cases. The case may be tried either by at least two – but usually three – lay magistrates, or by a District Judge who sits alone. The magistrates' courts must follow precedent but do not create it.

The Coroners' Courts

The coroners' courts are one of the most ancient parts of the English legal system, dating back to at least 1194. They are not, in modern function, part of the criminal courts, although for historical reasons they have an association with that branch of the justice system. They do not create precedent but are bound by the decisions of the High Court, and those above it.

Coroners were originally appointed as *custos placitorum coronae*, 'keepers of the pleas of the Crown'. They had responsibility for criminal cases in which the Crown had an interest, particularly a financial interest. As the role of coroner developed, however, particularly through the pioneering work of the nineteenth-century coroner Dr Thomas Wakley, the coroner became, in Wakley's phrase, 'the people's judge'. The coroner is the ultimate public safeguard in an area of unmatched importance: the official documentation of how people die. It was Wakley who originally campaigned for all suspicious deaths, deaths in police custody or prison, and deaths attributable to neglect, to be brought within the jurisdiction of the coroner. He was an energetic reformer who was also an MP and founder of the medical journal The Lancet.

Today there are 157 coroners' courts, of which 21 sit full-time. Coroners are usually lawyers, although about 25 per cent are medical doctors with a legal qualification. The main jurisdiction of the coroner concerns unnatural and violent deaths. Finds of treasure, known as treasure trove, are also occasionally dealt with in these courts; however, the Treasure Act 1996, which came into effect in 1997, introduced new rules relating to the reporting of finds and how they should be dealt with.

Under the Coroners and Justice Act 2009, the coronial system was reorganised. The Act establishes a Chief Coroner to lead the coroners service, with powers to intervene in cases in specified circumstances, including presiding over an appeals process designed specifically for the coroner system. The Act establishes a senior coroner for each coroner area (previously known as coroner districts) with the possibility of appointing area coroners and assistant coroners to assist the senior coroner for the area (in place of the existing deputy coroners and assistant deputy coroners). A senior coroner who is made aware that the body of a deceased person is within that coroner's area must as soon as practicable conduct 'an investigation' into the person's death if there is evidence that –

(a)   the deceased died a violent or unnatural death,
(b)   the cause of death is unknown, or
(c)   the deceased died while in custody or otherwise in state detention.

The general rule is that an inquest must be held without a jury. There are, though, some exceptions. A jury must be summoned where the deceased died while in custody or otherwise in state detention, and the death was violent or unnatural, or of unknown cause; where the death was as a result of an act or omission of a police officer or member of a service police force in the purported execution of their duties; or where the death was caused by an accident, poisoning or disease which must be reported to a government department or inspector. This includes certain deaths at work. Although a jury is not required in any other case, the coroner will be able to summon one in any case where he or she believes there is sufficient reason for doing so. Coroners sit with juries of between seven and 11 people.

The classifying of types of death, of which there are about 500,000 each year in England and Wales, is clearly of critical importance, not just to the state, politicians and policy-makers, but also to the sort of campaign groups that exist in a constitutional democracy to monitor suicides, drug-related deaths, deaths in police custody and prison, accidental deaths, deaths in hospitals, and deaths through industrial diseases. About 45 per cent of deaths a year are reported to coroners as unnatural, violent, reportable from certain industries, or from an unknown cause.

Deaths must be reported to a coroner if there is evidence that they occurred in an unnatural or violent way. The coroner will order a post-mortem and this may reveal a natural cause of death, which can be duly registered. If not, or in certain other circumstances, for example if the death occurred in prison or police custody or if the cause is unknown, there will be an inquest. In 2011, there were 500,000 registered deaths in England and Wales. The number of these reported to coroners was 222,371, resulting in 93,954 post-mortem examinations and 30,981 inquests.[13]

Having a reliable system that charts who is dying, and in what circumstances, is of considerable social value. It is important for us to know, for example, that there were 3,471 suicides in England and Wales in 2011, as this should inform public policy related to the health service, community services, custodial policy and the emergency services.

The European Court of Human Rights

In one respect this court could be placed at the top of the court structure, because although its judgments cannot directly change UK law, they can declare UK law (as decided by any UK court or even Parliament) to be incompliant with the European Convention on Human Rights (ECHR) and thus in need of adjustment. For an example, see the prisoner voting case of *John Hirst v United Kingdom* (2005) in Chapter 7.

The European Court of Human Rights (ECtHR) does not arise from the European Union. The court is based in Strasbourg. It was established as a result of the European Convention on Human Rights (ECHR), created in 1950. This set out a catalogue of civil and political rights and freedoms. It allows people to lodge complaints against states that have signed up to the ECHR, for alleged violations of those rights. Although founded in 1950, the court did not actually come into existence until 1959.

To start with, the number of cases coming forward was relatively few. But from 1980 they started to grow steadily. By 2001, the Court was receiving nearly 14,000 applications a year from people who felt they had a grievance against a signatory state. The Court is currently made up of 41 judges, one for every state signed up to the Convention. They are elected by the Parliamentary Assembly of the Council of Europe and serve for six years. Judges sit on the Court as individuals and do not represent their country. All the signatory nations, with the exception of Ireland and Norway, have incorporated the Convention into their own law. This means that domestic courts take full account of its provisions when considering a grievance. Only when domestic remedies are exhausted can an individual look to Strasbourg for help.

It is commonly but wrongly believed that the Convention and its institutions have been imposed upon a reluctant UK. However, the UK was one of the architects of the human rights agenda that grew out of the devastation of the Second World War. Indeed, the UK was one of the first members of the Council of Europe to ratify the Convention when it passed through Parliament in 1951. The main reason for the Convention was so that states would 'accept the principles of the rule of law and of the enjoyment of all persons within its jurisdiction of Human Rights and fundamental freedoms'. The Convention was engendered in the reaction to the spread of communism into Central and Eastern Europe after the Second World War, and the terrible human rights violations that Europe had witnessed during that war.

HUMAN RIGHTS

Human rights are a most important development – for the first time in human history people have been given rights by virtue simply of being human. The Human Rights Act came into force in England and Wales on 2 October 2000. Under section 3 of the Act, primary and subordinate legislation passed in the UK is given effect in a way that makes it compatible with various rights set out in the European Convention on Human Rights. British courts can, to achieve such compatibility, overrule previous case law. Every time the UK government passes a new law, it must declare at the beginning of the procedure that the law complies with the Human Rights Act. If the proposed law does not comply, the government must explain why and ask the legislature if it accepts the departure from the Act.

The Act makes it unlawful for a public authority to violate Convention rights unless, because of an Act of Parliament, it has no choice. There is no express definition of 'public authority' in the Act, but the term includes:

- government departments
- local authorities
- police, prison and immigration officers
- public prosecutors
- courts and tribunals
- non-departmental public bodies (NDPBs)
- any person exercising a 'public function'.

Cases can be dealt with in a UK court or tribunal; a complainant does not have to go to the European Court of Human Rights in Strasbourg.

The rights established via the Human Rights Act cover the following areas:

The right to life

People have the right to have their lives protected under the law. There are extremely few circumstances under which it is acceptable for the state to take someone's life. One such case, for example, would be if a police officer had to use violent force in self-defence.

Prohibition of torture

People have the absolute right not to be tortured or subjected to treatments or punishments that are inhumane or degrading.

Prohibition of slavery and forced labour

People have the absolute right not to be treated as slaves or forced to perform certain kinds of labour.

Right to liberty and security

People have the right not to be arrested or detained, except in limited cases, such as when a person is suspected or has been convicted of committing a crime. Arrests must be justified by clear legal procedures.

Right to a fair trial

People have a right to a fair and public hearing within a reasonable time from the moment of arrest or charge. Hearings are held before an independent and impartial tribunal established by law. In criminal trials, a defendant is presumed innocent until proven guilty beyond a reasonable doubt. The defendant has the opportunity to present a defence.

No punishment without law

People cannot be punished for an act that was not illegal at the time it was committed. Convicted people are also protected against later increases in the possible sentences for their offences.

Right to respect for private and family life

People generally enjoy the right of privacy in their homes and correspondence. However, this right may be limited under certain circumstances, such as during criminal investigations.

Freedom of thought, conscience and religion

People have the right to hold and to practise religious and political beliefs without interference from the state. This right includes all sorts of political views, and the state can impose restrictions only under rare circumstances, such as grave threats to individual safety or national security.

Freedom of expression

Individuals and groups have the right to express their opinions freely. This right applies even when the expression is disturbing to some people or is unpopular. The right does, however, have some limits. People are free to speak, write or print what they like, as long as they do not overstep the bounds set by law. The right does not protect people who commit crimes that involve such activities. They may not commit the crimes of sedition (causing rebellion), obscenity, blasphemy (abuse of God or sacred things) or criminal libel (spreading of false or damaging statements). They also may not commit the torts (civil wrongs) of libel or slander.

Freedom of assembly and association

People have the right to meet and assemble with others in a peaceful way, and to form organisations, such as trade unions and political parties.

Right to marry

People have the right to marry, have children and start a family. National law may still, however, govern how and at what age such events can take place.

Right not to be discriminated against

Under Article 14 of the ECHR, people have a right not to be discriminated against on any ground such as sex, race, colour, language, religion, political or other opinion, national or social origin, association with a national minority, property, birth or other status. This is not a standalone right: it is only engaged if one of the other human rights listed above has been violated in a way that is discriminatory. For example, if someone has not been able to have a fair trial because they are disabled and cannot access a court, the right to a fair trial would be violated in conjunction with the right not to be discriminated against.

Also incorporated into UK law are Articles 1–3 of the First Protocol to the ECHR, and Articles 1 and 2 of the Sixth Protocol. They cover rights related to the protection of property, the right to education, the right to free elections at reasonable intervals with secret ballots, and the abolition of the death penalty.

The Human Rights Act was carefully drafted to preserve the primacy of Parliament. This means that judges cannot contradict Parliament. If a judge finds that a piece of primary legislation is incompatible with the Act, he or she can make a 'declaration of incompatibility', but it remains for Parliament to decide what, if any, action to take. The Parliamentary Joint Committee on Human Rights reported that in 2011, there had been 27 declarations of incompatibility, none of which were the subject of an appeal.

FURTHER READING

Sir Carleton Kemp Allen, *Law in the Making*, Oxford: The Clarendon Press, 1964.

Jeremy Bentham, *An Introduction to the Principles and Morals of Legislation*, 1780, ed. J. H. Burns and H. L. A. Hart, New York: Oceana, 1970.

Lord Denning, *Landmarks in the Law*, London: Butterworths, 1984.

R.E. Megarry, *A New Miscellany-at-Law*, Oxford: Hart Publishing, 2005.

A.W.B. Simpson, *Leading Cases in the Common Law*, Oxford: Clarendon Press, 1995.

Case Technique

5

The key part of a case for the people involved in it is whether they win or lose. But from a general viewpoint, in the more important cases, the key part of a case is what it declares to be the law. This manufacture of law from the bench at the higher levels of the court system is sometimes called judicial legislation. Law reports vary considerably in length. Some of the older ones are no longer than one sentence. Many from later times run to over one hundred pages.

TITLES

The first thing to note about cases, before examining how the law is distilled from them, is their presentational style. Case names are written in a particular way, for example *Miller v Jackson* (1977). The '*v*' in the middle stands for versus, which is Latin for 'against'. Either side are the names of the parties. The first name is the person or organisation that brought the case. If it is a civil case, that person is called the claimant (formerly called the plaintiff) and the other party is called the defendant.

If a case concerns a dispute over a will, it can be titled *In re* (Latin for 'in the matter of') a person or item, for example *In re Thompson*, concerning the will of Mr Thompson. Sometimes the name of a ship is used as the title, for example *In re Polemis*, although such cases often have a longer title as well, such as *Re an Arbitration between Polemis and Furness Withy & Co* (1921). The use of longer Latin phrases in civil law was replaced under the Civil Procedure Rules 1998 by English phrases. However, older case titles still bear the Latin. One common reference is *ex parte*. It means 'from a party or faction' and indicates that an application by one side alone has been made to a court, without the presence of the other. The new phrase to describe such actions is 'without notice' applications. The words *ex parte* can also mean 'on behalf of ' and are used in some actions in which the person himself cannot proceed but has to ask the Crown to act, for example, in claiming that a court has acted wrongly, as in *R v Bow Street Metropolitan Stipendiary Magistrate, ex parte Pinochet Ugarte* (2000).

In a criminal case the person bringing the case is called the prosecutor and the other person is called the defendant. When the case begins with a single *R*, for example *R v Smith*, the '*R*' stands for *Rex* (King) or *Regina* (Queen) and shows that the case is a criminal prosecution being brought by the Crown, i.e. the state. Sometimes especially important cases are brought by the Attorney-General, the government's chief lawyer, or are prosecuted by the Director of Public Prosecutions, the head of the Crown Prosecution Service, in which case the title will be *Attorney-General v Smith* or *Director of Public Prosecutions v Smith* (sometimes abbreviated to *Att-Gen v Smith* or *DPP v Smith*). The way cases are referred to, or to use the technical word, 'cited', by lawyers – the letters and numbers – are explained later in this chapter.

Most types of law report carry a summary of the themes at the top of the report, followed by a note of the main facts of the case, and then a heading marked 'Held', meaning what the court decided. The summary of points and the decision are known as the headnote. There then follows the judgment of the judge (or judges), and at the bottom of the report the final outcome of the proceedings is recorded.

A law report of a case contains a narrative of the facts, and the legal discussion on which the judgment was based. The legal key to the case is not the actual decision in a case, such as 'guilty', or 'the defendant is liable to pay compensation', but its *ratio decidendi*, Latin for 'the reason for deciding'. This is the legal principle applied to the key facts that led to the judgment. It is an 'extracted distillate' (in the phrase of the former judge John Gray) and usually incorporates a combination of facts found and law applied by the Court in a previous case.

RATIO DECIDENDI

Consider the case of *Fardon v Harcourt-Rivington*. It went all the way to the House of Lords in 1932. Mr and Mrs Seaward Harcourt-Rivington (Seaward was the man's first name and it was the custom then to refer to a couple using the full name of the husband) of Langhan Street, London, left their car outside Selfridges department store in Somerset Street, off Oxford Street in London. In their car they left their large Airedale dog while they briefly visited a shop. For a reason that could not later be discovered, the dog became excited and started jumping around and barking furiously. It was not thought that the dog was suffering from dehydration or was overheated. The dog pawed the rear glass window, the window pane shattered, and a shard of glass flew off, unfortunately falling into the eye of a passer-by, Mr Oliver Fardon of Vivian Avenue in Wembley, Middlesex. Despite operations to remedy the injury, Mr Fardon eventually had the eye removed. His work as a mechanical draftsman, for which he earned £7 a week, ceased and he became unemployed. He sued the Harcourt-Rivingtons for damages.

Was the couple liable to pay compensation for the man's lost eye? A High Court jury said yes, and he was awarded £2,000. But this was overturned on appeal to the House of Lords. The House of Lords ruled that people should take care to guard against 'realistic possibilities'. They should only be liable, it said, if they caused others harm by doing something that could be reasonably foreseen as likely to cause harm. We are not liable if we fail to guard against 'fantastic possibilities' that happen to occur. The accident in this case, the judges ruled, was just such a 'fantastic possibility'. The couple therefore did not have to pay compensation. The reason for the decision in this case, the *ratio decidendi*, can therefore be expressed simply as follows: where harm was caused to a pedestrian by a dog smashing the window of the car that it was in, and where this sort of incident was not reasonably foreseeable, the defendants were not liable.

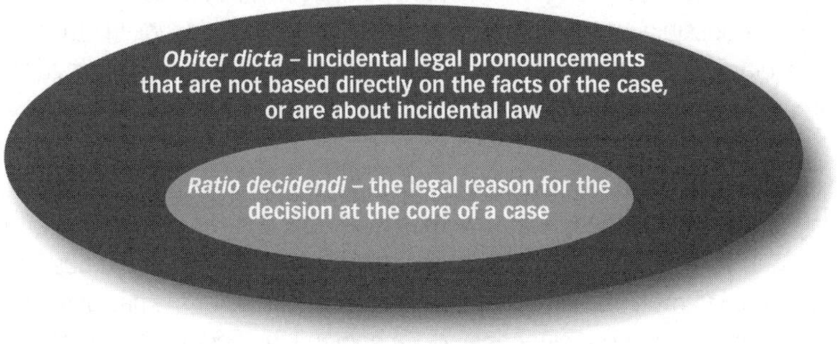

Obiter dicta – incidental legal pronouncements that are not based directly on the facts of the case, or are about incidental law

Ratio decidendi – the legal reason for the decision at the core of a case

Figure 5.1 The parts of a judgment

OBITER DICTUM

In a judicial judgment, any statement of law that is not an essential part of the *ratio decidendi* is, strictly speaking, superfluous; and any such statement is referred to as an *obiter dictum* (this is Latin for 'a word said while travelling' or 'a word said along the way'; *obiter dicta* in the plural). Although *obiter dicta* statements do not form part of the binding precedent, they are persuasive authority and can be taken into consideration in later cases, if the judge in the later case considers it appropriate to do so.

For example, in the *Harcourt-Rivington* case, one judge said that if you knew your dog had an excitable tendency or went mad in cars then you would be liable if it caused someone harm in a predictable way (not in the freakish broken-window scenario) and you would have to pay compensation. The judge did not need to rule on that in this particular case because the couple did not have a dog with a known excitable temperament. His observations were, therefore, made 'by the way' and can be referred to as an *obiter dictum*. In a future case involving a dog known by its owners to be excitable, a lawyer for an injured claimant could refer back to the judge's *obiter dictum* in the *Harcourt-Rivington* case and use it as 'persuasive' but not 'binding' authority.

The division of cases into these two distinct parts is a theoretical procedure. Unfortunately, judges do not actually separate their judgments into these two clearly defined categories and it is up to the person reading the case to determine what the *ratio* is. In some cases this is no easy matter, and it may be made even more difficult in cases where there are three or five judges and where each of the judges delivers their own lengthy judgment so there is no clear single *ratio* for the decision. It is possible for a case to have several *rationes decidendi*. In other cases, it may be difficult to ascertain precisely the *ratio* of the case and to distinguish the *ratio* from the *obiter dicta*.

Keeping to more straightforward examples, consider *Barnett v Chelsea and Kensington Hospital Management Committee* (1968). The full description of what happened in this case would run to many pages. This, though, is the basic story. William Patrick Barnett was employed as a night watchman at the hall of residence at the Chelsea College of Sciences and Technology in London. On 31 December 1965, following celebrations with some friends while at the hall of residence, he had to take his friend, who had become injured in an attack, to the hospital. After they returned they all drank some tea and after a while began vomiting violently. They returned to the hospital and recounted their symptoms, including continuous vomiting and cramp. The nurse telephoned the casualty officer, a doctor, to tell him of the men's complaint.

The casualty officer, who was himself unwell, did not see them but said that they should go home and call their own doctors. The men went away and Mr Barnett died on the afternoon of 1 January 1966 from what was later found to be arsenic poisoning. The coroner later recorded a verdict of 'murder by a person or persons unknown'. However, even if Mr Barnett had been admitted to hospital instead of being told to go home, by the time he arrived, which was approximately 8 a.m. on 1 January, it would still have been too late for him to have been saved, because the arsenic he had ingested at 5 a.m. could not have been counteracted within the time it would have taken to get him into a bed, give him the appropriate tests, get the results, and provide the treatment.

In this case, in which the dead man's widow was suing the hospital, the High Court decided that the defendant hospital management committee was not liable to pay damages to the deceased's wife and children. From a legal point of view, the important thing is the extraction of the principle on which this decision is based.

The name, age and sex of the victim are irrelevant because the law would apply just the same if any of these data were different. The location of the case is irrelevant because the same law would apply in Leeds as applied in London. The case was decided as it was because although the doctor was negligent in not seeing the patient, the death of the victim was not the result of that negligence. Even had the doctor seen the patient, he inevitably would have died because of the stage of his poisoning when he went to the hospital. Accordingly, the hospital was not liable. The hospital *did* owe a duty of care towards the patient, and it *was* in breach of that duty of care when its employee, the doctor, did not check the patient. But the breach of duty could not be said to be the cause of the victim's death. So, in future cases, the relevant law to guide us is that if a defendant owes a duty of care to another, and is in breach of that duty, he will only be liable if the breach was the cause of the victim's injury, loss or death. The *ratio* in the *Barnett* case can be expressed as follows:

> In failing to see and examine the deceased, and in failing to admit him to hospital and treat him, the hospital's casualty officer was negligent but the claimant had not discharged the onus of proving that the deceased's death was caused by the negligence (or, if the onus was on the hospital to show that Mr Barnett's death was not due to its negligence, they had done that), so the claimant's claim failed.

As noted before, judges, when delivering judgments in cases, do not separate and highlight the *ratio decidendi* from the rest of their judgment. This can lead to a lack of certainty in determining the *ratio decidendi*. This uncertainty is compounded by the considerable length of many reports of decisions in cases, and is further compounded if there are a number of separate judgments, as even if the judges involved agree on the decision of a case, they may not agree on the legal basis of the decision reached. It is for the judge deciding the case in which a precedent has been cited to determine the *ratio* of the authority and so work out whether he is bound by the earlier case or not. This factor provides later courts with a considerable degree of discretion in choosing whether to be bound or not bound by a particular authority.

The main mechanisms through which judges alter or avoid precedents are by overruling or distinguishing earlier cases. When a court contradicts the decision of the court below it in the same case, it is known as 'reversing' the earlier decision. When a court invalidates the decision of a lower court in a different earlier case, it is said to 'overrule' it.

OVERRULING

Within the system of precedent outlined in the last chapter, precedents gain increased authority with the passage of time. As a consequence, courts tend to be reluctant to overrule long-standing authorities, even though they may no longer accurately reflect contemporary practices or morals. While old precepts are very rarely useful in dentistry or computer science, they are sometimes seen as proper in law.

In addition to the desire to maintain a high degree of certainty and predictability in the law, another reason for judicial reluctance to overrule old decisions is that overruling operates retrospectively, so that the law being overruled is held never to have been the real law. If the Supreme Court in 2010 says that a 1998 Court of Appeal statement of the law was incorrect, then, technically, the 2010 ruling represents *what the law has always been and will be*, from before 1998 and after 2010.

In *Kleinwort Benson Ltd v Lincoln City Council* (1998), for example, the House of Lords overruled various earlier decisions and decided that, subject to some specific defences, the law should now recognise that there was a general right to recover money paid under a mistake, whether of fact or law. Lord Goff acknowledged the fact that, unlike legislation, which is always prospective unless otherwise stated by Parliament, judicial declarations about the common law often imply that the law as now stated has always been the law.

> The law as declared by the judge is the law applicable not only at the date of the decision but at the date of the events which are the subject of the case before him, and of the events of other cases in *pari materia*

[Latin for 'in like material', i.e. of equal relevance] which may thereafter come before the courts. I recognise, of course, that the situation may be different where the law is subject to legislative change. That is because legislation takes effect from the moment when it becomes law, and is only retrospective in its effect to the extent that this is provided for in the legislative instrument.[1]

In general, cases that have been decided according to an established principle will not be later re-tried if that principle is subsequently overruled by a higher court. Overruling, however, is not always and necessarily prospective. It can be retrospective in a way that allows people whose rights were determined according to previous declarations of the law to benefit from the newer declarations. So, for example, if a prison governor had calculated a prisoner's release date using a principle that was later declared by the Court of Appeal to be wrong, the prison governor could not, in an action for false imprisonment, rely on a defence that the imprisonment was lawful according to the law as understood by the courts at the time.[2]

The freedom of higher courts to overrule earlier lower courts (or even themselves sometimes; see Chapter 4) is an essential part of how a system of law must operate if it is to be living law. The courts have the capacity for pruning withered principles, and cultivating gradual organic growth in the law.

DISTINGUISHING

In comparison to the mechanism of overruling – which is rarely used – the main device for avoiding binding precedents is that of distinguishing. As previously stated, the *ratio decidendi* of any case is an abstraction from, and is based upon, the material facts of the case. This opens up the possibility that a court may regard the facts of the case before it as significantly different from the facts of a cited precedent and thus it may not find itself bound to follow that precedent. Judges use the device of distinguishing if, for some reason, they are unwilling to follow a particular precedent. The law reports provide many examples of strained distinctions where a court has quite evidently not wanted to follow an authority that it would otherwise have been bound by.

Lawyers and judges are always making fine distinctions. If a lawyer is ever faced with a case precedent from an authoritative law court that does not favour his or her client, then the only way around it is to try to put the current case outside the scope of the precedent.

An example of this occurred when a case in 1969, which looked at first sight as if it might have produced the same result as a similar case from 1967, was distinguished from the earlier decision. The case of *Bradford v Robinson Rentals Ltd* (1967) concerned an unusual injury suffered by a British employee in the course of his work: frostbite. He eventually won £2,500 damages against his employer.

Oliver Bradford, the claimant, who was 57 years old, was employed by the defendants as a radio service engineer. He travelled over his area in a motor van and his normal daily work involved frequent stops at customers' houses, during which he would carry out maintenance work inside. In January 1963, at a time when it was known to the defendants that the weather was likely to be very severe, he was sent on a journey to exchange a colleague's old Austin van for a newer one. The round journey, from Exeter to Bedford and back, was between 450 and 500 miles and would involve about 20 hours' driving. The old van and the new van were unheated, and the radiator of the old van was defective. The plaintiff expressed the view that the journey was hazardous and ought not to be undertaken by him. He was nevertheless instructed to go. As a result of cold on the journey, and despite precautions taken by Mr Bradford, he suffered injury by frostbite, which was unusual in England.

The court decided that the claimant had been called on to carry out an unusual task that would be likely to expose him to extreme cold and considerable fatigue, and thereby the defendants had exposed him to a reasonably foreseeable risk of injury. Although the injury that he in fact suffered was unusual, it was an injury of the kind that was foreseeable (namely, injury from exposure to cold), and, as liability did not depend on the precise nature of the injury suffered being itself reasonably foreseeable, the defendants were liable to the claimant for their negligence.

In 1967, William Tremain, also a worker from Devon, suffered an unusual injury at work, but, unlike Mr Bradford, he was not successful in his claim for damages. In the later case of *Tremain v Pike* (1969), the case of *Bradford v Robinson Rentals Ltd* (1967) was accepted as a valid precedent but distinguished from the situation in Mr Tremain's case. Mr Tremain, a herdsman employed on a farm in Devon owned by the defendants, Leonard Pike and Edwin Pike, alleged that he had suffered injury by contracting Weil's disease in the course of his employment by reason of the defendants' negligence.

Weil's disease is carried by rats but very rarely contracted by humans because of our low susceptibility to the disease. It is contracted by contact with rats' urine. Expert evidence disclosed that the risk of infection in 1967 was a remote possibility, that it was the only disease caused by rats that was not associated either with rat bites or with food contamination by rats, and that knowledge of the disease in this country was as rare as the disease itself. There was no evidence that the farmers knew or ought reasonably to have known of Weil's disease, and the first defendant had never heard of it.

Although there had been a considerable growth in the rat population on the farm early in 1967, the court was not satisfied that the defendants knew or ought reasonably to have known this, or that any more precautions against rat infestation were required than those which they had applied as a matter of routine. On the question whether the claimant's illness was attributable to any negligent breach of the defendants' duty of care to him, for which they would be liable, the court decided that an employer's duty of care to his employees was to take reasonable steps to avoid exposing them to a *reasonably foreseeable risk of injury*, and, on the facts of the case, the claimant's illness was not attributable to any breach of this duty. The court held that Weil's disease was a remote possibility that the employers could not reasonably foresee, and that the damage suffered by the claimant was, therefore, unforeseeable and too remote to be recoverable.

In the first case involving Mr Bradford, 'injury by cold' was a foreseeable result of sending someone on a 500-mile trip in an unheated van in freezing weather, so the fact that Mr Bradford suffered a rather extreme version of injury through cold (i.e. frostbite) did not stop him winning his case because it was of a type (i.e. injury by cold) that was foreseeable. In the second case, however, in ruling that Mr Tremain's claim could not succeed, the court distinguished his situation from that in Mr Bradford's case because although injury by rat bite would have been foreseeable (however extreme the victim's suffering might have been due to individual weakness), injury via rats' urine was not a foreseeable *type* of injury.

Consider another example of the art of distinguishing. In *England v Cowley* (1873), the court heard that an argument had arisen about household furniture which Mr England had sold to Miss Morely. She defaulted on payment and he was entitled to repossess the goods, which were by now in her house in River Terrace, Chelsea, London. When his bailiffs turned up to try to get the property back, they were prevented from doing so by Miss Morely's landlord. This man, Mr Cowley, was owed half a year's rent and wanted legally to seize some of her furniture himself the following day.

Mr England sued him for the civil wrong of conversion, which is 'dealing wrongfully with a person's goods in a way that constitutes a denial of the owner's rights or an assertion of rights inconsistent with the owner's'.

The court held that Mr Cowley had *not* committed a conversion because there was no 'absolute denial' of Mr England's legal title. Simply by not letting Mr England's bailiffs into the house, Mr Cowley was not committing conversion against Mr England's property.

In a later case, *Oakley v Lyster* (1931), there was a dispute about concrete left on land. Mr Oakley was a demolition contractor who, in 1925, pulled down an aerodrome on Salisbury Plain. Mr Lyster was a farmer on whose nearby land Mr Oakley had left 4,000 tons of stone materials from the demolition, having rented the space to do so. Mr Lyster, who had for years held his farmland on a lease, subsequently purchased the land, and afterwards claimed to own 'everything on it'. Was this the civil wrong of conversion? Had Mr Lyster committed conversion of Mr Oakley's stone materials? Mr Oakley asserted that it was a conversion.

The earlier case of *England v Cowley* was cited in argument by Mr Lyster's lawyer to suggest that Mr Lyster had not committed a conversion, but this time the person claiming there had been a conversion won his case. The court in 1931 disregarded the earlier authority (where the defendant had refused to allow the claimant to remove the furniture), because in this later farm case there was a distinguishing characteristic. Unlike Miss Morely's landlord in the earlier case, the farmer Mr Lyster *had* 'asserted his own title' to the rubble in a way that was inconsistent with Mr Oakley's rights. Mr Lyster had made this key assertion, expressing dominion over the property, through his lawyers. Mr Lyster's solicitors had written to Mr Oakley saying:

> We would inform you that Mr Lyster purchased this farm in January last, and the hardcore stacked thereon of course belonged to him . . . You must not, therefore, attempt to remove any of the hardcore, otherwise you will become a trespasser on our client's land.

The court agreed that this was an act of conversion, and Mr Oakley was awarded damages.

JUDICIAL DEVELOPMENT OF THE LAW

The law relating to psychiatric harm provides a good example of the way that case law has been developed by judicial ingenuity to keep pace with social changes. In what circumstances can someone who has suffered psychiatric injury as a result of having witnessed a terrible accident successfully sue the person whose negligence has caused the accident?

The leading case on recovery of compensation in such circumstances is *Alcock v Chief Constable of South Yorkshire Police* (1991), which arose from the Hillsborough Stadium disaster. At the FA Cup semi-final match at Hillsborough Stadium in Sheffield between Nottingham Forest and Liverpool in April 1989, 96 people were killed and over 400 physically injured in a crush that developed owing to poor crowd control by the police.

The Chief Constable admitted liability for those physically harmed. Many more people variously related to, or connected with, the dead and injured suffered psychiatric illness resulting from the shock of witnessing the event, seeing it on television, or identifying the bodies.

Sixteen claims were heard at first instance, of which ten succeeded in the High Court in 1991. Mr Justice Hidden held that brothers and sisters of the victims, as well as parents and spouses, could sue, but that grandfathers, uncles, brothers-in-law, fiancées and friends could not. He also decided that seeing the scene on television was equivalent to being at the scene itself.

Later in 1991, the Court of Appeal dismissed all the claims on the ground that, apart from rescuers, only parents and spouses could claim and that 'a perception through the broadcast of selective images accompanied by a commentary is not such as to satisfy the proximity test'. Ten claimants then appealed unsuccessfully to the House of Lords.

Where was the line to be drawn between sufferers of psychiatric harm who could sue those responsible for the disaster and those who could not? The House of Lords refused to prescribe rigid categories of the potential claimants in nervous shock claims. They ruled that there must generally be a close and intimate relationship between the claimant and the primary victim (for example, in the Hillsborough setting, someone who was crushed or asphyxiated) of the sort generally enjoyed by spouses, parents or children. The House of Lords ruled that siblings and other more remote relatives would normally fall outside such a relationship in the absence of special factors. But, for example, a grandmother who had brought up a grandchild since infancy might qualify. Therefore, claims by brothers, sisters and brothers-in-laws failed in *Alcock*, while the claim on the part of a fiancée was allowed. One of the judges, Lord Ackner, suggested that in cases of exceptional horror where even a reasonably strong-nerved individual might suffer shock-induced psychiatric injury, a bystander unrelated to the victim might recover damages.

The Lords went on to rule that a degree of proximity in time and space between the claimant and the accident is required. The claimant must therefore either actually be at the accident itself and witness it, or come across the aftermath in a very short period of time. Identifying a relation several hours after death is not sufficient to pass the legal test, and neither, generally, is witnessing the accident via the medium of television. Parents who watched the Hillsborough disaster on television had their claims rejected. Two of the lords, Lord Keith and Lord Oliver, did, however, recognise that there might be exceptional cases where simultaneous broadcasts of a disaster were equivalent to a personal presence at the accident. In the Court of Appeal, Lord Justice Nolan gave the example of a balloon carrying children at a live broadcast event suddenly bursting into flames.

The harm for which the person sues, the psychiatric illness, must be shown to result from the trauma of the event or its immediate aftermath. Psychiatric illness resulting from being informed of a loved one's death, however shocking the circumstances, is not recoverable. The approach taken by the House of Lords in *Alcock* was a very pragmatic one. They rejected the simple approach based on strict categories of those who could and could not recover damages and in what circumstances. In his judgment, Lord Keith said:

> ...as regards the class of person to whom a duty may be owed to take reasonable care to avoid inflicting psychiatric illness through nervous shock sustained by reason of physical injury or peril to another, I think it is sufficient that reasonable foreseeability should be the guide. I would not seek to limit the class by reference to particular relationships such as husband and wife or parent and child. The kinds of relationship which may involve close ties of love and affection are numerous, and it is the existence of such ties which lead to mental disturbance when the loved one suffers a catastrophe. They may be present in family relationships or those of close friendship, and may be stronger in the case of engaged couples than in that of persons who have been married to each other for many years.

It is common knowledge that such ties exist, and reasonably foresee-able that those bound by them may in certain circumstances be at real risk of psychiatric illness if the loved one is injured or put in peril. The closeness of the tie would, however, require to be proved by a plaintiff, though no doubt being capable of being presumed in appropriate cases. The case of a bystander unconnected with the victim of an accident is difficult. Psychiatric injury to him would not, ordinarily, in my view, be within the range of reasonable foreseeability, but could not perhaps be entirely excluded from it if the circumstances of a catastrophe occur-ring very close to him were particularly horrific.[3]

Thus, the *ratio decidendi* of this case, while being one that is reasonably clear, is nevertheless one whose precise application in future cases is difficult to predict.

In a subsequent case, *McFarlane v EE Caledonia Ltd* (1994), the Court of Appeal had to apply the general principle expounded by the Lords in *Alcock*. In this case, the claimant, Francis McFarlane, witnessed the destruction of a North Sea oil rig (the *Piper Alpha*) from aboard a support vessel that had been involved in attempts to rescue survivors of the explosion that tore apart the rig. The claimant was not himself involved directly in the rescue effort and was far enough away from the burning rig to avoid any personal danger to him. Even so, the events that he witnessed were horrific almost beyond imagining. He had to watch people in agony burning to death as the rig was devastated by fire and explosions. Although technically a 'bystander' to the incident – because he was neither a relative of any of the primary victims nor a rescuer – he does seem to fit within the last category of possible claimants described above by Lord Keith. His case, though, was rejected by the Court of Appeal, which suggested that practical and policy reasons militated against allowing him to recover damages. Lord Justice Stuart-Smith said:

In my judgment both as a matter of principle and policy the court should not extend the duty to those who are mere bystanders or witnesses of horrific events unless there is a sufficient degree of proximity, which requires both nearness in time and place and a close relationship of love and affection between plaintiff and victim.[4]

In *Henry White and others v Chief Constable of South Yorkshire and Others* (1998), the House of Lords decided that four police officers who were on duty at Hillsborough on the day of the disaster in 1989, which was the subject of the earlier *Alcock* case, could not recover damages (as employees or rescuers) for psychiatric injury suffered as a result of tending victims of an incident caused by their employer's negligence. It was admitted by the Chief Constable that the events were caused by the negligence of the police in allowing the overcrowding of two spectator pens. The question was how far compensation should go for alleged psychological injury. The four police officers had actively helped to deal with the human consequences of the tragedy and as a result suffered from post-traumatic stress disorder. Counsel for the police officers argued there was no justification for regarding physical and psychiatric injury as different kinds of damage. They also argued the case on conventional employer's liability principles as well as on the grounds that they were rescuers.

In a decision that seems distinctly mindful of social policy (as opposed to mechanical application of the existing rules), the House of Lords ruled, by a majority of three-to-two, that a recognition of the claims would have substantially expanded the existing categories in which compensation could be recovered for pure psychiatric harm and would have sat uneasily with the denial of the claims of bereaved relatives by the decision of the House of Lords in *Alcock v Chief Constable of South Yorkshire Police*.

Similar examples of judicial development of the law include the changing definition of domestic violence to include emotional as well as physical harm in the case of *Yemshaw v London Borough of Hounslow* and changing the meaning of 'spouse' to include unmarried homosexual partners in the case of *Ghaidan v Godin Mendoza*.

DISSENTING JUDGMENTS

In *Henry White and others v Chief Constable of South Yorkshire and Others* (1998), Lord Griffiths and Lord Goff delivered dissenting judgments – or speeches, as House of Lords judges' judgments are properly termed. They were broadly in favour of the claimants succeeding as rescuers. Although their speeches were judgments that would have allowed the claimants to succeed, in fact they had no effect in that case because the preponderant opinion – the majority of three Law Lords – decided against the claimants.

Judges deliver judgments dissenting (*dissentiente*) from that of the majority of judges when their analysis of the law is different from that of their fellow judges. It comes as a surprise to some people that it is not only lawyers who have different understandings of what the same law means, but that judges also might have divergent opinions. Dissenting opinions are sometimes adopted later by a higher court or by Parliament to represent the law. In an American case in 1937, Justice Clarkson said this before delivering his dissent:

> In those after years when this case, elevated to high authority by the cold finality of the printed page, is quoted with the customary 'It has been said' perchance another court will say, 'Mayhaps the potter's hand trembled at the wheel.' Possibly when that moment comes these words may give the court a chance to say, 'Yea, and a workman standing hard by saw the vase as it was cracked.'[5]

Lord Denning, who retired at the age of 83 in 1982, became known for his strongly argued dissents in cases, several of which subsequently became law, such as that concerned with the liability for negligent misstatements. In his book *The Discipline of Law* (1979), Denning recounts some of the dissenting judgments he delivered, which 'led to decisions by the Lords which might never have taken place except for my dissenting from previous precedents'.[6]

LAW REPORTING

Precedents cannot be cited to a judge by lawyers if there is not a good record of all the earlier cases and how they were decided. The operation of binding precedent, therefore, relies on the existence of an extensive reporting service to provide access to previous judicial decisions.

The professionalism and reliability of the doctrine of precedent, therefore, grew in tandem with the development of law reporting. The earliest reports of particular cases appeared between 1275 and 1535 in what are known as the *Year Books*. These reports are really of historical interest as they were originally written in a language known as Law French. As with the common law generally, the focus was on procedural matters and forms of pleading.

Reports known as 'private reports' were published between 1535 and 1865. They are known as private because they were produced by private individuals and cited by the name of the person who collected them. They were, however, published commercially for public reference. A problem with the old private reports concerns their accuracy. At best, it can be said that some were better – that is, more accurate – than others. Of particular importance among the earlier reports are those of

Plowden, Coke and Burrows; but there are many other reports that are of equal standing in their own right, with full and accurate reports of the cases submitted by counsel together with the reasons for decisions in particular cases. A substantial number of the private reports have been collated and published as the *English Reports*. The series comprises 178 large volumes – 176 volumes being reports and the last two volumes providing an index of all the cases reported. In addition, the volumes are accompanied by a useful chart to assist location of individual reports.

Publication of the private reports was slow and expensive. This situation was at last remedied by the establishment of the Council for Law Reporting in 1865, subsequently registered as a corporate body in 1870 under the name of the Incorporated Council of Law Reporting for England and Wales. The council was established under the auspices of the Inns of Court and the Law Society with the aim of producing quicker, cheaper and more accurate reports than had been produced previously.

The Law Reports are produced by the Incorporated Council of Law Reporting. They have the distinct advantage of containing summaries of counsels' arguments and, perhaps even more importantly, they are subject to revision by the judges in the case before they are published. Not surprisingly, the Law Reports are seen as the most authoritative of reports and it is usual for them to be cited in court cases in preference to any other report.

The current series of Law Reports, from 1891, is issued annually in four parts:

Appeal Cases	(AC)
Chancery Division	(Ch)
Family Division	(Fam); pre-1971, 'P' for Probate, Divorce, and Admiralty
King's/Queen's Bench	(KB/QB)

Delays in reporting can obviously mean that cases decided in one year are not reported until the following year. Since the start of the current series, individual volumes of reports carry the year of publication in square brackets together with a volume number if there is a need for more than one. Cases are cited, therefore, in relation to the year and volume in which they are published, rather than the year they were decided.

Weekly Law Reports (citation WLR) have also been published by the Council of Law Reporting since 1953. They are not, as the name might suggest, reports of cases decided in the current week, but they are produced much more quickly than the Law Reports. The need for speed means that these reports do not contain counsels' arguments, nor do they enjoy the benefit of judicial correction before printing.

The *All England Law Reports* (citation All ER) are produced by the legal publishers Butterworths, and although they do enjoy judicial revision, they do not contain counsels' arguments. They are published weekly and are then collated annually in volumes.

Various specialist reports are also published, including the *Industrial Relations Law Reports* (IRLR), *Family Law Reports* (FLR) and *Criminal Appeal Reports* (Cr App R). Although European cases may appear in the English reports, there are specialist reports relating to EC cases, such as the *European Court Reports* (ECR) and the commercially produced *Common Market Law Reports* (CMLR). Reports of the European Court of Human Rights in Strasbourg are provided in the *European Human Rights Reports* (EHRR).

In line with the ongoing modernisation of the whole legal system, the way in which cases are cited was changed in January 2001. Since then, a new *neutral* (i.e. non-commercial) system was introduced, and cases in the various courts are now cited as follows ('EW' means England and Wales):

Supreme Court	[year] SCUK case number
House of Lords	[year] UKHL case no.
Court of Appeal (Civil Division)	[year] EWCA Civ case no.
Court of Appeal (Criminal Division)	[year] EWCA Crim case no.
High Court	
Queen's Bench Division	[year] EWHC case no. (QB)
Chancery Division	[year] EWHC case no. (Ch)
Patents Court	[year] EWHC case no. (Pat)
Administrative Court	[year] EWHC case no. (Admin)
Commercial Court	[year] EWHC case no. (Comm)
Admiralty Court	[year] EWHC case no. (Admlty)
Technology & Construction Court	[year] EWHC case no. (TCC)
Family Division	[year] EWHC case no. (Fam)

Within the individual case, the paragraphs of each judgment are numbered consecutively, and if there is more than one judgment the numbering of the paragraphs carries on sequentially. Take, for example, the case of *Atkinson & Anor v Seghal*

(2003), which applied the decision made in *Alcock*. In *Atkinson & Anor* it was decided that the immediate aftermath of a fatal road accident, in which the claimant's daughter was killed, extended from the moment of the accident until the moment the claimant left the mortuary after seeing her daughter. The civil trial judge in the county court had not found for the mother. The mother's psychiatric shock, which had set in after the mortuary visit, had not, the judge said, been suffered in the 'immediate aftermath' of the accident as required by law if the sufferer was to be awarded compensation. The case was taken to the Court of Appeal by the claimant, and she won. The three judges ruled unanimously that the trial judge was wrong to have artificially separated the mortuary visit from the previous events on the evening of the death. The mortuary visit was a part of the immediate aftermath. It was not merely to identify the body but also to complete the story so far as the claimant was concerned. The defendant could be liable on the basis of what was seen at the mortuary. The neutral citation of the case is [2003] EWCA Civ 697. This case was decided in 2003 in the England and Wales Court of Appeal, Civil Division, and its case number is 697. The neutral reports do not have page numbers.

There is a particular punctilio about the use of round and square brackets in case citations. There are some exceptions in some law reports, but it is a useful generalisation to know. Square brackets are used where one needs the year of the case in order to be able to identify the relevant volume, and round brackets are used where the enclosed date is just a courtesy because one could identify the relevant book of law reports by its volume number alone. For example, to find *Attorney-General v Associated Newspapers Ltd & Ors* [1994] 1 All ER 556, you need to go to the 1994 volumes of the *All England Law Reports*, choose volume 1, and turn to page 556. By contrast, to find *Montriou v Jeffreys* (1825) 2 C & P, 113, you would not need to know its year of judgment, you would just need to go to the second volume of the Carrington & Payne reports, and turn to page 113. The final number in a case report is the page in the volume at which the particular case report begins. When a particular line or passage of a law report is being cited in a book, or in another law report, it is done by adding 'at' (not 'at page') to the end of the reference. So, *Attorney-General v Associated Newspapers Ltd & Ors* [1994] 1 All ER 556 at 568 is a reference to page 568 of the report that begins on page 556.

LAW ONLINE

As in other fields, the growth of information technology has revolutionised law reporting and searching for legal reports and regulations. Many of the law reports mentioned above are available on CD-ROM, on the internet, or on databases such as Justis, Lawtel, Lexis-Nexis and Westlaw UK. The database BAILII provides free access to case reports and judgments of the European Court of Human Rights are freely available on the Hudoc database. In addition, all of the laws of England and Wales are reproduced on legislation.gov.uk

If you are ever mystified by a legal citation – the letters and numbers after the name of a case – you need to look at a list of legal abbreviations. The easiest way to get a good list of legal abbreviations is to go to the University of Leeds CASE website, at <http://case.Leeds.ac.uk/ abbreviations.htm>.

NEWS REPORTING

It is also important to note that there has been a revolution in the way law and legal matters have been reported in the national press. Today there is an abundance of stories in all the newspapers, but this is a relatively recent phenomenon. It is a socially beneficial development, as it provides a way of making judges, lawyers, legal officials and legal policy formulators more accountable than they were when their conduct and views were largely shielded from public attention, scrutiny and debate. In March 2006, in a lecture at the University of London, Frances Gibb, Legal Editor of *The Times* and Queen Mary Visiting Professor in Legal Journalism, put this development in a clear setting:

> Let me give some historical context. *The Times* has always had a strong reputation in law reporting, because of just that – its law reports. Formal law reports, as you might know, have a long history, the earliest of which, the Year Books, date from the end of the thirteenth century . . .

> . . . But reporting of legal news and analysis is a relatively recent phenomenon that has developed in the last decade or two. When I was a general reporter for *The Times* in the early 1980s, there was perhaps one legal news story in the paper a week. It was not regarded as a mainstream job. Judges and lawyers were delighted if they found their names in the paper – but only on the court and social page or in the law reports. They certainly did not wish to find themselves the subject of news stories. The professional bodies – the Bar in particular – were low profile. There were no press offices, no press releases or press conferences. Judges tended not to speak to the press. It was almost a closed world.[7]

The reporting of law and legal developments in the context of public concerns and from a social perspective – a technique pioneered from the 1980s by Gibb – has done much to give law and the legal system the exposure to democratic debate that it deserves. Law affects us all, and, as Geoffrey Howe QC said in 1972, 'the law is everybody's law'.[8]

JUDGING THE SYSTEM OF PRECEDENT

For the legal system itself, and more generally for society, the doctrine of precedent carries various advantages and disadvantages.

The advantages of the system include consistency, certainty, efficiency and flexibility. Consistency in approach stems from the rule that 'like cases are decided on a like basis' and are not subject to the whim of the individual judge deciding the case in question. This aspect of formal justice is important in justifying the decisions taken in particular cases. Certainty of what the law is, or something akin to certainty, is enjoyed because lawyers and their clients are able, by looking at past decisions, to predict the likely answer to any legal question. So, once a legal rule has been established in one case, individuals can orient their behaviour with regard to that rule, relatively secure in the knowledge that it will not be changed by some later court. Efficiency is promoted because the doctrine of precedent saves the time of the judiciary, lawyers and their clients, as similar cases do not have to be repeatedly re-argued before the courts. Potential litigants save money in court expenses because they can apply to their lawyer for guidance on how their particular case is likely to be decided in the light of previous cases on the same or similar points. Additionally, some flexibility is built into the system because the discretionary judicial use of overruling, distinguishing and creative development of the law means that it should be very rare for a judge to make a manifestly unfair ruling on no better basis than the inescapable dictate of the law. As Lord Esher once noted, 'Any proposition the result of which would be to show that the common law of England is wholly unreasonable and unjust cannot be part of the common law of England.'[9]

The disadvantages of the doctrine of precedent include aspects of uncertainty, fixity and unconstitutionality that it can bring to the legal system. They arise from the same factors that generated the advantages. This is often the case when many things are evaluated: a small, light car might be easy to manoeuvre and to park, and might consume relatively little fuel, but it might be less strong and safe than a larger car, and hold fewer people. The uncertainty of the system of precedent comes from the fact that any certainty afforded by the doctrine of *stare decisis* is undermined by the huge number of cases that have been reported and can be cited as authorities. Certainty cannot come from a sea bobbing with so many relevant decisions. With so many rules and slightly different interpretations of them in thousands of cases, it is not always easy to see which interpretation of the law a court will give in your case. This uncertainty is increased by the ability of the judiciary to select from what is often a wide range of precedents, and to distinguish earlier cases on their facts where this would otherwise lead to an unjust result in the view of the judge.

The fixity of law promoted by the doctrine of precedent can sometimes be socially disadvantageous. The law in relation to any particular area may become solidified on the basis of an unjust precedent, with the consequence that previous injustices are perpetuated. An example of this is the long delay before the courts were willing to change the law to say that marital rape was a crime. Since the 1970s, arguments had been put to the courts on behalf of women raped by their husbands, but the law was only amended by the House of Lords in 1992. Another arguable disadvantage flowing from the system of precedent is that it can entail unconstitutional consequences. This refers to the fact that the judiciary might arguably be overstepping their theoretical constitutional role by actually making law rather than restricting themselves to the role of simply applying it. If they are not elected as law-makers, then why should they be allowed to make law? Judges are supposed only to make law interstitially – in the intervening spaces between rules. By filling in detail in applying the law, they make new, smaller rules. In truth, though, as we have seen, judges can innovate quite substantially.

FURTHER READING

J.A.G. Griffith, *The Politics of the Judiciary*, London: Fontana Press, 1997.

Lord Reid, 'The Judge as Law Maker', *Journal of the Society of Public Teachers of Law* 22, 1972.

A.W.B. Simpson, *Invitation to Law*, Oxford: Blackwell, 1988.

Gary Slapper and David Kelly, *The English Legal System*, 12th edition, Abingdon: Routledge, 2011.

Michael Zander, *The Law-Making Process*, Cambridge: Cambridge University Press, 2004.

Interpreting Acts of Parliament

6

Acts of Parliament are of unquantifiable importance. There are many thousands of them – Parliament produces more than two thousand pages of new statutory law a year – and there is no limit on the law that can be made by statute.

In the UK, there is no law of higher authority than an ordinary Act of Parliament. There is therefore no criterion by which an Act of Parliament can be judged as invalid, provided it has been properly passed using the correct procedure. Even an Act of Parliament passed to limit the life of governments to five years – such as the Parliament Act 1911 – is only an ordinary Act of Parliament, with exactly the same status as the Wild Mammals (Protection) Act 1996.

Any Act can be repealed and replaced with another Act proclaiming something different. An Act that begins, 'This Act is irrevocable and will have permanent standing in the UK' would be just as easy to repeal as any other Act. Some Acts of Parliament do take on a constitutional significance that is greater than others. The Human Rights Act 1998 is an example of this. In the case of *R v A (No 2)* Lord Steyn described the Human Rights Act 1998 as an Act of constitutional significance. However, this does not mean that Parliament could not repeal or amend the Human Rights Act 1998. The Supreme Court have indicated that there might be exceptional circumstances where, if Parliament enacted a law that was truly contrary to the Rule of Law or fundamental rights, the courts might refuse to apply it (*AXA General Insurance Ltd v The Lord Advocate* (2011)).

In one case in 1892, Lord Justice Kay said, 'Even an Act of Parliament cannot make a freehold estate in land an easement, any more than it could make two plus two equal to five.'[1] But that fairly reasonable limit on parliamentary power was subsequently rejected by Lord Justice Scrutton, who said in 1917, 'I respect-fully disagree with him, and think that . . . It can affect both these statutory results.'[2]

Sometimes the drafting of legislation is so plain and clear that it is almost painful. For example, consider the way that Schedules to the Brighton Corporation Act 1931 are defined in that legislation. They manifest what the former High Court judge Sir Robert Megarry describes as the style of pomp and circumstance. The Act simply could have noted that the word 'Schedule' appearing in the Act refers to 'a Schedule to this Act'; instead, however, what it actually said was:

'The First Schedule', 'the Second Schedule', 'the Third Schedule', 'the Fourth Schedule', 'the Fifth Schedule', 'the Sixth Schedule', 'the Seventh Schedule', 'the Eighth Schedule', 'the Ninth Schedule', 'the Tenth Schedule', 'the Eleventh Schedule','the Twelve Schedule', and 'the Thirteenth Schedule' mean respectively the First, Second, Third, Fourth, Fifth, Sixth, Seventh, Eighth, Ninth, Tenth, Eleventh, Twelth, and Thirteenth Schedules to this Act.[3]

Written not, perhaps, by the sort of person you would want to be asking for directions to the local railway station. The real problem comes, however, as the late Sir Robert observed, when drafting makes something difficult to understand. He cites the Teachers (Compensation) (Advanced Further Education) Regulations 1983, S.I.1983, No 856. They include this passage:

In these Regulations a reference to a Regulation is a reference to a Regulation contained therein, a reference in a Regulation or the Schedule to a paragraph is a reference to a paragraph of that Regulation or the Schedule and a reference in a paragraph to a sub-paragraph is a reference to a sub-paragraph of that paragraph.[4]

Writing clear, unambiguous laws to cover potentially very complicated issues is a substantial challenge. It is arguably impossible, philosophically, to write any legislation without at some time using language that is ambiguous. It is also very difficult to be prescient. When framing a rule, considerable foresight is required to anticipate all of the ways that people might behave and all the events that might develop in the future. Mr Justice Stephen once observed that:

It is not enough to attain to a degree of precision which a person reading in good faith can understand; but it is necessary to attain if possible to a degree of precision which a person reading in bad faith cannot misunderstand. It is all the better if he cannot pretend to misunderstand it.[5]

The way that the words written in the sections of statutes are interpreted by judges in law courts is very important. It is the law brought to life. Flicking through the music manuscript of an opera, or a concerto, and trying to imagine what it would sound like is a very different experience from sitting in an auditorium and hearing the music played by an orchestra. Judges animate the law in the way that musicians animate a manuscript.

At least, though, in music, the notes in a manuscript have a fairly objective and universal meaning. Musicians everywhere will understand the same thing by the note Middle C. Musicians will also know how to play ♫ or ♪ if those notes are printed on a stave. In music there is some room for interpretation, as different musicians can make individual choices in how to present a piece of music. In verbal language, however, there is more room for divergent interpretation. A word or phrase can mean different things, and its precise legal meaning is often only clarified when a court comes to declare its meaning. Take the expression 'public place'. In *David Lewis v Director of Public Prosecutions* (2004), a pub car park (private land) was ruled to be a 'public place' during licensing hours, for the purposes of drink-driving law.

Police officers discovered David Lewis driving his vehicle in the car park of the Black Bull pub in Ruislip, Middlesex. He was over the legal alcohol limit. The High Court ruled that it could be assumed, without proof, that a pub car park open to the public was a 'public place'. In 1947, in upholding the drink-driving conviction of a Mr Cartlidge, who had been caught in grounds adjoining the Fox and Hounds near Otley, Yorkshire, the High Court observed in *Elkins v Cartlidge* that a public place was 'a place to which the public have access'.

In other areas of law, however, the phrase 'public place' has been interpreted differently. In *Brannan v Peek* (1947), the High Court decided that the courts should not be confused by 'common parlance', and that a 'public house' was *not* a 'public place'. Mr Brannan was prosecuted under the Street Betting Act 1906 for taking racing bets in the Chesterfield Arms in Derby. The High Court decided that, under the Act, the pub was 'no more a public place than a draper's shop' because the public did not have a right of access to it – the invitation to guests could be withdrawn at any time. Mr Brannan was therefore not guilty of an offence under the 1906 Act.

Another case, *Cooper and others v Shield* (1971), concerned a group of nine young men accused of using threatening behaviour on the platform of West Kirby station. The court ruled that a station platform was not, as required by the Public Order Act 1936, a 'public place' because it was an integral part of a *building* – the station – and incidents in buildings (apart from public meetings) were beyond the scope of the legislation. Similar levels of debate in the case law have arisen in relation to the definition of a 'public body' for the purposes of the Human Rights Act 1998.

A DANGER DUE TO THE STATE OF THE PREMISES

A decision of the Court of Appeal provides a good illustration of how the application of a simple legislative phrase to a simple situation may have to go beyond solicitors and barristers and a judge in the county court before it is settled. The case of *Keown v Coventry Healthcare NHS Trust* (2006) concerned Martyn Keown, an 11-year-old boy who had been climbing the underside of a fire escape at the Gulson Hospital in Coventry when he fell to the ground and was injured. The fire escape reached the top of the three-storey building. It was in part of the hospital grounds that were used by the public as a means of going between the streets on either side.

The Occupiers' Liability Act 1984, section 1(1)(a) says that if someone who is legally a trespasser, like Martyn Keown, is to win damages after being injured on premises then, among other things, there must be a 'danger due to the state of the premises'. The trial judge held that there was such a danger. These seem like quite clear words, but in this case there was a dispute about how far, when you are considering if there was 'a danger', you are allowed to take into account the way in which people – even trespassers – might use the premises.

The NHS Trust submitted that the fire escape was not itself dangerous and that any danger was due to Martyn Keown's activity on the premises and not to the state of the premises. Mr Keown's counsel submitted that there was danger due to the state of the premises 'as found by' Martyn Keown, since the fire escape was amenable to being climbed from the outside with a consequent risk of harm from falling from a height. He argued that it constituted an inducement to children habitually playing in the grounds of the hospital. It was dangerous because children would be tempted to climb it. The healthcare trust appealed to the Court of Appeal against the county court decision that it was liable for the personal injuries suffered by a trespasser.

The trust won its appeal. Mr Keown was not entitled to damages. The trial judge in the County Court had found that Martyn Keown had not only appreciated that there was a risk of falling but also that what he was doing was dangerous and that he should not have been climbing the exterior of the fire escape. In the circumstances, the Court of Appeal held, it could not be said that Keown did not recognise the danger. The risk arose not out of the state of the premises, which were as one would expect them to be, but out of what Martyn Keown chose to do. Therefore, Martyn Keown had not suffered injury by reason of any 'danger due to the state of the premises' and did not pass that requirement in section 1(1)(a) of the 1984 Act. In his judgment, Mr Justice Lewison, sitting as a judge in the Court of Appeal, said:

> [T]here was nothing inherently dangerous about the fire escape. There was no physical defect in it: no element of disrepair or structural deficiency. Nor was there any hidden danger. The only danger arose

from the activity of Mr Keown [called 'Mr' as he was 21 when the case came to the Court of Appeal] in choosing to climb up the outside, knowing it was dangerous to do so.[6]

The judges of the Court of Appeal analysed relevant case law before coming to a judgment, and there are some subtle points of reasoning in the judgments. But the decision really turns on the ruling about what the statute's simple words mean when applied to the awful accident outside Gulson Hospital.

THE RULES OF INTERPRETATION

The principles according to which statutes are interpreted by judges are sometimes known as the 'rules of statutory interpretation'. Calling them 'rules' can be misleading, though, because they do not necessarily have to be applied by judges. They are more like guidelines than rules. They are the precepts judges can use when interpreting the meaning of words in a statute. Citizens in general, and lawyers' clients in particular, need to know how judges will interpret the words of statutes. Knowing the 'rules' that the judges will utilise is therefore very helpful. Such knowledge, however, is not determinative of the issues because there is no way of confidently knowing which guidelines the judges will use to help them. Applying different rules will produce different results.

According to the traditional theory of the division of powers, the role of the judiciary is simply to apply the law that Parliament has created. This view is, however, simplistic, because it ignores the extent to which the judiciary has a measure of discretion and a creative power in the way in which it interprets the legislation that comes before it.

In all legislation, ambiguous words and phrases create uncertainty that can only be resolved by judicial interpretation. That interpretation is a creative process and inevitably involves the judiciary in the process of creating law. The question arises, therefore, as to what techniques judges use to interpret legislation that comes before them. The usual answer is that they can make use of one of the three primary 'rules' of statutory interpretation and of a variety of other secondary aids to construction (from the verb 'to construe', a popular legal term for 'to interpret').

The three principal 'rules' of statutory interpretation often referred to in older cases are: (a) the literal rule; (b) the golden rule; and (c) the mischief rule. Commonly, the rules are not overtly applied by trial judges or appeal judges. The method of statutory interpretation used in a judgment is only labelled as, for example, 'the literal method' by lawyers or academics after the judgment has been published.

The Literal Rule

Under this rule, the judge considers what the legislation actually says, rather than considering what it *might mean*. In order to achieve this end, the judge should give words in legislation their literal meaning; that is, their plain, ordinary, everyday meaning, even if the effect of this is to produce what might be considered as an otherwise unjust or undesirable outcome. The 'literal rule' is based on the assumption that the words selected by Parliament to express its intention in passing the legislation were exactly what it wanted to express. As the legislative democratic part of the state, Parliament must be taken to want to effect exactly what it says in its laws. If judges are permitted to give unobvious or non-literal meanings to the words of parliamentary law, then the will of Parliament, and thereby of the people, is being contradicted. Lord Diplock once noted:

> Where the meaning of the statutory words is plain and unambiguous it is not for the judges to invent fancied ambiguities as an excuse for failing to give effect to its plain meaning because they consider the consequences for doing so would be inexpedient, or even unjust or immoral.[7]

In *Fisher v Bell* (1961), the Restriction of Offensive Weapons Act 1959 made it an offence to 'offer for sale' certain offensive weapons including 'flick-knives'. James Bell, a Bristol shopkeeper, displayed a weapon of this type with a sign 'Ejector knife – 4s' (i.e. shillings) in his shop window in the Arcade, Broadmead. The Divisional Court held that he could not be convicted because, giving the words in the Act their tight, literal legal meaning, Mr Bell had not 'offered for sale' the knives. In the law of contract, placing something in a shop window is not, technically, an 'offer for sale'; it is merely an 'invitation to treat'. It is the customer who, legally, makes an 'offer' to the shop when he proffers money for an item on sale. The position would have been different if the legislative phrase had been 'expose for sale'.

The Golden Rule

This rule, that 'law is never nonsensical', is used when the application of the literal rule will result in what appears to the court to be an obviously absurd result. An example of the application of the golden rule is *Adler v George* (1964). Under section 3 of the Official Secrets Act 1920, it was an offence to obstruct HM Forces *in the vicinity of* a prohibited place. Mr Frank Adler had in fact been arrested whilst obstructing such forces *within* such a prohibited place – Marham Royal Air Force Station in Norfolk. The court applied the golden rule to extend the literal wording of the statute to cover the action committed by the defendant. If the literal rule had been applied, it would have resulted in the absurdity that someone protesting near the base would be committing an offence while someone protesting in it would not.

The Mischief Rule

This rule was clearly established in *Heydon's Case* (1584). It gives the court a justification for going behind the actual wording of a statute in order to consider the problem that the particular statute was aimed at remedying. At one level, the mischief rule is clearly the most flexible rule of interpretation, but it is limited to using previous common law to determine what mischief the statute in question was designed to remedy. *Heydon's Case* concerned a dispute about legislation passed under Henry VIII in 1540, and a legal action against Heydon for 'intruding into certain lands, &c. in the county of Devon'. The Crown won in what was a complicated argument over land and rents. The court stated that it should consider the following four matters:

a   What was the common law before the passing of the statute?
b   What was the mischief in the law with which the common law did not adequately deal?
c   What remedy for that mischief had Parliament intended to provide?
d   What was the reason for Parliament adopting that remedy?

An example of the use of the mischief rule is found in *Corkery v Carpenter* (1951). On 19 January 1951, Shane Corkery was sentenced to one month's imprisonment for 'being drunk in charge of a bicycle' in public. The law report records that at about 2.45 p.m. one afternoon in Devon, the defendant was drunk and was 'pushing his pedal bicycle along Broad Street, Ilfracombe'. He was subsequently charged under section 12 of the Licensing Act 1872 with being 'drunk in charge of a carriage', as the legislation made no actual reference to bicycles. It is certainly arguable that a bicycle is not a carriage, but in any case, the court elected to use the mischief rule to decide the matter. The purpose of the Act was to prevent people from using any form of transport on the public highways while in a state of intoxication. The cycle was clearly a form of transport and therefore its user was correctly charged.

Apart from the supposed rules of interpretation considered above, the courts may also make use of certain presumptions. As with all presumptions, these are open to rebuttal. These presumptions include the following:

Presumption against Parliament Changing the Law

Since Parliament is sovereign, it can, of course, alter the common law by express enactment. But it must be express and explicit. The common law cannot be changed by a mere implication that it should. So, a statute is presumed not to make any change to the common law if it is possible to make an alternative interpretation that maintains the existing common law position. For example, before the Criminal Evidence Act 1898, a wife was regarded as incompetent to give evidence against her husband in a trial. To preserve the absolute sanctity of marriage, she could not be called as a witness, no matter what he was accused of doing, and however crucially useful her testimony might be. The 1898 legislation changed the law. She was thereafter regarded as competent to give evidence. However, that is as far as it went. In *Leach v R* (1912), the House of Lords held that the legislation could not be taken to have made a wife a 'compellable witness' – that is, someone whom the court could order, under threat of punishment, to give evidence. A competent witness (meaning someone who has the capacity to be a witness rather than someone who is a proficient performer) is a different legal category in law from a compellable witness, and the 1898 Act only explicitly moved the wife from being in neither category to being in the first of these categories. This rule has been applied in the human rights context to mean that there is a presumption that Parliament did not mean to infringe fundamental rights, unless there are express and unambiguous words in primary legislation to the contrary.

Presumption against Imposing Criminal Liability without Fault

Crimes are serious wrongs, so it is generally assumed that they cannot be committed by someone who does not have at least some form of guilty mind. This can be a very particular form of guilty mind, like an intention to produce harm, or a more vague form of guilty mind, like negligence. In law, the mental element of a crime is known as the *mens rea*. It is part of a longer Latin saying, *actus non facit reum nisi mens sit rea*, meaning 'an act does not make a person guilty unless his mind is guilty'. The states of mind it includes vary across the different sorts of crime known to the law.

However, it is possible for Acts to create offences – for example motoring offences – that do not require any *mens rea*, or guilty mind, in order for the defendant to be convicted. But it is right for society to be wary about the number of such offences, so the courts presume that a statute does not impose criminal liability without the need for proof of *mens rea* unless it specifies explicitly that that is what it is doing. In *Sweet v Parsley* (1970), Stephanie Sweet, the owner of Fries Farm in Gosford and Watereaton in Oxfordshire, was charged, contrary to section 5(b) of the Dangerous Drugs Act 1965, of being concerned in the management of premises which had been used for the purpose of smoking cannabis. The House of Lords decided that as she did not know her property was being used for that purpose, she could not be guilty of the offence with which she was charged. She was a sub-tenant of a farm who had let it to students but retained a room for her own occasional use. Lord Reid said, '[W]henever a section is silent as to the *mens rea* there is a presumption that . . . we must read in words appropriate to require *mens rea*.'[8] While Lord Pearce observed that:

> [B]efore the court will dispense with the requirement of *mens rea*, it has to be satisfied that Parliament so intended . . . . the wording of the particular section and its context may show that Parliament intended that the act should be prevented by punishment regardless of intent or knowledge.[9]

Presumption against Retrospective Operation

A statute is presumed not to operate retrospectively. It is, however, always open to Parliament to enact such legislation, as it did with the War Damage Act 1965. Property of the British-owned Burmah Oil Company was destroyed in 1942, on the orders of a military commander acting in furtherance of a government 'scorched earth policy'. This was done to prevent the Japanese army from taking the installations intact. In *Burmah Oil Co v Lord Advocate* (1965), the company won a substantial damages claim in the House of Lords, but then the government passed the 1965 Act to prevent the company from collecting damages. The Act provided that no one should be entitled to receive compensation in such a case whether before or after the passing of the Act, within or without the UK. In principle, this is no different from being convicted of driving a red car last year under legislation passed this year to prohibit such activity. In both cases (the oil company case, and the car case), law is being retrospectively applied to a situation which, when it occurred, was subject to a different law.

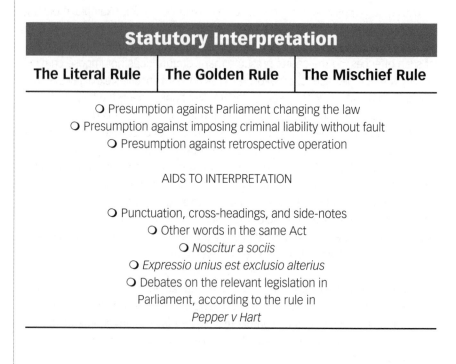

Statutory Interpretation

The Literal Rule	The Golden Rule	The Mischief Rule

○ Presumption against Parliament changing the law
○ Presumption against imposing criminal liability without fault
○ Presumption against retrospective operation

AIDS TO INTERPRETATION

○ Punctuation, cross-headings, and side-notes
○ Other words in the same Act
○ *Noscitur a sociis*
○ *Expressio unius est exclusio alterius*
○ Debates on the relevant legislation in
Parliament, according to the rule in
Pepper v Hart

OTHER AIDS TO INTERPRETATION

Other sorts of information can be used by a judge in court to determine the meaning of the words in an Act, and if there is an ambiguity in a word or phrase, to choose the preferable interpretation. These aids come from within the statute itself, and some particular principles of language. Looking at the whole of the statute, it is acceptable to presume that a word should be given the same meaning wherever it appears in the same statute.

Punctuation, Cross-headings and Side-notes

In *Director of Public Prosecutions v Schildkamp* (1969), Lord Reid made some important observations about how legislation can be interpreted. The case concerned a man called Jan Schildkamp who, as a director of a company called Fiesta Tours Ltd, had been prosecuted for fraudulent trading under section 332(3) of the Companies Act 1948. His conviction was eventually quashed. The particular meaning of the key section could have been elucidated by reference to punctuation, cross-headings (sub-headings under which sections are grouped) and side-notes (small margin notes beside the printed legislative sections, summarising the nature of the section). Lord Reid said:

> No one disputed that in construing a provision in an Act of Parliament one begins by considering its words in the context of the whole Act. And I think it is now clear that there is a very strong presumption that a provision in a consolidation Act does not alter the pre-existing law. The question which has arisen in this case is whether and to what extent it is permissible to give weight to punctuation, cross-headings and sidenotes to sections in the Act. Taking a strict view one can say that these should be disregarded because they are not the product of anything done in Parliament. I have never heard of an attempt to move that any of them should be altered or amended, and between the introduction of a Bill and the Royal Assent they can be and often are altered by officials of Parliament acting in conjunction with the draftsman.
>
> But it may be more realistic to accept the Act as printed as being the product of the whole legislative process, and to give due weight to everything found in the printed Act. I say more realistic because in very many cases the provision before the court was never even mentioned in debate in either House, and it may be that its wording was never closely scrutinised by any member of either House. In such a case it is not very meaningful to say that the words of the Act represent the intention of Parliament but that punctuation, cross-headings and side-notes do not.
>
> So if the authorities are equivocal and one is free to deal with the whole matter I would not object to taking all these matters into account provided that we realise that they cannot have equal weight with the words of the Act. Punctuation can be of some assistance in construction. A cross-heading ought to indicate the scope of the sections which follow it but there is always a possibility that the scope of one of these sections may have been widened by amendment.[10]

Other Words in the Same Act

In 1967, the Divisional Court ruled in *Gibson v Ryan* on what was meant by the word 'instrument' in section 7(1) of the Salmon and Freshwater Fisheries (Protection) (Scotland) Act 1951. James Gibson and another man had been found close to the River Tweed in Northumberland carrying an inflatable rubber dinghy and basket, each of which contained traces of salmon scales and blood.

Mr Gibson was convicted of being found in possession of 'an instrument which could be used in the taking of salmon or trout' contrary to section 7 of the Act. But his conviction was quashed on appeal. Turning from section 7 to section 10, Lord Justice Diplock noted:

> [S]o far as that s.(10) is concerned a distinction is drawn between instruments on the one hand, boats on the other hand, and baskets, on the third hand, if there is such a thing. One gets similar confirmation when one turns to section 19 . . .[11]

So, boats and baskets (what the men were caught with) were not 'instruments' (what they were charged with possessing), and so they were not guilty as charged.

* * *

Several principles of language are also used by the courts in the interpretation of statutes.

Ejusdem Generis

This is Latin for 'of the same type'. It signifies that where particular words describing a category or genus of persons or things are followed by general words, then, subject to any reasons for not thinking so, the general words will be confined to persons or things of the same class as the particular words. For example, the Betting Act 1853 prohibited the keeping of a 'house office, room, or other place' for betting. In *Powell v Kempton Park Race Course* (1899), the court had to decide whether a place within a racecourse known as Tattersall's Ring was covered by the words 'other place' in the phrase 'house, office, room, or other place'. The court decided it did not, because the words 'house, office, room' created a genus (type) of indoor places within which a racecourse – as it was outdoors – did not fall.

To take another example, in *Phonographic Performance Ltd v South Tyneside MBC* (2001), the claimant (PPL) demanded damages for infringement of its copyright in a number of musical recordings. A preliminary issue was whether the defendant council was entitled to the benefit of the exception contained in section 67 of the Copyright, Designs and Patents Act 1988. The council ran aerobics and keep-fit lessons for members of the public at two of its sports facilities. The recordings were played at these lessons. The council claimed that the lessons were, in the words of section 67:

> activities of, or for the benefit of, a club, society or other organisation (which was) not established or conducted for profit and (whose) main objects are charitable or are otherwise concerned with the advancement of religion, education or social welfare . . .

It argued, following that assertion, that its use of the recordings fell within the permitted exceptions to infringement activity.

The High Court held that as a matter of ordinary language, a local authority was not an organisation whose 'main objects are charitable or are otherwise concerned with the advancement of religion, education or social welfare'. To the same effect, application of the *ejusdem generis* rule meant that the meaning of the expression 'other organisation' was restricted by the earlier references to clubs and societies, so would exclude local authorities. The functions of a council were administrative and governmental, and did not naturally fall within any of the categories in section 67. The objects of the council were not concerned with 'social welfare' in the sense in which that expression was properly to be understood, namely the promotion of objects which were akin to charitable objects.

Noscitur a Sociis

A Latin phrase that means 'it is known from fellows or allies'. It signifies the principle that meaning of a doubtful word can be ascertained by reference to the meaning of the words associated with it. So in *Pengelley v Bell Punch Co Ltd* (1964), the Factories Act 1961, section 28, fell to be interpreted. The case arose from an industrial injury suffered by Edward Pengelley at the defendant's factory in Uxbridge, Middlesex. It was held that the word 'floors' within the expression 'floors, steps, stairs, passages, and gangways' (which the Act required to be kept free from obstruction) could not be applied to a part of the factory floor used for storage rather than passage, as the other words 'steps, stairs, passages, and gangways' are all locations designed for human movement.

Expressio Unius Est Exclusio Alterius

This is Latin for 'the expression of the one is the exclusion of the other'. This means that the express mention in a document of one or more members, or things, of a particular class may be taken as tacitly excluding others of the same class which are not mentioned. In *R v Inhabitants of Sedgley* (1831), words in the Poor Relief Act 1601 required interpretation. It was held that a section that imposed a poor rate on the occupiers of 'lands', houses, tithes, and 'coal mines' did not apply to mines other than coal mines, even though the word 'lands' would normally cover all kinds of mine. Lord Tenterden, the Chief Justice said, 'I take it to be now established as law, by the several decisions, that the expression of coal mines in the Statute . . . has the effect of excluding all other mines, according to the maxim "expressio unius".'[12]

Generalia Specialibus Non Derogant

A Latin phrase meaning 'general provisions cannot derogate from specific provisions'. Its significance was very well encapsulated by Mr Justice Stirling in 1887:

> [W]here there is an Act of Parliament which deals in a special way with a particular subject matter, and that is followed by a general Act of Parliament which deals in a general way with a subject matter of the previous legislation, the court ought not to hold that general words in such a general Act of Parliament effect a repeal of the prior and special legislation unless it can find some reference in the general Act to the prior and special legislation.[13]

In one case, for example, the maxim *generalia specialibus non derogant* was applied to prevent the Housing Act 1925 from overriding the special provisions of the London Open Spaces Act 1893, with regard to 30 acres of Hackney Marshes in London. The local authority was thus prevented from developing buildings on green land that had been allocated, under the principles of the general 1893 Act, for the recreational enjoyment of the public.[14]

HUMAN RIGHTS AND INTERPRETING UK LAW

The introduction of the Human Rights Act 1998 has had a significant effect on the English legal system generally, and its impact upon statutory interpretation has been extensive. Section 3 of the Human Rights Act requires all legislation to be read, so far as possible, to give effect to the rights provided under the European Convention on Human Rights. This section provides the courts with new and extended powers of interpretation. It also has the potential to invalidate previously accepted interpretations of statutes – which were made, by necessity without recourse to the European Convention on Human Rights. The Act brings the European Convention into UK law. An examination of some cases reveals how this power has been used by the courts.

A Rape Case

In *R v A sub nom R v Y* (2001), Lord Slynn began his speech in this way:

> In recent years it has become plain that women who allege that they
> have been raped should not in court be harassed unfairly by questions
> about their previous sex experiences. To allow such harassment is very
> unjust to the woman; it is also bad for society in that women will be
> afraid to complain and as a result men who ought to be prosecuted will
> escape.[15]

To help reduce that problem, section 41 of the Youth Justice and Criminal Evidence Act 1999 had restricted the circumstances in which a complainant in a sexual offences case could be asked questions about his or her sexual history. How that section of the statute was to be properly interpreted became the key issue in *R v A sub nom R v Y*.

In this case, the defendant, who had been charged with rape, had claimed that sexual intercourse with the complainant had been by consent and that they had been involved in a relationship for about three weeks. The issue was whether she could be questioned about that relationship in the trial. Relying on the provisions of section 41 of the Youth Justice and Criminal Evidence Act 1999, the trial judge ruled that the complainant could not be cross-examined, and that evidence about her alleged previous sexual relationship with the defendant could not be used. The defence invited the House of Lords to read section 41 of the 1999 Act in accordance with section 3 of the Human Rights Act 1998, so that section 41 of the 1999

Act could be given effect in a way that was compatible with the fair trial guarantee under Article 6 of the European Convention on Human Rights.

In reaching its decision, the House of Lords emphasised the need to protect women from humiliating cross-examination and prejudicial but valueless evidence about their previous sex lives. It held that, under section 41 of the 1999 Act, the trial court was placed under a restriction that seriously limited evidence to be adduced in cross-examination of a sexual relationship between a complainant and an accused. Under section 41(3)(b) of the 1999 Act, such evidence was limited to sexual behaviour 'at or about the same time' as the event giving rise to the charge that was 'so similar' in nature that it could not be explained as a coincidence. Therefore, it would not be possible to question on a continuous period of cohabitation or sexual activity or on individual events in the past. As a matter of common sense, however, a prior sexual relationship between a complainant and the accused could, depending on the circumstances, be relevant to the issue of consent.

If the defendant could not ask the complainant about what he alleged to be their previous sexual relationship, the defence of belief in consent would have no air of reality. A defendant had the right in a criminal trial to offer a full and complete defence. While women needed to be protected from humiliating cross-examinations and prejudicial but valueless evidence in respect of their previous sex lives, it was clear, the Lords ruled, that the restrictions in section 41 of the 1999 Act were *prima facie* (Latin for 'at first sight' or 'on first impression') capable of preventing an accused from putting forward relevant evidence that could be critical to his defence.

If construed in such a way, section 41 of the 1999 Act prevented the accused from having a fair trial and had to be declared incompatible with the European Convention on Human Rights. Section 41(3)(c) of the 1999 Act had to be read with Article 6 of the Convention in a way that would result in a fair hearing. Section 41(3)(c) of the 1999 Act should therefore be read, the Lords ruled, as permitting the admission of evidence or questioning relating to a relevant issue in the case, where it was considered necessary by the trial judge to make the trial fair.

If the section was approached in this way, a declaration of incompatibility could be avoided. The effect of this decision was that the test of admissibility of evidence of previous sexual relations between an accused and a complainant was whether the evidence was so relevant to the issue of consent that to exclude it would endanger the fairness of the trial under Article 6 of the Convention. If that test was satisfied, the evidence should not be excluded.

A Tenancy Case

The Rent Act 1977, by Schedule 1, paragraph 2, allows a surviving spouse to succeed to the tenancy of a flat if the other spouse dies. It reads:

> 2(1) The surviving spouse (if any) of the original tenant, if residing in the dwelling-house immediately before the death of the original tenant, shall after the death be the statutory tenant if and so long as he or she occupies the dwelling-house as his or her residence. (2) For the purposes of this paragraph, a person who was living with the original tenant as his or her wife or husband shall be treated as the spouse of the original tenant.

Should the words 'spouse', 'husband' and 'wife' in these paragraphs be interpreted to include only heterosexual survivors, and, if so, why? Why should a man or woman whose life partner was the same sex be treated differently as a rent-payer than they would be treated if their deceased partner had been a different sex? In *Ahmad Raja Ghaidan v Antonio Mendoza* (2004), the House of Lords held that it was possible under the Human Rights Act 1998, section 3, to 'read down' or interpret the Rent Act provision so that it was compliant with the European Convention on Human Rights. It ruled that it was necessary to depart from an earlier interpretation of the Rent Act provision enunciated in the case of *Fitzpatrick v Sterling Housing Association* (2001). Instead, the Rent Act should be interpreted as though the survivor of a homosexual couple living together was the surviving spouse of the original tenant.

The details of the *Ahmad Raja Ghaidan* case are as follows. In 1983, Mr Hugh Wallwyn-James was granted an oral residential tenancy of a flat in west London. Until his death in 2001, he lived there in a stable and monogamous homosexual relationship with the defendant, Mr Juan Godin-Mendoza. After the death of Mr Wallwyn-James, the landlord, Mr Ahmad Ghaidan, brought proceedings claiming possession of the flat. The Lords held that the Rent Act provision fell within the ambit of the 'right to respect for a person's home' guaranteed by the European Convention on Human Rights 1950, Article 8. It would be wrong to discriminate between heterosexual and homosexual couples in this context since the distinction on grounds of sexual orientation had no legitimate aim and was made without good reason.

However, in spite of this potential increased power, the House of Lords found itself unable to use section 3 in *Bellinger v Bellinger* (2003). The case related to the rights of transsexuals and the court found itself unable, or at least unwilling, to interpret section 11(c) of the Matrimonial Causes Act 1973 in such a way as to allow a male-to-female transsexual to be treated in law as a female. Nonetheless, the court did issue a 'declaration of incompatibility'. This is an action it can take under the Human Rights Act 1998 where a higher court judges an Act to be incompatible with a relevant part of the European Convention on Human Rights. Such a declaration does not change UK law but does allow Parliament to change the existing law, if it wishes to, using a 'fast track' method. The doctrine of parliamentary sovereignty is unaffected by the Human Rights Act because the courts do not have the power to 'strike down' legislation that is incompatible with human rights law. They have the power only to declare it incompatible.

THE EUROPEAN CONTEXT

The use of a 'purposive' interpretative approach by the courts is becoming something of a standard one since Britain has become more involved in Europe. Continental European legal technique, in both a European Union setting and a European human rights setting, has historically set much store by a purposive approach to interpreting legislation. In this context, the key question for the courts is: what was the purpose of the rule and the legislation or code of which it is a part?

There are comparisons here with the influence of EC Law. For example, in *Pepper (Inspector of Taxes) v Hart* (1993), the House of Lords abolished the long-established convention that the British courts do not look at Hansard (the transcript of everything said in Parliament) to discover the parliamentary intention behind legislation. The case arose from an issue of tax law, and concerned staff from Malvern College, a fee-paying school. The Lords ruled that the convention against allowing any reference to Hansard when interpreting statutes should be relaxed, so as to permit reference to parliamentary materials where: (1) legislation was ambiguous or obscure or led to absurdity; (2) the material relied upon one or more statements by a minister or other promoter of the Bill, together with such other parliamentary material as was necessary to understand such statements and their effect; and (3) the statements relied on were clear.

It is strongly arguable that this was a consequence of European law, where it is common to look for the purpose of a law in order to interpret that law, and to look for that purpose in the legislative history of the item in question. The community law doctrine of proportionality is also having a great influence. That doctrine, which is drawn from German administrative law principles, is a tool for judging the lawfulness of administrative action. It amounts to this: excessive means are not to be used to attain permissible objectives.

A good example of this approach can be found in the House of Lords decision in *White v White and Motor Insurance Bureau* (2001). Shortly after midnight, in the early moments of 5 June 1993, Brian White was going to a late-night party. He was a front-seat passenger in a Ford Capri. The car was being driven by his brother Shane along a country road a few miles outside Hereford. The car crashed and rolled over violently. Brian was very seriously injured. The accident happened at a quiet time of night, and no other vehicle was involved. Shane's driving was at fault. He lost control of the car coming out of a bend, by not driving safely and properly. Shane was at fault in another respect: neither he nor the car was insured. Indeed, he had not passed a driving test and, moreover, he was disqualified from driving. At the time of the accident Brian did not know his brother was unlicensed and, hence, uninsured, but he had known in the past that his brother was driving without a licence. The trial judge, Judge Potter, sitting as a judge of the High Court, said that while it would be going too far to say that Brian knew Shane was uninsured, it 'stands out a mile' that he ought to have known. He ought to have made sure one way or another and he made no effort to do so.

Brian had tried to get compensation from an organisation, the Motor Insurers' Bureau (MIB), which pays compensation in certain circumstances when a blame-worthy driver is uninsured. Whether Brian got the compensation depended upon the interpretation of the words 'knew or ought to have known' as they appeared in an MIB document. That document differed from the EEC Council directive on which it was based, because it included the phrase 'or ought to have known'.

The relevant UK law was made on a template of law from the EU, so some background to this is important. Part of the social and political purpose of the European Union is to make sure the same main law applies in each separate jurisdiction in matters that affect areas such as commerce, trade, industry and companies, in order to ensure fairness and equality across all member states. European directives are addressed to one or more member states, and require them to achieve specified results. Whether that is done by regulation or legislation is a matter for the individual states. The directive in this case was to ensure a uniformity of insurance practice across Europe.

This case went on appeal to the House of Lords. At issue was whether, when he got in the car, Brian 'knew or ought to have known' that his brother was uninsured.

If so, then the MIB would not pay. Lord Nicholls stated that when interpreting any document it was always important to identify, if possible, the purpose the provision was intended to achieve. That made it necessary to go to the relevant European directive which the English law implemented, on the approximation of the laws of the member states relating to insurance against civil liability regarding the use of motor vehicles. It was necessary to do so because the purpose of the 1988 MIB agreement had been to give effect to the terms of that directive. Article 1(4) of the directive provided for the setting up of bodies in member states to provide compensation for damage or injuries caused by uninsured vehicles. It then stated:

> However, member states may exclude the payment of compensation
> . . . in respect of persons who voluntarily entered the vehicle . . . when
> the body can prove that they *knew* it was uninsured. [italics added]

What was meant by 'knew' in the context of the directive? The general rule is that people who suffer loss or injury should get compensation. What the directive sought to do was permit countries to exclude from any compensation scheme people who had deliberately or knowingly driven while not insured.

The European Court of Justice had stressed repeatedly in cases that exceptions were to be construed strictly. In other words, any phrase that sought to exclude a category of person from getting compensation should be given the narrowest and strictest interpretation in order to keep those excluded to the smallest number. Here, a strict and narrow interpretation of what constituted knowledge was reinforced by the subject matter. Proportionality requires that a high degree of personal fault must exist before it would be right for an injured passenger to be deprived of compensation. In its context, knowledge that a driver was uninsured meant primarily possession of information from which the passenger drew the conclusion that the driver was uninsured. Most obviously, that occurred if the driver told the passenger so, but the information might be obtained in many other ways, for example if the passenger knew that the driver had not passed his test.

Knowledge of that character is often labelled 'actual knowledge'. There is one category of case so close to actual knowledge that the law generally treats a person as having knowledge. That is where a passenger has information from which he has drawn the conclusion that the driver might well not be insured but deliberately refrains from asking lest his suspicions should be confirmed. Such a passenger as much colludes in the use of an uninsured vehicle as one who actually knows. They should be treated alike. The directive was to be construed accordingly. Lord Nicholls was, however, in no doubt that 'knew' in the directive did not include what could be described broadly as carelessness or negligence. Typically, that would cover the case where the passenger had given no thought to the question of insurance, even though an ordinary prudent passenger, in his position and with his knowledge, would have made inquiries. A passenger who was careless in that way could not be treated as though he knew of the absence of insurance. As Lord Denning, Master of the Rolls, had said in another case, negligence in not knowing the truth was not equivalent to knowledge of it.[16] To decide otherwise would be to give a wide, rather than a narrow, interpretation to the exception permitted by the directive.

The circumstances of Brian White's accident came within that last category of case. The trial judge had rejected the idea that on the night in question any one of those involved had 'so much as bothered his head about such a matter as insurance'. His finding that Brian ought to have made sure that Shane was insured was no more than a finding of carelessness. Thus the accident fell outside the circumstances in which the directive permitted a member state to exclude payment of compensation.

In the event, the House of Lords used a purposive approach in interpreting the legislation. They looked at what purpose the relevant law was designed to achieve and, in the light of that, ruled that the Motor Insurance Board was bound to pay compensation to Brian.

The British approach to statutory interpretation will continue to change over time as a result of the Human Rights Act 1998, rather in the way that it has done as a result of the European Communities Act 1972. The tools of construction used in mainland Europe are different from those used in the English courts. In Europe, for example, the 'teleological approach' is concerned with giving the instrument its presumed legislative intent. Teleology is a philosophical term meaning that some things are better understood in terms of their purpose than their cause. This approach to the interpretation of statutes is less concerned with examining the words used in an Act with a dictionary to hand, and more concerned with divining the purpose of the law and deciding upon the meaning of its words in the light of that general purpose.

In modern times, the emphasis on identifying the true substance at issue has been seen in diverse areas. In tax law, new techniques have been developed in order to view the substance of a transaction overall to avoid focusing solely on the form of an isolated step within it. In the area of statutory control of leases, the courts are now keen to prevent any set form of words being used to obscure the reality of the underlying transaction. In the area of contract law there has been a move away from literal and semantic analysis and a greater emphasis on discerning the real intent of the parties.

STATUTORY INTERPRETATION, JUSTICE AND TRUTH

When the statutory rules that govern a situation produce an awkward result, judges must struggle to do justice between the parties in a dispute. Clearly, judges cannot just brush aside the democratically legislated rules to remedy what some might see as an injustice.

In *The Leeds Teaching Hospitals NHS Trust v Mr and Mrs A and others* (2003), a man's sperm was used mistakenly by a clinic to fertilise the embryo not of his wife but of another woman. He was confirmed as the legal father of the twins who were born to the other woman as a result.

Mr and Mrs A were white. They went to the clinic in order to have a baby through IVF treatment, i.e. *in vitro* (literally, 'in glass') fertilisation. The plan was that the husband would donate sperm, which would be used with his wife's eggs to create an embryo in a laboratory, and the embryo would then be implanted in Mrs A. At the same time, Mr and Mrs B, who were black, went to the hospital for the same reason. By mistake, sperm from Mr B was used with an egg from Mrs A. This meant that Mr A was not the biological father of his wife's twins.

At one point in the case, Dame Elizabeth Butler-Sloss quoted the thought of Lord Justice Thorpe in an earlier case. He said that 'the interests of justice are best served by the ascertainment of truth'. It is instructive to look at how the law sets out to achieve that aim. By studying the drama of effects and the application of law to them, it is possible to appreciate the difficulties of legislating in controversial areas, the challenges for those drafting such laws, what happens when a factual situation arises that seems not to have been imagined or planned for by the legislators, and how judges can resolve such awkward situations.

The ruling in the High Court was that Mr B (a stranger to Mr and Mrs A) had the right to help to bring up the children. Mr A would have to bring separate adoption proceedings to enforce his own parental status. Dame Elizabeth Butler-Sloss, president of the Family Division of the High Court, said that under the current law Mr B was the legal father but that the custody of the twins must remain with the white couple, Mr and Mrs A, stating, 'Everyone concerned with the problems which have arisen in this case agrees that the twins should remain with the family into which they were born, with Mr and Mrs A.' She noted that the mistake leading to their birth could not be rectified. She also said that they had inherited two cultures, and observed that '[t]heir biological mother and their biological father are not married and cannot marry. They may not be able during their childhood to form any relationship with their biological father.'

Some decisions for the law are potentially more agonising than others, but matters concerning the fate of children are among the most challenging. A biblical story (1 Kings III, 16–28) provides a good example. When he was faced with two women arguing passionately over which of them was the rightful mother of a baby, King Solomon threatened to cut the baby in two with a sword. To save the life of the baby, one of the women then instantly gave in and said the other woman should have the child. Solomon declared the woman who wanted the child's life saved to be the real mother, and he was recognised as a great judge. The Bible states that his people stood in awe of him, 'for they saw that he had the wisdom of God within him to administer justice'. The administration of justice no longer requires or permits stunts being pulled with a sword. The most intense disputes involving children have to be resolved by courts using only legal principles, rules and reasoning.

Legislation

Both families in the Leeds case had sought treatment within the provisions of the Human Fertilisation and Embryology Act 1990.

What did the Act say about Mr B's situation, in which he had become the biological father of twins who were not from his wife? The short answer is 'nothing', because it had not envisaged it. The preamble (the introductory paragraph at the beginning of an Act, describing its aim) to the 1990 Act sets out the purpose of the legislation with the words:

> An Act to make provision in connection with human embryos and any subsequent development of such embryos; to prohibit certain practices in connection with embryos and gametes; to establish a Human Fertilisation and Embryology Authority; *to make provision about the persons who in certain circumstances are to be treated in law as the parents of a child*; and to amend the Surrogacy Arrangements Act 1985. [italics added]

A clear purpose of the 1990 Act is to make provision for certain persons to be treated as parents. The main question in the Leeds case was whether the facts fell within the scope of the 1990 Act, so as to give Mr A the status of father of the twins.

It was section 28 of the 1990 Act which was crucial in determining the case. It defines the meaning of 'father' for the purpose of the Act. Would Mr A, who wanted to be a father but whose wife's twins were created with the sperm of Mr B, be the legal father? The Act says:

> 28 (1) This section applies in the case of a child who is being or has been carried by a woman as the result of the placing in her of an embryo or of sperm and eggs or her artificial insemination.
>
> (2) If –
>
>> (a) at the time of the placing in her of the embryo or the sperm and eggs or of her insemination, the woman was a party to a marriage, and
>>
>> (b) the creation of the embryo carried by her was not brought about with the sperm of the other party to the marriage, then, subject to subs. (5) below, the other party to the marriage shall be treated as the father of the child unless it is shown that he did not consent to the placing in her of the embryo or the sperm and eggs or to her insemination (as the case may be).
>
> (3) If no man is treated, by virtue of subs. (2) above, as the father of the child but
>
>> (a) the embryo or the sperm and eggs were placed in the woman, or she was artificially inseminated, in the course of treatment services provided for her and a man together by a person to whom a licence applies, and
>>
>> (b) the creation of the embryo carried by her was not brought about with the sperm of that man, then, subject to subs. (5) below, that man shall be treated as the father of the child . . .

The court was invited, as per the ruling in *Pepper (Inspector of Taxes) v Hart* (1993), which allowed such research, to use Hansard (the record of all parliamentary debates) to help it interpret what Parliament had intended by the words in section 28. Dame Elizabeth declined, however, on the basis that the meaning of the words in the 1990 Act, whatever was intended by the MPs who passed the Act then, had now to be shaped in the light of the Human Rights Act 1998.

Judgment

Dame Elizabeth took careful notice of the fact that the whole scheme of the 1990 Act was based upon the principle of consent. Her scrupulous approach is difficult to categorise simply as one of the standard styles of statutory interpretation like the 'golden rule' or the 'mischief rule', although to say that the 'literal' approach was taken, interpreting the statutory words in their literal sense, is probably the most accurate tag to apply. She noted with approval[17] what Lord Justice Hale said in *Mrs U v Centre for Reproductive Medicine* (2002):

> The whole scheme of the 1990 Act lays great emphasis upon consent. The new scientific techniques which have developed since the birth of the first IVF baby in 1978 open up the possibility of creating human life in ways and circumstances quite different from anything experienced before then. These possibilities bring with them huge practical and ethical difficulties. These have to be balanced against the strength and depth of the feelings of people who desperately long for the children which only these techniques can give them, as well as the natural desire of clinicians and scientists to use their skills to fulfil those wishes. Parliament has devised a legislative scheme and a statutory authority for regulating assisted reproduction in a way which tries to strike a fair balance between the various interests and concerns. Centres, the [Human Fertility and Embryology Authority] HFEA and the courts have to respect that scheme, however great their sympathy for the plight of particular individuals caught up in it.

However, the real challenge in this case came from the fact that, in Dame Elizabeth's words:

> The present situation where the sperm of a man has been placed in the eggs of a woman by mistake was not in the minds of those drafting the Bill or in Parliament's mind when it passed s.28. Miss Hamilton [counsel for Mr and Mrs A] accepted that the present situation was not contemplated by the legislators, but submitted that the court is not bound to

assume that parliamentary counsel [who draft legislation] could foresee every possibility that might arise. Otherwise . . . there would never be any problem of statutory interpretation for the court to resolve.[18]

Dame Elizabeth ruled that on the proper interpretation of section 28(2), Mr A did *not* consent to the placing in his wife of the embryo that was actually placed – because it was from another man. Accordingly, section 28(2) did not apply. That was the provision dealing with *husbands*, whose consent was needed for them to become legal fathers of children born through IVF treatment.

The next provision, section 28(3), Dame Elizabeth ruled, was aimed at couples who were not married. Consequently, Mr A could not class himself under section 28(3) and become the legal father by contending that the phrase 'for her and a man' in section 28(3)(a) covered husbands. In this context 'man' meant partner but not husband. So he could not become the legal father using the rules in any way.

The Human Rights Act and the European Convention on Human Rights

The Human Rights Act could not remedy the situation. Dame Elizabeth ruled that Article 8 (right to respect for private and family life) of the Convention (ECHR) was engaged by the facts in the case but that they were not violated in respect of Mrs B, who had neither a blood nor factual relationship with the twins. Mr B was the biological father of the twins, but in circumstances in which he had no opportunity to forge any relationship with them. Although he was clearly not a consenting sperm provider other than in a treatment process with his wife, it was, on the facts of this case, only the use of his sperm that connected him with the twins. In *M v the Netherlands* (1993), the European Commission declared inadmissible a case on stronger facts than the *Leeds* case. In the *M* case, the biological father agreed to be a sperm donor to a lesbian couple and after the birth of the child visited regularly and babysat on occasions. When he sought greater contact with the child after the couple had broken off contact with him, his application to the courts was dismissed. On his application to the European Court, the Commission rejected it out of hand and stated:

Family life . . . implies close personal ties in addition to parenthood . . . The Commission considers that the situation in which a person donates sperm only to enable a woman to become pregnant through artificial insemination does not of itself give the donor a right to respect for family life with the child.[19]

Dame Elizabeth recognised that the human rights of Mr and Mrs A were 'engaged' (the legal word for 'technically eligible for evaluation') in this case, and that her draft ruling that Mr B was the legal father constituted an interference with those rights. Should she therefore try to 'strain the language of s.28(3) in order to meet the rights of Mr and Mrs A', or grant a 'certificate of incompatibility' under section 4 of the Human Rights Act 1998 (what a judge is obliged to do if a UK statute is incompatible with the law incorporated into the British system by the 1998 Act)? She decided that neither option was needed because there were satisfactory alternative remedies available in the case, namely the granting of a 'residence order' that would give Mr A parental responsibility, and, later, the legal adoption of the twins by Mr and Mrs A. Thus, Dame Elizabeth concludes:

> In my judgment the interference with the exercise of the rights of Mr and Mrs A under article 8(1) is in accordance with the law. It can properly be cured by the legal remedies available in our domestic law. The interference is necessary in a democratic society and pursues the legitimate aim of protecting the rights and freedoms of others, in this case the twins. It is proportionate in its aim to provide the necessary protection of the twins whose rights and welfare must predominate . . .[20]

A cursory read of the case facts and the decision could prompt the conclusion that the law did not produce justice in this case. The man who wanted to be regarded as the father, as it was his wife who gave birth (the husband of Mrs A, who had the twins), was not the father according to this case. He was left to apply to adopt the twins. However, from a conventional legal point of view, many people will agree this is the best result that could have been achieved using the law as it stood. In the same way that even the best medicine and surgery cannot solve all human health problems, so also is the law unable to conjure happiness out of all situations.

Our Parliament, like all legislatures, produces laws that do not cover every possible scenario. A case inadvertently not covered by a statute is sometimes referred to by the Latin tag *casus omissus*. In one case recorded in 1949, Lord Justice Denning noted that:

> Whenever a statute comes up for consideration it must be remembered that it is not within human powers to foresee the manifold sets of facts which may arise, and, even if it were, it is not possible to provide for them in terms free from all ambiguity. The English language is not an instrument of mathematical precision . . .[21]

Straining the words of an Act so that they stretch over the facts of a particular case might produce justice in that case, but such stretching would also entail two controversial consequences. First, the decision might set a precedent that would apply to other, more contentious cases. Second, such judicial inventiveness in stretching the meaning of parliamentary words must be posited on the general premise that judges can depart from what Parliament has said if to do so is, in the eyes of the court, in the interests of justice. That would allow unelected judges a great deal of creative leeway.

FURTHER READING

Rupert Cross, John Bell and George Engel, *Statutory Interpretation*, Oxford: Oxford University Press, 1995.

Lord Denning, *The Discipline of Law*, London: Butterworths, 1979.

Colin Manchester and David Salter, *Exploring the Law: The Dynamics of Precedent and Statutory Interpretation*, London: Sweet & Maxwell, 2006.

Gary Slapper and David Kelly, *The English Legal System*, 12th edition, Abingdon: Routledge, 2011.

Imagine a very large fruit basket filled with every type of fruit. If you were asked to divide its contents into different categories, there would be various ways in which you could approach that task. There would be no right way of doing this. It would all depend on what the person asking you to make the categorisations had as their criterion for division. You could divide all the fruit into groupings such as citrus and non-citrus, or tropical and non-tropical. Or you might divide the fruits according to colour, putting all those that are orange in one category, all those that are green in another, and so on. You could divide up the contents of the basket according to the shape of the fruit, or its country or continent of origin.

So, if there was an orange in the basket it could be placed in one of several categories depending on how the division was made. Similarly, classifying law can be done in various ways. The quantity of law that applies in the UK today is very considerable. It is contained in thousands of voluminous tomes of law reports of decided cases judged over many centuries, statutes and regulations passed by Parliament, and a gigantic quantity of European law and European human rights law.

Taking this law as a whole, it can be divided according to whether it has originated from judicial pronouncement (judge-made law) or legislation (from Parliament). Equally, it can be divided according to whether it is private law (law that applies to people in respect of the private relations they might have as citizens or organisations, for example contract law) or public law (law that applies to everyone at large, for example criminal law).

Very commonly, a great many laws, and several types of law, will be relevant to a single transaction or relationship or event. For example, consider the awful case of a lorry travelling at speed along a motorway, crashing into a car that had stopped on the hard shoulder, killing one of a number of people standing near the car, and then smashing through the barrier and plunging down an embankment on to a railway line in front of an oncoming train. All sorts of laws could be applied to such a dreadful situation including the following:

- A criminal charge of dangerous driving against the lorry driver.
- A criminal charge of causing death by dangerous driving against the lorry driver.

- A charge of 'corporate manslaughter' against the haulage firm, if defective brake pads and discs had been fitted to this lorry, along with others in the fleet owned by the haulage company, and it knew of this danger.
- A civil claim in the tort of negligence by the dependants of the person who was killed, against the lorry driver and his or her employer.
- A civil action in the tort of negligence for nervous shock by people who witnessed the horror of the carnage at its scene.
- A civil action for economic loss in the tort of negligence against the lorry driver and the haulage firm brought by the train company, or companies, whose business was disrupted for days following the accident and the blocked train lines.
- The accident might well have prevented a number of scheduled events with a commercial significance from taking place, for example if a group or orchestra had been travelling on the train and was unable to arrive at a large auditorium to play on a scheduled night (as part of a busy world tour that would not be repeated). Various civil actions for breach of contract might follow, i.e. by the promoters of the events against the performers and their insurers for no performance. Insurance-related claims might follow, in which case the law relating to the frustration of contracts and so called 'Acts of God' might be applicable.

These last four claims would, if successful, be likely to be paid by the defendant's insurance companies.

The following sections deal with the ways in which the law might be divided.

COMMON LAW AND CIVIL LAW

These terms are used to distinguish two distinct legal systems and approaches to law. The use of the term common law in this context refers to all those legal systems which have adopted the historic English legal system. Foremost among these is, of course, the United States. The English jurist, and first Vinerian Professor of English Law at Oxford, Sir William Blackstone (1723–80) produced a comprehensive treatise on the common law called *Commentaries on the Laws of England*, first published in four volumes from 1756 to 1759. Courts in the United States often quote Blackstone's *Commentaries* as the definitive source of common law. The writers of the US Constitution were readers of Blackstone and used the same terms and phrases in the US Constitution as Blackstone used in his Commentaries.

Many commonwealth, and former commonwealth, countries retain a common law system. By contrast, the term 'civil law' refers to those other jurisdictions which have adopted the European continental system of law derived essentially from ancient Roman law, but owing much to the Germanic tradition.

One principal distinction to be made between common law and civil law systems is that the common law system is largely case-centred and heavily reliant on judicial interpretation of general principles, allowing scope for a policy-conscious and pragmatic approach to the particular problems that appear before the courts. The law can be developed on a case-by-case basis. On the other hand, the civil law system tends to be a codified body of general abstract principles which control the exercise of judicial discretion. In reality, both of these views are extremes, with the former overemphasising the extent to which the common law judge can impose his discretion and the latter underestimating the extent to which continental judges have the power to exercise judicial discretion. The European Court of Justice, founded, in theory, on civil law principles, is, in practice, increasingly recognising the benefits of establishing a body of case law. Although the European Court of Justice is not bound by the operation of the doctrine of *stare decisis*, it still does not decide individual cases on an individual basis without reference to its previous decisions.

COMMON LAW AND EQUITY

This division reflects the way in which law developed within the English legal system. Both common law and equity are types of law, in the sense that they are applied by judges in law courts. But they are different types of law, and so their applications, 'grammars' of operation and vocabularies are distinct.

As the common law progressed, there developed a formality among judges, typified by a reluctance to deal with matters that were not or could not be processed in the proper form of action. Such a refusal to deal with injustices, because they did not fall within the particular procedural and formal constraints, led to much dissatisfaction with the legal system. In 1374, for example, a man with an injured hand sued a surgeon in London for worsening the injury. The claimant lost, however, because contrary to precise requirements, he had not shown on his writ of 'Trespass on the Case' (a form of legal action) that the incident had been committed 'with force of arms' and 'against the peace'.[1] Another source of dissatisfaction was with the legal action to recover land of which a person had been dispossessed, the writ of Novel Disseisin, which could not be used by a lease-holder, even if his lease was for 1,000 years. A modern analogy would be with a company or government department that refused to deal with your complaint because none of its existing forms was suitable, even though you obviously had suffered a wrong. The common law courts were also perceived to be slow, highly technical and very expensive. A trivial mistake in composing the technical legal arguments of a case (a procedure called 'pleading a case') could lose a good argument. How could people obtain justice, if not in the common law courts? The response was the development of equity.

Claimants (then called plaintiffs) unable to gain access to the common law courts directly appealed to the sovereign, and such pleas would be passed for consideration and decision to the Lord Chancellor, who acted as 'the king's conscience'. As the common law courts became more formalistic and more inaccessible, pleas to the Chancellor correspondingly increased and eventually this resulted in the emergence of a specific court constituted to deliver 'equitable' or 'fair' decisions in cases which the common law courts declined to deal with. As had happened with the common law, the decisions of the courts of equity established principles which were used to decide later cases. So it should not be thought that the use of equity meant that judges had discretion to decide cases on the basis of their personal idea of what was just in each case.

An almost obsessive attention to words is, however, sometimes something that principles of equity cannot correct. The law generally governs people with a precise application of words and legal forms; for example, if you attack someone in writing publicly, the form of words you use might amount to libel. You are also, in general, strictly bound by the words you agree to sign to in a contract. Hence, Portia's admonition in *The Merchant of Venice* (Act IV, Scene i):

> This bond here gives you no drop of blood; the words expressly are 'a pound of flesh'. If in cutting off the pound of flesh you shed one drop of Christian blood, your land and goods are by the law to be confiscated . . .

From medieval times, only a limited range of claim forms, or 'writs', was available, and litigants had to be very careful about choosing the correct form for their complaint, and filling it in properly. Litigation could be struck out if there was a spelling mistake on the form. Errant use of Latin was irretrievable, as was the omission of a single punctuation mark. The moral justice of a case was often subordinate to its orthography. So, the omission of a single down-stroke or contraction sign, or an error of Latin, were fatal mistakes. One writ, for example, was invalidated because *inundare* (meaning 'to overflow or flood') was misspelled as *inumdare*.

The pursuit of propriety with such apparent pettifogging still happens today. Consider the following case. In 2004, Vincent Ryan was given a fixed penalty notice by a car park attendant in Ipswich, Suffolk. He was ordered to pay a £30 penalty, even though he had purchased a ticket, because he had left the ticket upside down on his dashboard – the penalty notice had been marked 'not displaying a valid parking ticket'. The need for punctiliousness, though, sometimes favours the citizen. In 2003, the speeding conviction of the footballer Dwight Yorke was quashed by the High Court because he did not personally fill in the official form to confirm that he was the driver of the vehicle. A missing signature rendered the form inadmissible in evidence.

Historically, there were a number of important conditions which a person seeking justice from the Court of Equity had to meet:

- He had to show that he could not receive justice in the common law courts.
- He had to show that he himself was without blame. This was called coming to the court with 'clean hands'. By contrast, claimants using the older common law courts did not have to show they were acting in a morally blame-free way.
- He had to show that he had not delayed in bringing his case before the court.

The division between the common law courts and the courts of equity continued until they were eventually combined by the Judicature Acts 1873–75. Prior to this legislation, it was essential for a party to raise his action in the appropriate court; for example, the courts of law (as opposed to courts of equity) would not implement equitable principles. The Judicature Acts, however, provided that every court had the power and the duty to decide cases in line with common law and equity, with the latter being paramount in the final analysis.

The development of equity did not stop centuries ago. The innovation of major principles has occurred several times in recent history. One example was discussed in Chapter 4 on Case Law: the case of *Central London Property Trust v High Trees Ltd* (1947). It holds that a person who is already in a contract, and who has made a promise by which he intentionally modifies his contractual rights against another party, will not be allowed to resile from such a promise. Normally, to be enforced, any promise needs to be given in exchange for something of value (in law known as 'consideration'), but equity here does not make such a requirement. Mr Justice Denning's doctrine of 'promissory estoppel' has affected hundreds of thousands of such situations ever since, either because people take legal advice before they try to go back on such a promise (made within an existing contract), or they just try to go back on their word and so learn about the principle through a lawyer once things have gone wrong.

Another example of an innovation of equity was the invention of the Mareva injunction in *Mareva Compania Naviera SA v International Bulkcarriers SA* (1975). A Mareva injunction is a court order restraining a person from using his property as he sees fit. It was designed to stop defendants from avoiding the payment of substantial damages to claimants by moving their assets out of the country. It was first used against foreign defendants but was then developed by the High Court to apply to UK defendants, and was given statutory effect in the Supreme Court Act 1981. These injunctions are now called 'freezing injunctions'.

COMMON LAW AND STATUTE LAW

As we have seen, the common law is the law that has been created by judges through the decisions in the cases they have heard. The judge and jurist Oliver Wendell Holmes Jr very aptly summed up the way such development works in his book *The Common Law* (1881). He noted:

> The life of the law has not been logic: it has been experience. The felt necessities of the time, the prevalent moral and political theories, intuitions of public policy, avowed or unconscious, even the prejudices which judges share with their fellow-men, have had a good deal more to do than the syllogism in determining the rules by which men should be governed.[2]

Statute law, on the other hand, refers to law that has been created by Parliament in the form of legislation. Although there has been a significant increase in statute law in the twentieth and twenty-first centuries, the courts still have an important role to play in creating and operating law generally and in determining the operation of legislation in particular.

PUBLIC LAW AND PRIVATE LAW

Public law is the law that applies to public institutions, or everyone at large, whereas private law is the law that applies to citizens in their relations with each other. Public law includes the law governing the government, the constitution of the UK, the administration of public authorities, and criminal law. Private law includes the law of contract, and the law affecting neighbours. This division, therefore, runs across others mentioned in this chapter. For example, the law of contract is here mentioned as forming part of private law, but I will examine it in more detail later in the chapter, as part of civil law. Here, we shall examine only constitutional and administrative law, which forms part of public law.

Constitutional and Administrative Law

Constitutional law concerns the relationship between the individual and the state examined from a legal viewpoint. One leading legal textbook on the subject describes it in this way:

> Law is not merely a matter of the rules which govern relations between private individuals (for example between employer and employee or between landlord and tenant). Law also concerns the structure and powers of the state. The constitutional lawyer is always likely to insist that the relations between the individual and the state should be founded upon and governed by law ... But when, within a community, political decisions are taken by recourse to armed force, gang warfare or the might of industrial muscle, the rules of constitutional law are either non-existent or, at best, no more than a transparent cover for a power struggle that is not conducted in accordance with anything deserving the name of law.[3]

The United Kingdom does not have one written document which is 'the constitution'. What amounts to the constitution in the UK is a diverse collection of guidelines and rules. It was described in 1733 by Henry Bolingbroke as 'That assemblage of laws, institutions and customs, derived from certain fixed principles of reason, directed to certain fixed objects of public good, that compose the general system, according to which the community have agreed to be governed.'[4]

Recent years have seen a rapid development of major parts of the UK constitution. As Professor Vernon Bogdanor has pointed out, the years since 1997 can be characterised 'as a veritable era of constitutional reform'.[5] The reforms include the independence of the Bank of England; devolution, proportional representation for election of devolved bodies in Scotland and Wales and for the European Parliament; the Human Rights Act 1998; the Freedom of Information Act 2000; and measures involving reform of the House of Lords.

Administrative law concerns particular branches of activity involving the state. It is defined by A.W. Bradley and K.D. Ewing in their *Constitutional and Administrative Law* (2007) in this way:

> It is a branch of public law concerned with the composition, procedures, powers, duties, rights and liabilities of the various organs of government that are engaged in administrating public policies . . . [it] includes in one extreme the general principles and institutions of constitutional law . . . and at the other the detailed rules contained in statutes and administrative regulations that govern the provision of complex social services (such as social security), the regulation of economic activities (such as financial services), the control of immigration, and environmental law.[6]

Much of administrative law is concerned with the process of judicial review. Judicial review is the procedure by which prerogative (coming from the inherent power of the court, and not subject to restriction) and other remedies have been obtainable in the High Court against inferior courts, tribunals, and administrative authorities from which there is no formal appeal process. So, where there is no procedure for an appeal to reconsider the merits of a case, it is very important that the decision-making panel's approach is impeccably fair. The primary purpose of judicial review is to control any actions of these bodies that might be made in excess of their proper powers (*ultra vires*) or on the basis of some unreasonable way of coming to a decision.

In cases of judicial review, an applicant will be proceeding against a public authority or part of the government asking for an official decision to be reviewed by a judge in respect of the propriety with which the decision was taken. In these cases, judges can issue court orders of a mandatory, prohibiting or quashing variety (in earlier cases before 2000 these were known as orders of *mandamus*, prohibition and *certiorari* respectively), although judicial review remedies are all discretionary, which means that even if an individual wins their judicial review claim against a public authority, the judge may refuse to grant them any relief.

Judicial review has expanded dramatically as a part of law in recent history, particularly in the context of immigration and asylum. In 1981, 552 applications for judicial review were made at the High Court, whereas in 2011, a total of 11,200 applications were made.

The case of *John Hirst v United Kingdom* (2005), decided by the European Court of Human Rights (ECtHR), provides a good illustration of public law in action. In this important judgment the Strasbourg judges ruled by 12 to 5 that the denial of the right of 48,000 sentenced prisoners in Britain to vote amounted to an abuse of the right to free elections. The ruling challenged the 1870 Forfeiture Act, which introduced the Victorian punishment of 'civic death'. The idea was that upon imprisonment an inmate ceased to have any civil status. The court merely 'challenged' the 1870 Act because it cannot cancel British legislation.

Mr Hirst first brought the case to ensure that MPs took an interest in what happened in their local prisons. The ECtHR ruled that voting was a protected human right and not a privilege, and awarded Mr Hirst £8,000 in costs and expenses. The Court did not state that all prisoners must now be given the right to vote, but it did rule that the UK government was wrong not to have considered fully the legal basis of its ban on prisoners voting, and whether the ban applied regardless of the gravity of the offence for which a prisoner had been convicted.

Protocol 1 to Article 3 of the European Convention on Human Rights (ECHR), to which the UK is a signatory, obliges the state 'to hold free elections at reasonable intervals by secret ballot, under conditions which will ensure the free expression of the opinion of the people in the choice of the legislature'. The ECtHR ruled that Protocol 1, Article 3 of the ECHR had been violated where UK domestic legislation imposed a restriction on the right of prisoners to vote. Rights guaranteed under Protocol 1, Article 3 were crucial to establishing and maintaining the foundations of 'an effective and meaningful democracy governed by the rule of law', and the right to vote was a right and not a privilege. Any limitations on the right to vote had to be imposed in pursuit of a legitimate aim and be proportionate.

The ECtHR further ruled that section 3 of the Representation of the People Act 1983, which prevented prisoners from voting, could be regarded as pursuing legitimate aims, namely to prevent crime by sanctioning the conduct of prisoners, and to enhance civic responsibility and respect for the rule of law.

But there was no evidence that Parliament had ever sought to assess the proportionality of a blanket ban on voting in elections. It was unacceptable for the UK to work on the assumption that none of its 75,000 prisoners should have the vote. (The UK government had said the ban affected only 48,000 prisoners because those prisoners who could vote, including those detained on remand, or in prison for contempt of court or defaulting on payment of fines, should be deducted from the full prison population of 75,000. The ECtHR said that, nonetheless, the ban was still too indiscriminatory.) The UK courts did not, the ECtHR ruled, undertake any assessment of the proportionality of the measure itself. Section 3 of the 1983 Act deprived all prisoners of their right to vote. It affected a significant category of people and was indiscriminate. It applied automatically to convicted persons in prison, irrespective of the length of their sentence and irrespective of the nature or gravity of their offence and their individual circumstances. Such a general, automatic and indiscriminate restriction fell outside any acceptable 'margin of appreciation'. A margin of appreciation is a concept used by the ECtHR by which a signatory state is allowed some freedom to regulate its activities. In the circumstances, there had therefore been a violation of Protocol 1, Article 3.

Although the ECtHR ruling will require legal changes by the UK government before it has any effect, it will eventually mean that prisoners' rights and interests will become more politically important as those fighting for seats in the House of Commons seek to gain prisoners' votes. Many prisons are in marginal seats (political constituencies in which no political party has a clear primacy in popularity), and 600 or 700 votes from prisoners could swing the result. Any candidate, however, seen to be according too much attention to such votes might be opposed by a rival seeking, by denying any promises to the prisoners, to win extra votes from other parts of the constituency. Whatever the outcome of such debates, the discussion will be lively.

CRIMINAL LAW AND CIVIL LAW

The difference between criminal and civil law is a particularly important distinction and is explored here in detail. Criminal cases are generally brought by the state for offences ranging from graffiti to murder. If the defendant is found guilty, he or she is punished. Civil cases are brought by citizens or organisations and the aim is usually to get compensation or a court order to make someone do something or stop doing something.

The Criminal Law

Ultimately, all justice systems hinge on their criminal codes because the criminal law is the portion of the law underpinning the legal system and enforcing its edicts. Behind every private law court order is the force of a criminal sanction for disobedience of the order. Testimony in all civil, family and private law matters is upheld ultimately by criminal laws against contempt of court, perjury and perverting the course of public justice. There are many types of law, but failing to obey a court which tries to enforce any of these types of law is ultimately a crime.

What is the distinguishing characteristic of a crime? Why is one type of wrong determined to be a crime, and another a civil wrong? The truth is that there is no scientific way of differentiating wrongs on that basis. It is impossible to be definitive about the nature of a crime because the essence of criminality has changed throughout history. As Glanville Williams observes in his *Textbook of Criminal Law* (1983):

> [A] crime (or offence) is a legal wrong that can be followed by criminal proceedings which may result in punishment.[7]

Lending money and charging interest was, anciently, the crime of usury. Now if done successfully it might earn a banker a knighthood. Cocaine used to be a legal narcotic used both for recreational purposes and toothache; now it is illegal. A crime is therefore anything that the state has chosen to criminalise. As Lord Atkin said in a case in the early 1930s:

> The domain of criminal jurisprudence can only be ascertained by examining what acts at any particular period are declared by the State to be crimes, and the only common nature they will be found to possess is that they are prohibited by the State and that those who commit them are punished.[8]

In an attempt to escape from the circularity of these definitions of crime, some writers have sought to explain its nature in terms of the seriousness of the conduct it prohibits. Thus Glanville Williams eventually concedes:

> [A] crime is an act that is condemned sufficiently strongly to have induced the authorities (legislature or judges) to declare it to be punishable before the ordinary courts.[9]

This is a little more helpful but it still leaves unanswered the following question: 'condemned sufficiently strongly' by whom? The principle connects with the thinking of the nineteenth-century French writer Emile Durkheim. He remarked on the way that collective 'social consciousness' can be enhanced by the condemnation and punishment of deviance. People like to stick together to condemn what they see as wrong, and this behaviour strengthens their togetherness. Criminal law therefore bolsters social solidarity. Durkheim said that:

> It is this solidarity that repressive law expresses . . . Indeed, the acts which such law forbids and stigmatises as crimes are of two kinds: either they manifest directly a too violent dissimilarity between the one who commits them and the collective type; or they offend the organ of the common consciousness. In both cases the force shocked by the crime and that rejects it is thus the same. It is a result of the most vital social similarities, and thus its effect is to maintain the social cohesion that arises from these similarities.[10]

The significant point about this view of the criminal law is that it is so widely shared by those who write about and operate the criminal justice system. There are many variants on this outlook. Some writers, for instance, do not share Durkheim's analysis of the criminal law as necessarily enhancing social solidarity, but the perception of criminal law as something concerning serious wrongs whose commission has a deleterious effect on society is very common. For example, in one edition of the leading theoretical text *Criminal Law*, the writers Smith and Hogan acknowledge the view of Sir Carleton Allen, who wrote:

> Crime is crime because it consists in wrongdoing which directly and in serious degree threatens the security or well-being of society, and because it is not safe to leave it redressable only by compensation of the party injured.[11]

The *public* nature of crimes is evidenced by the fact that, technically, any citizen is permitted to bring a prosecution after a crime. He or she does not have to establish a *personal* interest, as is necessary in civil proceedings. Each year there are about two million prosecutions, of which about 20 per cent are brought by someone other than the Crown Prosecution Service. These include shops, the education welfare service, utility companies and transport organisations. About 2 per cent of prosecutions are brought by private individuals.

By contrast to the general principle that anyone can prosecute for a crime, in civil law a litigant needs to show a particular status. For example, in *Holmes v Checkland* (1987), an opponent of cigarette smoking was denied 'standing' to restrain the BBC from broadcasting a snooker championship sponsored by a tobacco company, since he was no more affected than anyone else. He could only proceed with the aid of the Attorney-General. The word 'standing' in this context comes from the Latin phrase *locus standi*, 'a place to stand', which was used in older cases to denote that someone, by virtue of being personally affected by a matter, was in a position to sue.

There are only minimal controls over who can prosecute for a crime for the public good. There is provision in section 24 of the Prosecution of Offences Act 1985 for the High Court, on the application of the Attorney-General, to restrain a vexatious prosecutor. A vexatious prosecutor means someone who by the serial nature of their prosecutions or the evident malice of them is denied the facility in future. Another control is that if a private prosecution is regarded as inappropriate by the governmental legal authorities, the Attorney-General can take it over, for the sole purpose of dropping it. That process is called *nolle prosequi* (Latin for 'not to wish to proceed').

However, if a citizen begins a prosecution, he or she may not discontinue it at will: as was decided in *R v Wood* (1832), it is not only his concern but that of all citizens. If a prosecution succeeds and sentence is passed, a pardon cannot be granted by the instigator of the prosecution; it can only be granted by the Crown.

The current system of state prosecutions is not several centuries old. The huge rise in the level of crime arising from the rapid social and economic changes of the late eighteenth century coincided with a growing inadequacy of the magistracy as a form of administrative control and the absence of any professional police force. The main responsibility for law enforcement rested with the private citizen, whose sense of duty must have been sadly dampened by the realisation that the costs of bringing a criminal to justice had to be met out of his own pocket.[12]

After 1752, legislation making provision for payment of prosecution costs was passed, but these payments were never adequate and did little to encourage the private individual to prosecute. Prosecuting societies began to arise, and were themselves signs of the struggle to control lawlessness. By 1839, there were more than 500 prosecuting societies in existence. These were local, voluntary organisations which funded and organised both police officers and the prosecution of apprehended people. In Acton, London, for example, at the beginning of the nineteenth century, a society was set up 'on the initiative of a local bricklayer'. The 'principal inhabitants' of the district met in a church to organise watchmen and the funding of prosecutions.[13]

Modern civil police forces were being formed in England and Wales from 1829, but none of the legislation setting up these police forces referred to any prosecutorial role for the police. When the police did start to prosecute, it was in their capacity as private citizens. As the police began to prosecute more, so the prosecuting societies died away. Perhaps the first call for a public prosecution system was a proposal in 1534 from Henry VIII. He regretted that laws were not enforced 'unless it be by malice, rancour and evil will', and then he suggested that 'better it were that they had never been made, unless they should be put in due and perfect execution.'[14] To remedy the imperfect execution of the law, Henry unsuccessfully proposed that Sergeants of the Common Weal act as prosecutors.

The nineteenth century saw a number of proposals for a formal prosecuting agency, but none was successful. The campaign did succeed in creating the office of the Director of Public Prosecutions, first in 1879, and then on a fresh basis in 1908; however, those Acts specified that nothing in them should interfere in the right of any person to institute any criminal proceedings. Succeeding legislation has, though, gradually eroded the general right of private prosecution by requiring, in some cases, the consent of the DPP or the Attorney- General before a prosecution can be launched, or by confining the right to prosecute to particular agencies. Thus, although in theory the private individual is free to prosecute anyone, this right is substantially circumscribed by different pieces of legislation. Prosecutions continued to be brought by local police forces and their solicitors until 1986, when the first national prosecuting agency for criminal cases, the Crown Prosecution Service, was established under the Prosecution of Offences Act 1985.

In *Gouriet v Union of Post Office Workers* (1977), the right to undertake a private prosecution was described by Lord Diplock as 'an important constitutional safeguard', and by Lord Wilberforce as 'a valuable constitutional safeguard against inertia or partiality on the part of authority'.[15]

In his *Commentaries on the Laws of England*, William Blackstone contended that the distinction between private wrongs and crimes was:

> [T]hat private wrongs, or civil injuries, are an infringement or privation
> of the civil rights which belong to individuals, considered merely as
> individuals; public wrongs, or crimes and misdemeanours, are a breach

and violation of the public rights and duties, *due to the whole commu-nity, considered as a community, in its social aggregate capacity.* As if I detain a field from another man, to which the law has given him a right, this is a civil injury, and not a crime; for here only the right of an indi-vidual is concerned, and it is immaterial to the public, which of us is in possession of the land: but treason, murder and robbery are properly marked among crimes; since besides the injury done to individuals, they strike at the very being of society; which cannot possibly subsist, where actions of this sort are suffered to escape with impunity. [Emphasis added][16]

The nineteenth-century writer Jeremy Bentham presents a very similar view. Under the heading 'Reasons for Erecting Certain Acts into Offences', he writes in *The Theory of Legislation* that the criterion of whether conduct should be made a criminal offence should be 'utility' rather than the inherited prejudices of custom. Conduct is to be weighed, he suggests, so as to determine whether the good that results from it is outweighed by the bad; a task facilitated by the distinction between evils of the first, second and third orders:

Am I to examine an act which attacks the security of an individual? I compare all the Pleasure, or, in other words, all the profit, which results to the author of the act, with all the evil, or all the loss, which results to the party injured. I see at once that the evil of the first order surpasses the good of the first order. But I do not stop there. The action under consideration produces throughout society danger and alarm. The evil which at first was only individual spreads everywhere, under the form of fear. The pleasure resulting from the action belongs solely to the actor; the pain reaches a thousand – ten thousand – all. This dispropor-tion, already prodigious, appears infinite upon passing to the evil of the third order, and considering that, if the act in question is not suppressed, there will result from it . . . the dissolution of society.[17]

Civil Law

Sometimes words carry different meanings according to the settings in which they are used. For example, the word 'rich' can mean quite different things depending upon what sentence it is within. The person possessing great financial or finan-cially quantifiable wealth can be described as rich. A food or diet can be described as rich if it contains a large proportion of fat or eggs, or even spice. A voice is rich if it is mellow or deep. And if it is said that a person's assertion or statement 'is rich coming from you', then rich means highly amusing or ludicrous. As we have seen earlier, the phrase 'civil law' can also mean different things depending on the context in which it is used.

Civil law can be used to mean code law (in which the law is contained in coherent and encyclopaedic codes, as in France), so distinguishing it from common law, as practised in the UK. In other circumstances, 'civil law' can be used to refer to Roman law, which formed the basis of legal practice in much of continental Europe. Most commonly though in the UK, 'civil law' is used to refer to the sort of law used in civil proceedings. Common examples include cases for breach of contract, for nuisance, for negligence, and for defamation. Such civil proceedings have the object of declaring or enforcing a right for the advantage of a person or company, or of recovering money or property.

This can be contrasted with the action in law called a *criminal prosecution*, which we have examined earlier, and with a *public or administrative* law action. Criminal actions are brought on behalf of the state to condemn a crime (something affecting society at large). Similarly public or administrative law actions are aimed at securing a benefit for the general public, for example by stopping a nuisance which is disturbing the public at large.

In civil proceedings, the person or organisation bringing the action is known as the claimant (before the Civil Procedure Rules 1998 came into effect in 1999, a claimant was known as a plaintiff). If this litigation, often called a civil action, succeeds, the defendant will be found liable and judgment for the claimant might require the defendant to pay compensation (damages) to the claimant or to comply with a court order to carry out the terms of a contract (an order of specific performance), or to do something or to refrain from doing something (an injunction).

Important areas of civil law include contract law, tort law, trusts law, land law and family law

Contract Law

A contract is a legally enforceable agreement. In very early human societies, where people lived in small family or tribe communities, and everybody knew everyone else, it was unnecessary to have any framework of rules dealing with exactly at what point and in what circumstances an agreement was made, and how it should be enforced. The more complicated a society becomes, though, and the more the number of transactions increases, the more it needs to have a sophisticated law of contract. The UK now has a population of 63 million, and each week it makes tens of millions of contracts. You make a contract every time you buy something in a shop, or on the internet, or every time you buy a train or bus ticket. One leading writer on contract has put it this way:

> Contracts come in different shapes and sizes. Some involve large sums of money, others trivial sums. Some are of long duration, while others are of short duration. The content of contracts varies enormously and may include contracts of sale, hire purchase, employment and marriage.[18]

If you read a book on the law of contract you will discover there are many hundreds of possible points of contention concerning whether a contract has been properly made by two or more parties who have clearly consented to all of the same points in an agreement. Disputes can arise over whether the behaviour of one party is a breach, or tantamount to a breach, of the agreement, whether an agreement based on a mistake or misrepresentation should still enjoy the protection of the law of contract, and what remedies are available where a contract has been broken.

Here is an example of a contract case. Under general principles in contract law, if there is to be an enforceable agreement, then an acceptance of an offer must be communicated to the person who has made the offer. If I am to accept your offer, I must communicate my acceptance to you. In *Entores v Miles Far East Corp* (1955), the court was concerned with the technicality of precisely where a deal for '100 tons of Japanese cathodes' had been completed, because other matters swung on the issue of the city in which the deal had been made. The court had to consider at what point an acceptance made by telex (a precursor of the fax machine) in Amsterdam was 'communicated' to the person receiving the message in London. Was it communicated when it was typed in by the sender or when it was printed at the other end? The Court of Appeal decided the deal was made in London when the telex message was printed out in that office.

Lord Justice Denning said that if an oral acceptance is drowned by an overflying aircraft, so that the person making an offer cannot hear the acceptance, then there is no contract at that point. If two people are negotiating on the phone and one makes an acceptance to the other but the line goes dead so the acceptance is not heard, then again there is no contract because the acceptance has not been communicated. Where, however, the acceptance is made clearly and audibly but the person to whom it is said does not hear, a contract is concluded unless the person who has made the offer clearly says to the person making the acceptance that he did not hear what was said.

In the case of 'instantaneous communication' such as telephone or, as here, telex, the acceptance is ruled to take place at the moment when the acceptance is received by the person who has made the offer and at the place where the person who has made the offer is situated.

Another example of a contract case is *DWR Cymru Cyf v Edgar* (2004). In this case, the issue was whether an agreement which is supposed to be 'for ever and at all times' really means that it cannot be terminated by either party giving reasonable notice at any time until the end of the Earth. The High Court held that 'for ever' might not mean exactly that in all circumstances. In 1909, Colonel Jones Evans made a deed with Pwllheli Borough Council in Wales. The basis of the agreement was that the council would be able to draw water from the colonel's land 'for ever', while he would be entitled to the supply of clean water from them 'for ever'. The later legal dispute was between people who inherited the legal rights of that first agreement. The claimant (Welsh Water Ltd, who succeeded to the council's rights) wanted to give reasonable notice that it would be stopping the agreement because new regulations governing the cleanliness of the water that it supplied, and the huge increase in the quantities of water that it was being asked to supply, made it highly uneconomic for the supply to continue to be granted freely. More-over, the claimant had ceased to take water from under the land originally owned by the colonel, and was therefore no longer taking any benefit from the old agree-ment. Because circumstances had changed so much since the original agreement had been made, and because the water company was not taking any benefit as envisaged in the original agreement, the words 'for ever' could not in this agree-ment be taken to mean 'in perpetuity', and the agreement could be broken.

Tort Law

Tort law covers a wide range of civil wrongs which, broadly speaking, are the ways in which you can cause injury, damage or loss to someone or some organisation, apart from breaking a contract that you have with them. The unusual word 'tort' is an old French term meaning 'wrong'. It comes from the Latin word *tortus*, which means 'twisted' or 'crooked'. A person who commits a tort is known in law as a tortfeasor.

One of the largest areas of civil action within tort is the wrong of negligence. The case load for the courts is heavy. Over 12,000 negligence actions were heard by the courts in 2009. Civil actions for the tort of negligence include litigation arising from car accidents, sporting accidents and medical accidents. Actions in negligence are often brought against car drivers, health authorities, local education authorities, and sometimes against professionals such as accountants, doctors and lawyers. Other torts include defamation (libel and slander), private nuisance, assault, false imprisonment, trespass and 'passing off'. Passing off occurs where, through icons or logos or website styles, a business is conducted in a way that misleads the public into believing that its goods or services are those of another, more famous business.

The liability of the owners and occupiers of land for injury caused to visitors on their land or premises is another area of tort. Similarly, liability for damage caused by animals or defective products is within the compass of tort.

One major text on tort explains the aims of the law of tort in this way:

> The aims of the law of tort have changed throughout its history: appeasement, justice, punishment, deterrents, compensation, and loss spreading can be counted amongst them . . . at different stages of development of tort law one of its functions may have been more prominent than the rest. Moreover, each in its historical setting reveals something about the socio-economic and philosophical trends of the day.[19]

Negligence is a very developmental area of tort law. In 1932, in *Donoghue v Stevenson*,[20] Lord Macmillan made a momentous declaration about the law of civil negligence. He said, '[T]he grounds of action may be as various and manifold as human errancy; and the conception of legal responsibility may develop in adaptation to altering social conditions and standards.' And thus has the law developed.

The case of *Barber v Somerset County Council* (2004) illustrates the way in which the courts have applied old principles so as to develop the law. The House of Lords held that a local authority was in breach of its duty to its employee to take reasonable care to avoid injuring his health, when it had become aware that his difficulties at work were having an adverse effect on his mental health but had taken no steps to help him. Mr Alan Barber had been employed by the local authority as a teacher. In September 1995, there was a restructuring of staffing at the school at which he was employed, and he was told that in order to maintain his salary level he would have to take on further responsibilities. He worked between 61 and 70 hours a week, and often had to work in the evenings and at weekends. In February 1996, he spoke of 'work overload' to the school's deputy headteacher, and in March and April consulted his GP about stress at work, and made enquiries about taking early retirement. In May, he was absent from work for three weeks, his absence certified by his GP as being due to stress and depression. On his return to work, he met with the headteacher and the two deputy headteachers, and discussed the fact that he was not coping with his workload and felt that the situation was becoming detrimental to his health.

He was not met with an entirely sympathetic response, and no steps were taken by the school to assist him. Between August and October, he again contacted his GP about stress on a number of occasions. In November 1996, after losing control and shaking a pupil, Mr Barber left the school and did not return. By then he was unable to work as a teacher, or to do any work other than that of an undemanding part-time nature.

The House of Lords decided in favour of Mr Barber and endorsed damages of £72,000. Mr Barber, an experienced and conscientious teacher, had been absent for three weeks with no physical ailment, such absence having been certified by his GP as being due to stress and depression. The duty of his employer to take some action had arisen in June or July 1996 when Mr Barber had seen members of the school's management team, and continued so long as nothing had been done to help him. The senior management team should have made enquiries about his problems and discovered what they could have done to ease them, and the fact that the school as a whole was facing severe problems, with all the teachers stressed and overworked, did not mean that there was nothing that could have been done to help Mr Barber.

Trusts Law

The trust is a mechanism of great significance. It is an arrangement by which a person who makes a trust (called the settlor) transfers property to one or more trustees, who will then hold that property for the benefit of another or others. The trust property can include money for the benefit of one or more people called the beneficiaries, or *cestuis que trustent*. These beneficiaries are entitled to enforce the trust, if necessary, by a legal action.

The arrangement is called a trust because it is based on confidence – something which Chief Justice Coke described in 1628 as 'a confidence reposed in some other'.[21] It developed from a form of medieval tax dodging known as the 'use', under which the person using the land began to be given rights over it or arising from its use against the actual owner of the land. For a trust to be recognised by the courts, it must be certain in three respects: there must be certainty of an intention to create a trust; there must be certainty of the property which is intended as the property of the trust; and there must be certainty of its objects, in other words those who will or may benefit under the trust.

In the UK there are over 70,000 discretionary trusts (trusts where the trustees have a discretion as to who, within a class of beneficiary chosen by the settlor, should receive trust money or property and how much each should receive), with an aggregate value of over £10 billion. People take out life policies to be held on trust for their spouses and children; assets of unincorporated clubs are held on trust for club members; and the funds of trade unions, usually vast sums of money, are held on trusts. Many people also come into contact with charitable trusts, such as those for the relief of poverty or the advancement of education.

If a trust is created by a will, then the settlor is called a testator (someone who makes a will) and the trustee is called an executor. An example of a trust case is *Re Golay's Will Trust* (1965). By his will, dated 29 October 1957, the testator Adrian Golay directed his executors to:

> Let Tossy – Mrs F Bridgewater – enjoy one of my flats during her lifetime and to receive a reasonable income from my other properties; she is, if she so wishes, to wear any of my jewellery, car, etc., until her death.

The issue in this case was whether the direction by the testator to allow 'reasonable' income made it void for uncertainty. It was held by Mr Justice Ungoed-Thomas that this trust was successful because the court was used to making objective assessments of what was reasonable. He said:

> In my view the testator intended by 'reasonable income' the yardstick by which the court could and would apply in quantifying the

amount so that the direction in the Will is not in my view defeated by uncertainty.[22]

Each year, the Chancery Division of the High Court deals with about 300 cases involving wills and trusts.

Land Law

Land law, sometimes known as the law of real property, concerns much more than simply who owns large tracts of land. It regulates the ownership, and lesser interests like the leasehold interests, of every house, flat, building, office, car park, school, university, wood, lake, shopping centre, beach and beach hut in the country. One respected text on the subject explains the reach of the land law in this way:

> Since land provides the physical base for all human activity, there is no moment of any day in which we lie beyond the pervasive reach of land law. The law of the land has something to say to us, whether we are relaxing in our homes or sitting in a lecture theatre, cooking a meal in a bed-sit or engaging in a spot of D-I-Y, simply walking in the countryside or rushing along a footpath to catch a bus for a shopping expedition to the local mall. Our presence in each of these locations has a distinct significance for the land lawyer, for land law constantly describes our jural status in relation to land and its other users.[23]

Land law is a very technical and complex subject, for two main reasons: the nature of land, and the history of the law. First, land is permanent property, and so lends itself to the creation of various concurrent and consecutive interests. In other words, land can be owned or controlled by several different interests at once (concurrently) and passed on as an inheritance to different people in succession after specified events like the death of a property holder (consecutively).

Land can be transferred, commercially, for long periods like 99 or 999 years, in a way that would not really be suitable for other forms of property such as books or cars. So, 37 Eleanor Crescent, Westfield, can be owned by Alan, leased by Alan to Ben, sub-leased by Ben to Charlotte, and mortgaged by any of them to secure repayment of the loan advanced by the mortgage company. At the same time, the plot of land on which the house sits may be subject to a restrictive covenant preventing Alan, and anyone claiming through him, from building anything else on it. And again, Alan by his will may direct that the house is to be held on trust for his widow during her life and then for his eldest child during his life, and then for all his grandchildren absolutely in equal shares. Such possibilities generate a very complicated matrix of rules.

The second factor which engenders complexity in the rules of land law is the long historical evolution of this area of law. Unlike consumer law, or negligence law, or traffic law, land law has been developing from the earliest parts of history – as soon as people began in a very primitive way to exercise rights over certain places. This was probably when people settled on land and cultivated crops. Development during the last 300 years has been especially complicated with the development of commercial capitalism and urbanisation. In 1603, the population of Britain was about four million people, whereas in 2013 it is 63 million. The land inhabited has remained the same – 200,000 square kilometres. More recently, there has been an enormous increase in the ownership of land by ordinary people. It has more than doubled over the last 30 years, from 20 per cent to over 70 per cent.[24]

A couple of cases can illustrate a little of the ways in which land law is applied. In *Elitestone Ltd v Morris* (1997), the status of a chalet was at issue. In English law, buildings, and other constructions integrally linked to the land, become part and parcel of that land. Elitestone Ltd, a property company, was the freehold owner of land known as Holt's Field in Murton, near Swansea. The land was divided into 27 lots. Mr Morris was the occupier of a chalet or bungalow on lot number 6. He had lived in it since 1971. He claimed to be a protected tenant, but he could only be so if his bungalow was part and parcel of the land. It was a wooden bungalow resting on concrete pillars attached to the claimant's land. Elitestone wanted possession of the land. The property company lost its claim in the House of Lords. The reasoning of the decision was this. The chalet could be used only *in situ* (Latin for 'in its place') and could not be removed to another location without being demolished. The House of Lords held that the bungalow was not a 'fixture' (and thereby entitled to protection) as such because it rested without attachment on concrete pillars, but it must nevertheless be taken to have been intended to accede to (in the sense of 'join with'), and to become part and parcel of, the land as it could not have been intended to be personal property because it could not be moved.

By contrast, in *Chelsea Yacht & Boat Ltd v Pope* (2000), a houseboat with easily removable plug-in or snap-on service connections was held not to have become part of the land to which it was moored. The houseboat was moored to a pontoon and to the bank and bed of the river, in which it took the ground at half tide. It was let to the defendant by an agreement which closely followed a form appropriate for the letting of a dwelling house and which described the parties as landlord and tenant and the houseboat as a 'single-storey vessel'. A dispute about the security of tenure required the courts to decide whether the agreement was a tenancy under which a dwelling house is let within the terms of the Housing Act 1988, and thus a tenancy which afforded the defendant some protection against being evicted.

The defendant, Justin Pope, occupied this houseboat, called the *Dintymoore*, at Mooring 21, 106 Cheyne Walk, London SW10. The House of Lords held that the degree of annexation here did not require the houseboat to be recognised as part of the land. The object or purpose of the attachment of the houseboat was not to enable it to be used as a home for its occupant but to prevent it from being carried by the tide up or downstream and to provide services to it. Mr Pope was therefore not within the protection of the Housing Act 1988 and was subject to the eviction order from the claimant property company.

Family Law

Lawyers specialising in family law deal with a very wide range of matters, including law about engagement, marriage, invalid marriages, bigamy, forced marriages, protected occupation of property by a spouse, relationships and disputes about property, informal separations, separations by written agreements, judicial separation, adultery, desertion, gay and lesbian relationships, mediation, fostering, adoption and childcare orders.

The scope of family law has changed dramatically during recent history. The Introduction to an authoritative family law textbook published in 1976 explained the field of the subject in this way:

> The word 'family' is one which it is difficult, if not impossible, to define precisely. In one sense it means all blood relations who are descended from a common ancestor; in another it means all the members of a household, including husband and wife, children, servants and even lodgers. But for the present purpose both these definitions are far too wide . . . if a man and a woman are not married to each other, the fact that they are cohabiting has little effect on their rights *inter se* [between themselves] or with respect to third persons.[25]

However, now, as we have seen, the scope of family law is much wider. Under the Human Rights Act 1998, Article 8 of the European Convention on Human Rights (which guarantees a right to respect for private and family life, home and correspondence) was introduced into English law. The only limitations that can be placed on the protection of family life in this setting are those which are 'in accordance with the law and necessary in a democratic society'. Additionally, a government can limit the protection of family life in the interests of other factors such as national security, public safety, health or morals, and the rights and freedoms of others. One text has expressed the modern scope of the subject in the following way:

> The family relationships falling clearly within family life are the relationships of husband and wife, parent and child, siblings, grandparents and their grandchildren, adoptive parent and child, cohabitants (where stable and presumably of some long-standing), parents and illegitimate child and foster parent and child.[26]

It is, though, sometimes extremely difficult to translate the rights into a form of justice. For example, the same author also notes:

> Respect for family life includes the right of each member to consortium of every other member, which also encompasses the right of each member to live in the chosen residence of the family unit. There follows the right not to have the family unit disrupted by the removal of any members by, for example, removal from the country or the removal of a child into the care of a public authority.[27]

In *Re B (Children)* (2005), the court had to decide, following the break-up of a marriage, which parent the children should reside with – the mother wishing to relocate to her home country of Holland, or the father wishing to relocate to Dubai. The parties had married in 1995 and they had two children. Both adults had substantial connections with Dubai. The mother had lived there in her childhood. The father was working there, and both the children were born there. However, they moved to Norfolk in 2000, and in 2001 to Middlesbrough. The marriage broke down in July 2002 and the father returned to Dubai. A judge sitting at Middlesbrough County Court had found that both parties were able to care for the children, but concluded that it was in the children's best interest for them to live with their father in Dubai. The mother appealed and argued that the judge had failed to give sufficient weight to the strength of the children's attachment to her as a result of her care throughout their lives, including the period from the parties' separation to the hearing itself. The Court of Appeal dismissed the mother's appeal and found that, although the judge had made little comment about the strength of the mother's past care of the children, this was a case in which both parents were able to satisfy the children's physical, emotional and educational needs and, accordingly, it was impossible to say that the judge had misdirected himself.

FURTHER READING

John N. Adams and Roger Brownsword, *Understanding Law*, London: Sweet and Maxwell, 2006.

Peter Cane and Joanne Conaghan, *The New Oxford Companion to Law*, Oxford: Oxford University Press, 2008.

Wade Mansell, Alan Thomson and Belinda Meteyard, *Critical Introduction to Law*, Abingdon: Routledge, 2004.

Gary Slapper and David Kelly, *English Law*, Abingdon: Routledge, 2009.

Raymond Wacks, *Law: A Very Short Introduction*, Oxford: Oxford University Press, 2008.

The Jury

8

In the English legal system, over a million crimes are dealt with by courts every year yet virtually no one who is found guilty is found guilty by the state. Over 99.99 per cent of convictions are made by lay magistrates or jurors. That state officials should not be the deciders of criminal guilt is a key characteristic of a civilisation.

The vast majority of crimes, over 95 per cent, are dealt with by magistrates – ordinary people who are not paid a salary for their judicial work. The more serious crimes are tried in Crown Courts in front of a jury so, again, it is ordinary people, not anyone working for the state, who decide: guilty or not guilty. This system of justice by the people for the people is the mark of a democracy. The only exception is where full-time, salaried, district judges in cities decide whether the defendant is guilty.

British life has given to the world a number of prized institutions. Schemes, techniques and innovations developed in Britain have been so successful that they have been mimicked and adapted all over the globe. Scores of nations now boast civil services based on Whitehall, legislatures modelled on the Houses of Parliament, co-operative societies modelled on that of Rochdale, and bands modelled on the Beatles. Not to mention football, cricket, rugby and golf. But one of the most universally emulated British institutions is that of the trial before a jury. Some commentators have even called for right of an accused to be tried by a jury to be formalised into a human right.

The jury, over 800 years old in Britain, is generally seen as a desirable feature of the British constitution. In 1956, Lord Devlin referred to it as 'the lamp that shows that freedom lives', observing that 'the first object of any tyrant in Whitehall would be to make Parliament utterly subservient to his will; and the next to overthrow or diminish trial by jury', because no tyrant could afford to leave a citizen's freedom in the hands of ordinary people.[1] For the eighteenth-century jurist Sir William Blackstone, the jury was a 'sacred bulwark of the nation'[2] and, for Alexis de Tocqueville, the nineteenth-century French writer (who studied the jury in America):

> It invests each citizen with a kind of magistracy, it makes them all feel the duties which they are bound to discharge towards society, and the part which they take in the Government.[3]

Above all else, the jury has been lauded as an unbeatable contributor of 'common sense' to the otherwise technical and expert-ridden legal system.

One distinguished British academic, Alan Macfarlane, speaking of the legal system, has said this:

> If there is one central feature which makes it excellent above every-thing else it is the jury system. Now this is because in almost all legal systems, particularly in the more serious cases, you have a confronta-tion between power and the citizen, between the state and the citizen. And the state has everything at its control, and the citizen is very weak and there is nothing to protect him or her against the power of the state. So if the state says you are guilty, you are guilty. How can you defend yourself? A notable example is of people who were brought before Stalin's courts. There was no defence. The prosecutor would wear you down and then you would finally confess.
>
> Now . . . it is one thing to grind down a person who is already accused of an offence . . . it is an entirely different thing to persuade twelve free, moderately affluent, literate citizens who have been told to behave as well as possible, and to judge it fairly . . . to say to them, 'Look, there is no evidence but I want you to throw that person in jail.' You can't do it! So it immediately acts as a filter in the protection against the citizen and it is one of the major reasons why this country alone for long periods has been a democracy of a sort.[4]

The jury, however, can trace its origins to before the British version that became the one commonly used throughout the world. In classical Greek times, the courts were very large, and in the fourth century BC would often include a great many jurors – 201 was the minimum number for a private action, and 501 was the minimum number for a public action. They were drawn from a pool of 6,000 citizens over the age of 30 who put their names forward to be selected for one year as members of the panel from which jurors were chosen by lot on a day-to-day basis as needed.

The reason for the odd number was that, after listening to speeches made for both sides, the jurors, or *dikasts*, would vote on the verdict. They would use a small bronze wheel about two inches in diameter with a short axle that was either solid or hollow. The jurors would vote using the wheel with a solid axle to acquit, and with a hollow axle to condemn.

The voting of jurors occurred immediately after the speeches, without delibera-tion. Aristotle implies that jurors were discouraged from conferring,[5] although there was sometimes loud discussion while queuing for the votes. If the defendant was found guilty, and if the penalty was not fixed by law, this initial vote was followed by a second, to choose between a penalty proposed by the prosecutor, and an alternative proposed by the defendant.

A majority of one was all that was needed to carry a decision. Socrates was famously found guilty of impiety by 281 votes to 220 and sentenced to death in 399 BC. In Socrates' case, the prosecution proposed death, Socrates a derisory fine, and the jurors voted for the death penalty by 321 to 180.

Most worrying, however, is the fact that voting took place after hearing the speeches from the claimant or prosecutor, the defendant, and witnesses, but without the expert intervention of a lawyer. However, as one classicist has noted:

> A . . . singular feature of the Athenian courts is the complete absence from their working of professionals or experts. It arose, doubtless, from the wish to make the administration of justice democratic: if all citizens were to be able to take part, the whole legal system must be designed to be run by amateurs, and, if all citizens were in principle to have equal influence, it was necessary to inhibit the growth of a profes-sional corps of advocates or magistrates, since if some are amateurs and others professionals the professionals will always get the upper hand and your democracy will turn into an oligarchy. This fundamental principle was applied to everyone involved in a lawsuit or trial at Athens.[6]

THE LAW OF JURIES

Juries are bodies of persons convened by process of law to represent the public at a trial or inquest. They must discharge their duties on oath (religious) or affirmation (secular). The word 'jury' (from the Latin *jurata*) denotes a 'sworn body', in other words a group of people who have given a sworn undertaking to find the truth. Trial by jury is also sometimes called trial *per patriam* or *per pais*, meaning 'by the country' (more accurately, in this context, 'by the community'), as opposed to trial by ordeal. Trial by ordeal, an ancient way of settling a serious accusation, involved an accused person being put through physical tests by which his guilt or otherwise might be determined. For example, he might be made to carry a red-hot iron and declared innocent if his burns healed within three days.

The law concerning juries is consolidated in the Juries Act 1974. It has also been significantly amended by the Criminal Justice Act 2003. That Act abolished the former categories of ineligibility for jury service (except in the case of mentally disordered persons) and of 'excusal as of right' from such service. Under the Mental Health Discrimination Act 2013, the blanket ban on 'mentally disordered persons' from serving on a jury has been repealed. 'Excusal as of right' meant that certain classes of people, including MPs and doctors, could be excused from service without the need to refer to any particular reason. The Act also allows for trials on indictment without a jury in certain circumstances, although this change has not yet been implemented. Trial juries are used in Crown Court trials, and can be used in some High Court and some county court cases. Juries are also used in some coroners' inquests, and these are called juries of inquiry.

WHEN JURIES ARE USED

Juries are used in all three main parts of the legal system: the criminal process, the civil process, and the coronial process (in coroners' inquests). Juries are required in all serious criminal cases where the defendant pleads not guilty – called trials on indictment. These take place in the Crown Court. The question of 'fitness to plead' (is the accused sane enough to understand a trial?) and, where the accused is found unfit to plead, the question of whether the accused did the act or made the omission charged, are also determined by a jury. To resolve a case, and to close an inquiry, it is important to determine whether an accused actually committed the crime, even if he or she cannot be conventionally punished for it if they are insane.

In 2010, a major empirical study found that juries virtually always acted in a fair way. The research was conducted by Professor Cheryl Thomas, at University College London. *Are Juries Fair?* is the most in-depth study into the issue ever undertaken in this country.[7] The study involved a two-year survey of more than 1,000 jurors at Crown Courts and a separate study of over 68,000 jury verdicts. In the report, sensitive issues about jury decision-making were examined for the first time.

The report reveals that:

- all-white juries do not discriminate against defendants from black and minority ethnic backgrounds;
- juries almost always reach a verdict and convict two-thirds of the time;
- there are no courts where juries acquit more often than convict.

The study also shows that:

- jurors want more information about how to do their job;
- written instructions improve jurors' legal understanding of cases;
- some jurors use the internet to look for information about their case;
- some jurors find media reports of their case difficult to ignore.

The study recommends that all sworn jurors be issued with written guidelines explaining what improper conduct is, including use of the internet, and how and when to report it. The study also recommends that judges consider issuing jurors with written instructions on the law to be applied in each case.

In 2013, the trial of Vicky Pryce, who was charged with perverting the course of justice, demonstrated some of the problems with jury trials that this research high-lighted. In that case members of the jury passed questions up to the trial judge which indicated that they had fundamentally misunderstood the trial process and their role within it. One of their questions was whether or not they were able to rely on evidence that had not been presented in court, to which the answer was a firm 'no'. As a result of this lack of understanding, Mr Justice Sweeney ordered a re-trial.

The Criminal Justice Act 2003 contained provisions allowing for trials in cases of serious crime to take place without juries. The provision was to act as a safeguard against 'jury nobbling' – where jurors are intimidated or bribed into voting for an acquittal. Non-jury trials had been used in Northern Ireland in the 1970s during a period of civil strife when there were fears of jury nobbling, but outside of that situation cases of serious crime had been tried by juries for over four centuries. The power provided for in the 2003 Act was not used until February 2010.

Peter Blake, John Twomey, Barry Hibberd and Glen Cameron were tried for a violent £1.75 million armed robbery at Heathrow in 2004. The decision to allow the juryless trial was taken by the Court of Appeal in 2009 after an investigation by the police found that 'approaches' had been made to two members of the jury in the third trial of the men. The court decided that a serious attempt at jury tampering had taken place. It was also found that there was a real and present danger that jury tampering would recur if there were a further jury trial. In deciding to order a juryless trial, the Court of Appeal noted that the alternative of providing the jury with round-the-clock protection would still leave their families vulnerable and that such protection would cost £6 million as opposed to the £1.6 million for a judge-only trial.

In the juryless trial, the judge acts as both judge and jury: he resolves matters of law and has to do 'mental gymnastics', as one barrister put it,[8] if he excludes evidence as inadmissible – trying to put it out of his mind and to pretend that he has never seen it. In a jury trial, the jury is sent out by the judge when there are technical legal arguments about controversial evidence and does not hear any evidence that has been excluded or even know that it has been excluded. After less than three months (about half the time a jury trial for such a complex case would have lasted) the defendants were found guilty by the single judge and given a range of sentences from life imprisonment to 15 years' imprisonment.

In civil cases, in the Queen's Bench Division, there is a right to a jury under section 69 of the Supreme Court Act 1981 if:

1   a charge of fraud is made against the party applying for a jury; or
2   a claim in respect of libel, slander, malicious prosecution or false imprisonment is in issue; or
3   any question or issue of a kind prescribed is raised [but none has yet been so prescribed].

However, this right is waived if the judge thinks that a trial fulfilling any of the above conditions requires a prolonged examination of documents or accounts or any scientific or local investigation which cannot conveniently be made with a jury.

In all other cases, it is at the discretion of the court or a judge to order trial with or without a jury. Such an order is rarely made. For example, the fact that a case involves issues of integrity and honour, not merely credibility, might be a weighty consideration in ordering trial by jury at the request of the party whose integrity and honour were impugned, but issues of integrity and honour do not of themselves guarantee the ordering of a jury trial.[9]

A jury will not be ordered in claims for personal injury unless there are exceptional circumstances.[10] Trial by jury is normally inappropriate for any personal injury claim because the jury would be required to assess compensatory damages, and it would be unlikely to achieve compatibility with the conventional scale of awards. Take, for example, the case of *H v Ministry of Defence* (1991), which involved allegations of negligence arising from an awful series of events. A 27-year-old soldier had treatment for a congenital condition, and was given a test that resulted in his penis becoming infected. He eventually underwent an emergency penectomy (removal of the penis) while he was under anaesthetic for a skin graft. The House of Lords ruled that the facts, while unusual and very distressing, were not sufficiently exceptional for a jury to be empanelled. However, it was held that where personal injuries have resulted from conduct that amounted to a deliberate abuse of authority, there might be a claim for exemplary damages (an award higher than would be required for compensatory purposes), which might make the case suitable for jury trial.

It was decided in the Court of Appeal in 1964, in *Sims v William Howard & Son Ltd*, that in actions for damages for personal injuries it was desirable to have some uniformity in the amounts of damages awarded for very similar injuries. If trial was before a judge alone, such uniformity could be achieved or the amount could be corrected on appeal, but this was not so if trial was before a jury. It was ruled that the desirability of uniformity of awards in such cases was a factor that should be taken into consideration in deciding on the mode of trial. Lord Justice Pearson said:

> Counsel for the defendants has suggested that it would be suitable to have trial by jury if it is to be expected that there will be a strong conflict of evidence, or if questions of honesty or dishonesty, for instance if it is suggested that the plaintiff is malingering about his accident, pretending to be unable to work when he can work or pretending not to be working when in fact he is working. Those are illustrations of cases in which special circumstances would arise and would make it right to order trial by jury.[11]

In this case, the claimant had suffered severe injuries in an industrial accident when a great weight from a crane fell on him, but there was nothing to suggest that the case should be taken out of the category in which trial by judge alone was suitable.

In the Chancery Division a jury is never used. The same is true in the Family Division. Trial by jury in a county court is not permitted in respect of specified proceedings (like some housing cases), and in all other proceedings in a county court the trial must be without a jury unless the court otherwise orders one on application by a party. Trial by jury is thus now rare in county courts.

In certain circumstances a coroner is obliged to empanel a jury, under section 7 of the Coroners Act 2009. Coroners sit with juries of between 7 and 11 people in cases involving deaths in prison or police custody, and the cause was unnatural or unknown or the death was caused by police conduct or certain types of accident or disease. The coroner also has the power to call juries in other cases where there is sufficient reason for him to do so.

Most inquests (96 per cent) are held without juries, but the state has been insistent that certain types of case must be heard by a jury in order to promote public faith in government.

When, in 1926, legislation permitted inquests to be held without juries for the first time, it was specified that certain types of death still required jury scrutiny, including deaths in police custody, deaths resulting from the actions of a police officer on duty, and deaths in prison. This was seen as a very important way of fostering public trust in potentially oppressive aspects of the state.

In an inquest held with a jury, the verdict must record who died, and where, when and how they died. The verdict is technically called a 'conclusion'. Official notes to the form on which the conclusion is entered suggest the types of conclusion that should be adopted. They are:

(1) deaths from natural causes, industrial diseases, dependency on drugs or non-dependent abuse of drugs, want of attention at birth, and, where appropriate, lack of care or self-neglect;
(2) suicide, deaths from an attempted or self-induced abortion, accident or misadventure, execution of sentence of death, lawful killing, and an open verdict;
(3) deaths as a result of murder, manslaughter, or infanticide;
(4) still-births.

The choice of conclusion is, however, not restricted to the forms, and conclusions can be (although very rarely are) longer and more descriptive.

The tradition that a jury comprises 12 people is ancient and well established.[12] The tradition became statutory before 1729,[13] but is no longer always carried out in practice: the Juries Act 1825, section 26, which laid down that a jury must consist of 12 men (or women from 1919, when the Sex Disqualification Act permitted women to sit as jurors), was repealed in 1972.[14]

A county court jury must consist of eight people[15] and a coroner's jury must consist of not less than seven nor more than 11 people. In the High Court and the Crown Court, juries may consist of any number of people, although not above 12, provided, in the case of the Crown Court, there are at least nine.[16]

MAJORITY VERDICTS

There is no minimum time for which a jury must deliberate in both civil and criminal matters, although it should not reach any verdict before having heard all the evidence. The verdict of a jury in proceedings in the Crown Court or the High Court need not be unanimous if: (1) where there are not fewer than 11 jurors, ten of them agree; or (2) where there are ten jurors, nine of them agree. The verdict of a complete jury of eight in a county court need not be unanimous if seven agree. In a coroner's court, a majority verdict may be accepted if the minority consists of not more than two people.

While there is no minimum time for which civil or criminal juries must deliberate (and they can therefore return a unanimous verdict a short time after retiring), there is a time requirement in trials if the jury is divided and wants to deliver an 11:1 or 10:2 majority verdict. This part of the law is governed by section 17 of the Juries Act 1974. No court may accept a majority verdict unless it appears that the jury has had such period of time for deliberation as seems to the court reasonable, according to the nature and complexity of the case, and the Crown Court may not accept such a verdict unless it appears to the court that the jury has had at least two hours and ten minutes for deliberation.[17] Nor may the Crown Court accept a verdict of guilty by a majority unless the foreman has stated in open court the number who respectively agreed and dissented. These provisions do not affect any practice in civil proceedings, by which a court may accept a majority verdict by consent of the parties or by which the parties may agree to proceed with an incomplete jury.

A judge may urge a jury to avoid disagreement if it can do so without violating its convictions, and may in civil trials point out the inconvenience and expense which would result if a new trial became necessary. However, if a judge were to tell the jury that it was the duty of the minority to give up its independent judgment to that of the majority, and to reach agreement even if it had not changed its own convictions, this would amount to a misdirection.[18]

Slightly different considerations apply in criminal trials, where the trial judge may give the direction set out in *R v Watson* (1988):

> Each of you has taken an oath to return a true verdict according to the evidence. No one must be false to that oath, but you have a duty not only as individuals but collectively. That is the strength of the jury system. Each of you takes into the jury box with you your individual experience and wisdom. Your task is to pool that experience and wisdom. You do that by giving your views and listening to the views of others. There must necessarily be discussion, argument and give and take within the scope of your oath. That is the way in which agreement is reached. If, unhappily, ten of you cannot reach agreement you should say so.[19]

This direction should be given after a jury has had time to consider a majority direction or as part of the summing-up. Trial judges should not depart from the precise wording of the direction.[20]

JUDGES AS JURORS

There is some debate about whether it is good or bad for the legal system (or for society at large) if judges, in their capacity as citizens, serve on juries. Section 321 of the Criminal Justice Act 2003, following a recommendation from the Auld Review of the Criminal Justice system,[21] had the effect of removing certain classes of person (like judges and lawyers, and those concerned with the administration of justice) from the category of those ineligible to serve on juries. Judges, lawyers and police officers are now quite eligible to serve on juries. Guidance about the operation of the rule is set out in a *Practice Direction* of 2005, which notes:

> Jury service is an important public duty which individual members of the public are chosen at random to undertake. The normal presumption is that everyone, unless mentally disordered or disqualified, will be required to serve when summoned to do so.[22]

In 2004, the Lord Chief Justice wrote to judges, explaining how they should respond to certain events. The letter says, for example, 'Judges should avoid the temptation to correct guidance they perceive to be inaccurate as this is outside their role as jurors.' The Lord Chief Justice also noted that judges who sit as jurors can ask the presiding judge questions.[23]

The first judge to be called to serve as a juror was Lord Justice Dyson in June 2004. He did not serve then, but since that time some judges, and many barristers, have served.

In 2004, the Department of Constitutional Affairs, supporting the change in the law that had been made, issued a statement, in which it said:

> The American experience where, in a number of states, judges, lawyers and others holding positions in the criminal justice system have sat as jurors for some time, is that their fellow jurors have not allowed them to dominate their deliberations. In England and Wales, a large number of people with extensive knowledge of the criminal justice system – legal academics, law students and civil servants working in criminal justice – currently do jury service. There is no evidence to suggest that the involvement of any of these groups in jury service has been a problem.[24]

Under the old system, every year about 480,000 people were summoned for jury service but fewer than half (200,000) were eligible. The new rules of eligibility, which also mean that MPs and medical professionals can serve, are expected to significantly reduce the number of people avoiding service. According to a story told by Anthony Scrivener QC, there is only one certain way to avoid jury service. He cites the case of one juror who managed to get a rapid rejection. As the usher brought the jurors in, he confided to her, 'I always find them "not guilty".'

There is no agreement among scholars about why the traditional number of jurors is 12. However, 12 features in many social stories – there were 12 Apostles, 12 tribes of Israel – and in many units of measurement: 12 pennies to the shilling, 12 months in a year, and 12 inches to the foot. Unlike most other numbers, 12 enjoys its own name, 'a dozen'. In keeping with this figure, let me explain some important aspects of the jury by telling 12 diverse jury tales.

TALE 1: THE SEANCER'S TALE

Of the 6,000 appeals that are made each year to the criminal division of the Court of Appeal, few are more bizarre than the case of Stephen Young. The case raises important questions about the way juries work, the contempt laws, the criminal justice system, and even some theological and philosophical points to vex the clergy and academics.

In 1993, Stephen Young, aged 35, was unanimously convicted by a jury at Hove Crown Court of two murders. He was convicted and jailed for life. It later came to light, however, that during the time the jury was out, three of the jurors who were wavering about the proper verdict, used a Ouija board to consult with one of Mr Young's alleged victims. They held a seance to ask the victims who killed them. A juror claimed that they conjured up the spirit of Harry Fuller, who was killed with his wife Nicola. The spirit allegedly confirmed that the defendant was their killer. Using the board, the jurors had spelled out the name of the victims, the type of gun referred to in the evidence, and the message 'Vote guilty tomorrow'. The appeal against conviction was based on the ground that there was a 'material irregularity' in the deliberations of the jury, that is to say that they reached their decision not on the basis of the evidence but on conversations with the deceased. The Court of Appeal agreed and ordered a new trial, at which Mr Young was again convicted.

This case raises questions about section 8 of the Contempt of Court Act 1981, which effectively prevents jurors from talking about how they came to their decisions. It makes it a criminal offence of contempt of court 'to obtain, disclose or solicit any particulars of statements made, opinions expressed, arguments advanced or votes cast by members of a jury in the course of their deliberations'. How the jury makes its decision is a private matter for the jurors. In the case of Mr Young, the Court of Appeal was able to review what happened because the activity at issue had taken place not while the jury was formally deliberating but while staying at a hotel to which they had been sent for the night. The reason behind the prohibition on jurors telling anyone what went on in the jury room, or which way jurors decided, is a bit like that behind the secret ballot: it precludes bribery and blackmail. It makes little sense for someone to offer inducements or threats to a juror to decide in a certain way if that juror's decision cannot be checked. Also, as a government report observed in 1965, 'if such disclosure were to be made, particularly to the Press, jurors would no longer feel free to express their opinions frankly when the verdict was under discussion, for fear that what they said later might be made public.'[25]

Disclosure of jury secrets was formally made a specific offence, however, only in 1981, by the Contempt of Court Act; before that, the courts examined each case on its merits to see if the disclosure at issue amounted to a contempt.

The rule has generated a number of problems. It has meant that there is no proper empirical research on how juries decide cases. To what extent is prejudice on the basis of, say, race, sex or class a significant feature of how juries discuss and decide cases? The problems have really been highlighted in complex fraud trials lasting many weeks or months. It would be a challenge for even trained experts to sit diligently listening to the complicated twists of some financial scam, for hours every day, for a period of months, while all the time taking detailed notes and remembering names, dates and figures. Jurors, of course, are not selected for such skills, and there is evidence that many have been deciding such cases on alarmingly capricious criteria. A provision in the Criminal Justice Act 2003, not yet implemented, will permit trial without jury (but before a judge and specialist panel) in cases of serious and complex fraud.

In 1994, the House of Lords ruled on a major contempt-of-court case arising from an article in the *Mail on Sunday* in 1992 which gave the views of jurors who had sat in a case known as the Blue Arrow fraud trial at the Old Bailey. The trial had gone on for exactly one year. Four of the defendants were convicted by the jury and later sentenced to prison, although their appeals eventually succeeded because the trial judge had made an error when summing-up to the jury. Clive Wolman, the *Mail on Sunday*'s city editor, ran a story which included the views of jurors in that case. One juror, for example, said that another one had shown a complete lack of understanding about the case, had at first only wanted to drag the case out, and then had only agreed with the verdict because he wanted to go home. There was some evidence that the paper's editors were aware they would be breaking provisions of the Contempt of Court Act in publishing the article but considered that violation of the contempt laws would be outweighed by the public interest in exposing such a ridiculous and dangerous aspect of the legal system.

The newspaper publishers, the editor and the journalist were convicted and fined £30,000, £20,000, and £10,000 respectively. Their defence – that they had not 'disclosed' the jury secrets, because the jurors had originally given interviews to an American researcher – was rejected by the House of Lords, which preserved the strict application of the Contempt of Court Act by saying that newspaper publication was 'disclosure' even if a juror had earlier divulged the secrets to a researcher.[26]

Even before section 8 of the 1981 Act, it was an established rule of law that, on appeal, a court could not look at what went on in the jury room. In a case in 1922, Lord Justice Warrington said:

> [T]he court does not entertain or admit evidence by a juryman of what took place in the jury room either by way of explanation of the grounds upon which the verdict was given, or by way of statement as to what he believed its effect to be.[27]

The Court of Appeal decision in the Stephen Young case therefore raises some critical questions. Supposing the jurors in the hotel had sought advice not of a spirit through a seance but from God through prayer – a reasonable possibility, remembering the gravely consequential decision they had to make. Would such a course of action invalidate their decision? They would, after all, be consulting something non-corporeal and making a decision based on something other than the facts of the case. The divine and 'superstitious' oracles are both equally unprovable and rely on the faith of the juror. Can the law hold that consulting God for guidance is permissible but consulting any other non-corporeal entity is not allowed? If so, what will the court say is the validating element in religious faith in contradistinction to superstitious faith?

The court could avoid such a quandary by saying that jurors must be guided by absolutely nothing other than the evidence given in court. That option, however, would prevent religious people from receiving divine guidance when many must often be in great need of it. This would be an awkward decision from judges with the courts' motto *Dieu et mon droit* (God and my right) on a shield above them.

Let us now turn to another case involving the supernatural.

TALE 2: THE ASTROLOGER'S TALE

In July 1998, a juror at Newcastle upon Tyne Crown Court was barred from the trial of a man charged with grievous bodily harm after he requested the defendant's star sign in order to reach a verdict. The juror, a man in his 20s, had written a note to the judge asking for the accused's exact time and date of birth so that he could draw up an astrological chart to see what it foretold. After consulting with barristers, Judge Esman Faulks discharged the juror on the grounds that consulting such a chart fell outside the terms of his oath to consider only the facts before the court. The juror had said that he needed the information because he was unable to come to a decision without drawing up a chart and was puzzled as to why the judge frowned upon this.[28]

In 1993, the Royal Commission on Criminal Justice recommended a loosening of the terms of the Contempt of Court Act to permit some research into how juries deliberate. The government has not taken up this idea. In the United States, jurors are allowed to disclose their own votes but not to refer to the views or voting of other jurors. There are those who believe, though, that if ever jury secrecy was abandoned here, trial by jury would eventually go the same way. Others think it is perverse not even to permit research into the system.

Perversity provokes various responses, although rarely does it prompt people to dance in the streets. But that is what occurred one afternoon in 1996 outside Liverpool Crown Court, as the following tale demonstrates.

TALE 3: THE PEACE CAMPAIGNER'S TALE

The jubilation came after a jury acquitted Lotta Kronlid, Joanna Wilson and Andrea Needham of £1.5 million worth of criminal damage to a British Aerospace (BAe) Hawk jet, despite clear evidence that they had committed the damage alleged. They, and a fourth woman, Angela Zelter, were also acquitted of conspiring to damage the jet. While incredulity, dismay and panic ran through the corridors of the government and BAe, supporters of the defendants' Christian peace campaign group celebrated with jigs in the street. After the verdict, a government minister sought urgent talks between the Home Office and the Attorney-General, observing that 'the ramifications of the case are ... very important in terms of future security, jobs and the question of being able to do damage and getting off with it.'[29] Each year, many trials, most quite mundane, result in apparently perverse jury verdicts.

Is trial by jury a desirable institution or an expensive and dispensable anachronism which, after six centuries of evolution, cannot effectively adapt to its latest environment? Most Crown Court defendants plead guilty, and where acquittals take place, most are directed by the judge, although the jury must agree to acquit. During the period 1992–2006, most 'not guilty' verdicts recorded in the Crown Courts were not reached by juries acting alone, that is, without judicial direction to acquit. Where juries do reach a verdict without such a suggestion, acquittals have steadily declined from 45 per cent of contested cases in 1992–93 to 38 per cent in 2005–06.[30] Judges' acquittals, by contrast, have risen. In practice this means the judge has ruled at the end of the prosecution's case (in the absence of the jury) that there is insufficient evidence for the jury to consider and invites the jury to acquit. As the defendant is in the jury's charge, their verdict is required before the defendant can be acquitted. There are two types of such acquittals: (1) ordered decisions, entered when a trial is due to start because the prosecution says it cannot proceed; and (2) directed acquittals, when the judge stops the trial because of a legal problem, for example if key evidence is inadmissible. In 2005, juries found 5,927 defendants not guilty, whereas 13,894 defendants were acquitted by judges. Juries convicted 12,099 people, while 60,252 pleaded guilty.

Some academic writers such as Penny Darbyshire have argued that the jury is not really randomly selected, and even when it does warrant such a label, it is not thereby representative of the population. She says:

> Random selection from the community is unlikely to produce a cross-section, unless some form of stratified sampling is used, which is not the case in summoning a jury. Random selection may throw up juries which are male, all Conservative, all white.[31]

Further, Darbyshire argues, the extent to which juries have convicted people subsequently proved to have been not guilty shows that the institution does not merit the eulogies it normally receives from many constitutional writers. She has called the jury 'an anti-democratic, irrational and haphazard legislator, whose erratic and secret decisions run counter to the rule of law'. The defendants in a string of notorious miscarriages of justice – such as the cases of the Birmingham Six, the Guildford Four, Stefan Kiszko, Judith Ward and the Cardiff Three – were all originally convicted by juries.[32] If one looks at a range of cases during any given period, there is undoubtedly an unpredictability about those that resulted in a defiant jury verdict. A defiant verdict is one that goes against the decision to which the evidence, the existing law and the judge's summing-up clearly point. Some-times such jury verdicts appear to have been made when jurors take into account some non-legal factor like a social or political one, or one concerning the perceived sense of a prosecution.

The three women who admitted breaking into a British Aerospace plant near Preston, and using hammers to damage Hawk ZH955, argued that their otherwise criminal acts were subject to the lawful excuse that they were preventing a greater crime: genocide. Committing a crime to prevent a (usually) greater crime is permitted under section 3 of the Criminal Law Act 1967, which provides that a person may use 'such force as is reasonable in all the circumstances in the prevention of crime'. Genocide is a crime under English law by virtue of the Genocide Act 1969, which includes killing members of national, ethnic, racial or religious groups with intent to wholly or partly destroy that group.

The peace activists, members of the organisation Ploughshare, pointed out that the Hawk jet was due to be sold, as one of a consignment of 24, by British Aerospace to the Indonesian government. They contended that the aircraft would be used against the civilian population of East Timor as part of a genocidal attack on the people of that island. This former Portuguese colony was forcibly annexed by Indonesia in 1975, and Amnesty International had estimated that almost 200,000 East Timorese people (about a third of the population) had since been killed by the Indonesian government. The women had left a video film explaining their actions in the cockpit of the aircraft. The film included footage of the Dili massacre in 1991, in which 291 civilians were gunned down by Indonesian troops at a memorial service in Santa Cruz. The Indonesian government gave assurances that the Hawks would not be used against the East Timorese, and the British government said that an export licence had been granted because the Indonesian assurances had been accepted.

Lord Devlin stated in 1966 that 'each jury is a little parliament'. If that is so, the government was given a serious jolt by the microcosmic Commons in Liverpool Crown Court.

The right to return a verdict at variance with the one preferred by the authorities is an important constitutional asset and something heroically won. Next we will turn to another tale of heroic defiance.

TALE 4: THE RECUSANT'S TALE

One great victory for the English jury came in 1670 in a case which established the jury's right to follow its own conscience even to the extent of disregarding the letter of the law and the directions of the judge. It is known as *Bushel's Case*[33] and concerned two Quakers, William Mead and William Penn, who had been charged with conducting a 'seditious assembly' (a meeting assembled to do an unlawful act, such as commit violence or damage or to provoke disorder). They had been preaching in Gracechurch Street near London Bridge, despite laws aimed at suppressing Nonconformism. The meeting was orderly as the Quakers were peaceable people opposed to all violence. The jury refused to convict, and the judge angrily locked them up for two nights without meat, drink, fire, tobacco or – heaping indignity upon discomfort – chamber pot. The case was named after Edward Bushel, the jury foreman. The court eventually refused to accept the jurors' verdict of not guilty. The jurors were, on the fifth day of proceedings, all punished by a 40-mark fine (a mark was a seventeenth-century coin valued at 13 shillings and 4 pence), and were then imprisoned pending payment. Four of the men, led by Bushel, refused to pay, and so spent months in prison. The Lord Chief Justice, Sir Robert Vaughan, eventually decided that they should be released, asserting 'the right of juries to give their verdict by their conscience'. It was stated that jurors might use their own thinking 'to give their verdict contrary to the sense of court'.[34] In the eighteenth and nineteenth centuries, it was this right that helped juries save many petty criminals from the gallows.

Other instances of 'perverse verdicts' include the case of Cynthia Payne, to which we will now turn.

TALE 5: THE MADAME'S TALE

In 1987, Cynthia Payne was found not guilty of charges, under the Sexual Offences Act 1956, of controlling prostitutes. It was alleged that Ms Payne organised sex parties for gain in a suburban house, in Ambleside Avenue, Streatham. Some of the alleged clients were senior police officers, ex-squadron leaders, and senior citizens who used walking sticks and wheelchairs. Sex was said to have been paid for with money or even luncheon vouchers.

Each day of the trial the jury had to sit passively and consider scenes of tumultuous partying and risqué conduct recounted by police officers who had assumed various false identities and disguises in order to collect evidence. Day one of the trial, for example, concerned the events that occurred when the police finally raided the house. Some of the action seemed appropriate for a *Carry On* film from the 1960s. One elderly gentleman was perched on the edge of Cynthia Payne's bath with a woman at his knee, more or less. When the police burst into the room, she sprang to her feet, the court was told, and the gentleman toppled backwards into the bath with his legs in the air and his trousers around his ankles.

The detailed and often lurid evidence that the undercover police gave in court was the source of some hilarity in the public gallery and some very strained attempts from members of the jury to retain expressions of due solemnity as they considered the evidence. Although the trial judge stated in his summing-up to the jury that the case was 'a criminal trial, not a form of entertainment', the jury seemed to disagree: they acquitted Ms Payne in the teeth of all the evidence.[35]

In a grimmer context, another perverse jury verdict was given in the case of Stephen Owen, whose story is told in the next tale.

TALE 6: THE AVENGER'S TALE

Stephen Owen's 12-year-old son Darren was run down and killed by a lorry driver called Kevin Taylor, who, it emerged, had never taken a driving test, had a long criminal record for drink-driving and violence, and was blind in one eye. He was reputed not to have shown any remorse for killing the boy.

Darren had been riding his bicycle through Sittingbourne High Street in Kent in 1989. He was crushed under the wheels of the 30-ton lorry. Following this event, Taylor was convicted of a driving offence and given an 18-month sentence, from which he was released after 12 months. He promptly returned to unlawfully driving his lorry.

In outrage and grief, and having met with no response from letters to all sorts of authorities, the dead boy's father got a shotgun and fired at the lorry driver, injuring him. Mr Owen was prosecuted in 1992 for a variety of offences, including attempted murder, but despite all the evidence against him, was acquitted by the jury. Mr Justice Hidden had said to the jury at Maidstone Crown Court that they should not allow their 'understandable sympathy' to cloud their judgement about whether the father had committed an offence when he had fired a sawn-off double-barrelled shotgun at point-blank range at Mr Taylor. But they still acquitted Mr Owen, even though he had admitted his actions. Mr Owen was also acquitted of five other charges of wounding Taylor and his girlfriend. Mr Owen left the court to loud cheers and he said, 'Thank God for British justice.'[36]

The jury might have promoted public confidence in the criminal justice system through public participation, but such a benefit is limited by two considerations. First, juries are only as good as the evidence upon which they have to deliberate, so misleading evidence from forensic scientists or police officers can and has fooled the system. Second, 95 per cent of criminal cases are tried without juries in magistrates' courts. Juries can be helped by the evidence that experts give in court, but not by experts among themselves giving professional points of view in the jury room, because lawyers and experts in the case will not have had the chance to respond to whatever the expert juror might assert. This point was at issue in the next case.

TALE 7: THE EXPERT'S TALE

In medieval times, jurors were selected because they knew the defendant or the circumstances of a case and were sworn to testify about the events. Today, jurors are randomly chosen, and if a juror knows someone connected to the case, or is associated with the events leading to the case, he will not be permitted to act as a juror in the case. One question thus arising is, as a juror, how far are you permitted to use your own expert knowledge of an aspect of a case to inform jury discussion?

Consider the case of *R v Fricker* (1999). On 7 March 1998, while on patrol, police officers had seen the defendant, Clive Fricker, parked in a Mazda car in Sheridan Road in Horfield, Bristol. They looked in his car and saw three tyres, for which Mr Fricker could give no adequate explanation. The prosecution alleged that the tyres were stolen, but as there was no evidence to prove that they were stolen, the defendant was charged with attempting to handle stolen goods.

After the jury had retired to consider their verdict, they sent a note to the judge in the following terms:

> One of the jurors is a tyre specialist. The code 088 on the tyre signifies the tyre was manufactured in the eighth week of 1998. The defendant claims to have had the tyres in his house around this period – certainly very little time for the tyres to have gone through normal purchase before being acquired by the defendant. May we take this into consideration?

The judge was of the view that the juror could take to the jury room his particular knowledge, providing he was warned that he should be sure of the accuracy of his knowledge before the whole jury relied upon it.

The judge relied on a precedent in which it was held as legitimate for one justice to draw on specialist medical knowledge in forming an opinion on the facts and to inform colleagues about how such knowledge caused him to look at the evidence.[37] However, it was held on appeal in the *Fricker* case that where a juror had specialist knowledge of matters forming the background of the case against the defendant, and had communicated that information to other members of the jury who had then come to a verdict, the judge was obliged to discharge the jury because the defendant would have had no opportunity to challenge what amounted to entirely new evidence, or to have put forward his own explanation. It was wrong that any jury should have been permitted to have introduced entirely new evidence into the case when neither party had any notice of it. Accordingly, the appeal was allowed, and Mr Fricker's conviction was quashed.

Not all juries, however, are well supplied with experts. They can, perhaps, sometimes be the weaker for that. There is some evidence that juries can be easily fooled. There are studies that suggest good liars can fool even citizens who think they have a fair idea of what sort of mannerisms betray a perjurer. The studies show that compared with truth-tellers, liars typically make fewer hand gestures, move their heads less, speak more slowly and sit more rigidly. They betray their anxiety, however, by shifting their feet or tapping their fingers. In addition, liars tend to relax their facial muscles and affect pleasant expressions, as if aware that observers are watching their faces for signs of deceit. In one experiment involving 715 people, a truthful speaker was judged to be lying by 74.3 per cent of the subjects and a lying witness was judged to be truthful by 73.7 per cent.[38]

Some observers of the jury might be less inclined to see it as a noble institution composed of liberty-conscious individuals, and more in the terms favoured by Mark Twain, who said that 'The jury puts a ban upon intelligence and honesty, and a premium upon ignorance, stupidity and perjury.' Twain's is an extreme view, however, and not a popular one. Yet there is occasionally some evidence to show that the foibles and shortcomings present in any population, and the errors we are prone to as human beings, are just as extant in the juries composed from the general population. The next tale is a case in point.

TALE 8: THE BONDED JUROR'S TALE

On 30 January 1998, the jury at a trial at Lewes Crown Court in East Sussex had been considering its verdict for four hours when the judge was told 'the foreman has handcuffed himself'. Four men, accused of planning a jewel robbery, were on trial. After hearing that the gang had planned to use a pair of handcuffs on a Brighton shop assistant before raiding the safe, the foreman of the jury – a middle-aged man – decided to experiment with the evidence while deliberating a verdict. Unfortunately, after he had locked his hand in the handcuff, and realised that he had clamped it so tightly that the blood supply to his hand had become restricted, it became evident that the police had not brought a key for the handcuffs to the trial.

Judge Simon Coltart quickly sent for the fire brigade, but then he was faced with the problem that the law prevented anyone, including the fire and rescue officers, from entering the jury room or speaking to jurors. The matter was further complicated when the fire officer in charge of the rescue operation realised that his sister-in-law was on the jury. As the red-faced and white-handed foreman sat in pain, and fire and rescue officers waited outside the court for orders, legal minds wrestled with the tricky issues raised. Finally, barristers agreed that the courtroom should be cleared. All 12 jurors then trooped back into the jury box and the trapped foreman was freed with bolt cutters.[39]

Sometimes, though, even something as venial as a cough from a juror can have disastrous consequences, as in the following case.

TALE 9: THE COUGHER'S TALE

On 15 April 1999, a defendant at Cardiff Crown Court was mistakenly sentenced to two years in prison because a juror happened to cough at an inopportune moment. Unable to stifle a tickle at the back of his throat any longer, the juror coughed just as the foreman was announcing the verdict of not guilty, with the result that the noise drowned out the word 'not'. Only the word 'guilty' was audible to the judge. Judge Michael Gibbon, thinking that the defendant, Alan Rashid, had been found guilty of the charge of making a threat to kill, promptly jailed him for two years, thanked the jury for their efforts during the two-day trial, and released them.

The puzzled jurors assumed that Mr Rashid was being sentenced for other offences of which they were unaware, until on the way out of the building one juror asked an usher why Mr Rashid had been sent down after being found not guilty. The official realised there had been a blunder and called everyone back into court. A confused Mr Rashid, who minutes earlier was being consoled in the cells, was led back to the dock, told by the judge that he was free to go after all, and left.[40]

A cough, though, is a relatively minor indiscretion compared with that of a juror at Southwark Crown Court on 2 August 1999. Tired of her duties of listening to and evaluating masses of evidence, the middle-aged woman filled a lemonade bottle with vodka, took it to court, and slowly got sozzled. She did this after having listened to evidence in a case for more than two months, just before the jury was sent to a private room to consider its verdict. She had become so tipsy that her fellow jurors were forced to write a note to the judge protesting that she was making it impossible for them to concentrate.

The judge immediately ordered them into court, where he watched in amazement as the juror had to be helped to her seat. He then ordered the jury to cease deliberations and go home so the woman could sleep off the effects of the drink. Judge David Elfer said, 'It is plain to those who have dealt with her that she is profoundly drunk and nothing can be achieved without her having a very long sleep.' Barristers in the case expressed their concern about her remaining on the jury, but the judge said that he would allow her to continue. It was the forty-first day of the trial. Jury trials cost about £8,000 a day to operate, and the jury had been sent out to decide complicated matters that would determine whether five defendants were guilty. The cost of another trial would have been considerable.[41] The counts in the indictment in the case, a case so nearly derailed by alcohol, chiefly concerned conspiracy to cheat the Customs and Excise of duty on wines and spirits.

Turning from alcohol to cigarettes, the next case presents an example of another sort of challenge to jury deliberations.

TALE 10: THE SMOKER'S TALE

On 8 November 1993, at the Central Criminal Court in London, Judge Hawkins QC was forced to order a retrial when two jurors nearly came to blows after one had accused the other of burgling his flat. The row had been simmering from the very start of the trial (a trial, almost needless to say, for burglary) when, during a break for legal submissions, one juror accused the other of smoking in a no-smoking area.

Two days later the accuser arrived in court in a foul mood because his home had been burgled. He immediately blamed the other juror, calling him 'a swine', and claiming that the other juror had taken his name and address from a label on his rucksack. As tempers threatened to boil over, the two jurors were paid off with expenses and told their services were no longer required. A court official said, 'The man had a cast-iron alibi and was obviously being picked on as a scapegoat. There was no way the pair could be left to reach a verdict when there was such bad feeling between them.'[42]

Speaking of the jury, Sir William Blackstone once said, in his acclaimed legal treatise *Commentaries on the Laws of England*, 'The liberties of England cannot but subsist so long as this palladium remains sacred and inviolate.'[43] A palladium means a 'safeguard', and comes from the word for the wooden image of Pallas that protected the citadel of Troy. Not all great lawyers, though, have been as prepared as was Blackstone to repose complete faith in the jury. Louis Blom-Cooper QC, for example, believes that decisions now made by lay jurors should be made by appointed experts, as 'You wouldn't want a butcher to take out your appendix.'[44]

Would people specially trained in matters of criminal justice produce better results than do ordinary people? Today, people who work in the criminal justice system can sit as jurors. This raises the question of whether such people might be biased against defendants, a question examined in the next case.

TALE 11: THE CRIME FIGHTERS' TALE

Are people whose jobs concern the fight against crime likely to be biased jurors? In a case in 2005, the Court of Appeal decided that a fair-minded and informed observer would not conclude that there was a real possibility that a juror was biased merely because the juror's occupation meant that he or she was involved in the administration of justice.[45] The court decided that the presence of serving police officers and a prosecuting solicitor (an employee of the Crown Prosecution

Service) on separate juries in 2004 and 2005 had not offended against principles of fairness and there were no circumstances in the cases to give rise to concerns of bias.

The court was hearing together three separate appeals from defendants whose complaint about their trials was the same. The appellants each appealed against their convictions on the grounds that the jury in their respective trials (at the Central Criminal Court, Woolwich Crown Court and Warrington Crown Court) had contained members who were employed in the criminal justice system. The appellants all argued that a trial had to be fair, and had to be seen to be fair; for that to happen the tribunal conducting the trial had to be free from actual or apparent bias, and the presence of the police officers and the CPS employee on the respective juries offended against that principle.

Resisting the appeal, the Crown (i.e. the prosecution) argued that:

(1) the Criminal Justice Act 2003 (which allowed police officers and criminal justice personnel to sit as jurors) had been made by the democratically elected legislature for the legitimate purpose of maximising the pool of responsible and professional people available to perform the important civil function of serving on a jury. It was a valid Act and could not be subverted by a judicial decision;
(2) there was no actual partiality established by any of the jurors in the three cases;
(3) the summoning officer and the judge had a discretion to excuse or discharge a person from serving on a jury; and
(4) there were sufficient safeguards, such as the random selection process and the guidance given to jurors to inform the judge if they recognised anyone involved in the case.

The court decided there were few reasons why police officers, members of the CPS, or other persons involved in the administration of justice in general, should be excluded from the obligation of the public generally to shoulder the important responsibility of sitting on a jury. Those reasons – that they might know more than other jurors about the workings of the court system, that they might play an unduly dominant role in the jury's deliberations, and that they might not approach the case with the same open-mindedness of someone unconnected with the legal system – did not justify disqualifying individuals from jury service by reason of their occupation alone.

Jurors, the Court of Appeal noted, were selected randomly, they took an oath to determine the case on the evidence, and they were advised about their role and the importance of informing an official if they knew anyone involved in the case. Lord Woolf said:

> The fact that there are 12 members of the jury of which at least 10 must be agreed is a real protection against the prejudices of an individual juror resulting in unfairness to a defendant. In addition, it is to be hoped and expected, that those who are employed in the administration of justice [like police officers and CPS lawyers] will be particularly careful not to act in a manner which is inconsistent with their duty as members of the jury and in particular, to exercise the independence of mind which is required of all jurors and to be on their guard to reach their verdict only on the evidence in accordance with the directions from the trial judge.[46]

Not all jury issues are as grave. A good example of a lighter tale is the following one, recounted by Sir John Mortimer QC.

TALE 12: THE OPTIMIST'S TALE

The tale concerns an indecency case. A woman witness was giving evidence and was asked what the man in the dock had said to her. She was too embarrassed to repeat it in open court, so the judge asked her to write it down. She did, and what she wrote was 'Would you care for a screw?' This document was passed around the jury until it reached juror number 12, an elderly gentleman who was fast asleep. Sitting next to him was a fairly personable young lady. She read the note, nudged her neighbour and, when he was awake, handed it to him. He woke with a start, read it and, with apparent satisfaction, folded it and put it carefully away in his wallet. When the judge said, 'Let that be handed up to me', the juryman shook his head and replied, 'It's purely a private matter, my Lord.'[47]

A VERDICT

Sir William Blackstone argued that the jury was such a desirable part of the legal system that the liberty of subjects depended on its being free not just from outright attacks but from more insidious ways by which its role might be diminished, for example:

> [by] secret machinations, which may sap and undermine it; by introducing new and arbitrary methods of trial, by justices of the peace, commissioners of the revenue, and courts of conscience. And however convenient these may appear at first (as doubtless all arbitrary powers, well executed, are the most convenient), let it be again remembered, that delays, and little inconveniences in the forms of justice, are the price that all free nations must pay for their liberty in more substantial matters . . .[48]

Many things have changed since Blackstone published that in 1769. The country is now a large industrial nation, with a population of 63 million and nearly 2 million criminal cases a year: no one could argue that all the magistrates' court cases (currently dealing with 95 per cent of prosecuted crime) should revert to jury trials. But that is not a good reason for a government to start to shift some of the serious crimes currently tried before juries into the jurisdiction of non-jury courts. The jury is still an indispensable bastion of liberty. Sir John Mortimer QC has characterised its great virtue in this way:

> Juries are not composed of perfect people – they are not meant to be. They are meant to be people like us, full of imperfections. Our peers. Those of us who appear in criminal trials are always impressed by the jury's care, attention and sense of responsibility, and by verdicts which show, when there are a number of charges to consider, an astute awareness of the strength of the evidence on various complicated counts.[49]

The jury system is costly, and difficult to run smoothly. The managerial demands across the country are huge. Every year, the system necessitates the bringing together in small groups of 400,000 diverse people, whose ordinary routines are subject to all the normal pressures and vicissitudes of life. It requires each juror to act with great caution and immense concentration because so much is at stake, not just for all the people in the immediate drama of the case, but also for all those who stand to be indirectly affected by their verdicts. Arguments for any further diminution in the scope of jury work should be assessed with great care.

FURTHER READING

Stephen Adler, *The Jury: Disorder in the Court*, New York: Main Street Books, 1995.

Penny Darbyshire, 'The Lamp That Shows That Freedom Lives – Is It Worth the Candle?' Crim LR 740, 1991.

Lord Denning, *Landmarks in the Law*, London: Butterworths, 1984.

Sir Patrick Devlin, *Trial By Jury*, The Hamlyn Trust, London: Stevens, 1956.

Trevor Grove, *The Juryman's Tale*, London: Bloomsbury, 1998.

Ministry of Justice Research Series 1/10. London: Ministry of Justice, 2010.

Cheryl Thomas, *Are Juries Fair*. Ministry of Justice Research Series 1/10. London: Ministry of Justice, 2010. Online. Available <http://www.justice.gov.uk/publications/docs/are-juries-fair-research.pdf> (accessed 30 July 2010).

Language and Law

9

All professions and social groups, such as football fans or horticulturalists, have their particular and specialist vocabularies and styles of language. The language of judges and lawyers might be notorious for being technical, laden with Latin, and archaic, but the relationship between law and language is even more interesting and important than the relationship between other occupations and their languages or codes. This is because the actual business of law is transacted and executed in language.

Medicine has its own specialist vocabulary and medics speak and write to each other using medical argot, but the actual business of medicine is to do with the human body, medicines and medical procedures. Medicine is done physically. Architects have their own specialist vocabulary and use language in their own particular way, but their business is to do with building materials and buildings. Lawyers, too, have their own specialist language but, by contrast, their work, its materials and products, are words and language: the words in sworn documents (deeds), Acts of Parliament, regulations, advocacy and court judgments. This chapter looks at both legal vocabulary (the language used by judges and lawyers in the course of their work) and also some examples of legal work where aspects of ordinary language are themselves the issues in question.

Language is dynamic. Every year many words fall out of the dictionary and new ones are added. English has evolved an extraordinarily eclectic vocabulary. Whereas French offers about 100,000 words, English offers around one million words including word combinations and vocabulary used in electronic and broadcast media.

Juridically, the English language has become the best instrument box in the world. The word 'law' comes from an Old Icelandic word for 'something laid or fixed', although law's lexicon, like the general one, is unfixed and constantly developing. Every year some words become obsolete while others are born. So 'rixle', meaning 'to rule', has gone, but a 'clickwrap', a mouse-made contract, is arriving. Lawyers and judges often struggle against the accusation that they use a superfluity of words. Chief Baron Kelly once told a witness, 'You must give me an answer, in the fewest possible words of which you are capable . . . ' That, though, was his opening phrase in a 121-word sentence of instruction.

Even though language is changing all the time, anyone moving into the study or practice of law moves into an area heavily laden with a linguistic inheritance. In subjects such as science and the social sciences, much of current vocabulary and phrasing originated in modern times. In law, though, much of the language has been inherited from earlier ages. This is an inheritance of some considerable influence. As the esteemed legal historians Pollock and Maitland have observed, 'Language is not a mere instrument which we control at will; it controls us.'[1]

Verbal precision is not always possible when social factors cause obfuscation. Occasionally however, court definitions are evidently at variance with aspects of ordinary life. Consider this example. Does the working class still exist? In a case in 2003, Mr Justice Etherton was asked to rule whether a 1929 legal covenant on a piece of land, restricting its use to benefit the poor and in particular 'for the housing of the working classes', was now invalid. In court it was argued that 'It is not possible to say today with any degree of certainty or precision what is meant by the working classes.'[2] The Court of Appeal, faced with a similar argument in 1955, unanimously ruled that the working class in Britain had been abolished (*Guinness Trust (London Fund) v Green* (1955). This is very strange. If the working classes have been abolished, then who is making steel, cars and ships, and repairing the roads, and driving the buses, trains and lorries? Where does our food come from? These tasks are not being performed by the aristocracy. In a survey a few years ago, 80 per cent of respondents described themselves as 'middle class'. Thus, social attitudes can affect legal definitions. Whether a particular fruit is or is not a lemon will not depend on changing attitudes. However, what is meant by something like 'the working classes' can, in law, change even to the extent of ceasing to have a referent.

Verbosity is a fault often alleged against lawyers. Why does legal language often resort to pairs of words when plainly one would suffice? Why is law sprinkled with so many phrases such as 'each and every', 'last will and testament', and 'null and void'? There are various explanations. In medieval Britain, law was conducted in three languages (Anglo-Saxon, Norman French and Latin), and phrases were sometimes aggregations of words lifted from the different traditions. Lawyers were also often paid by the folio, so it did not hurt them to be a little fuller in expression than might be strictly necessary. The additional embroidery of a Latin phrase could also lend an authoritative air to an argument: 'If that phrase had not been in Latin,' said Lord Shaw in a case in 1923, 'nobody would have called it a principle.'[3]

LATIN AND THE LAW

'I'm off to the local radio station now,' I once said to a legal colleague. 'I'm going to speak about the public irritation with legal language.' 'Good for you,' he replied. 'Is that something you have done heretofore?'

Law is closely associated with Latin for several reasons. For centuries, while law was being developed in Britain, Latin was the official language used in court documents. Additionally many principles that matured into law in Britain were derived from those used in Roman law. Principles were also developed by medieval jurists at a time when Latin was the language of scholarship. The use of a language alien to over 95 per cent of the population certainly fuelled the observation by George Bernard Shaw that a profession is a conspiracy against lay people. Study of Latin is, however, expanding. There has been a growth recently in Latin study in schools, and in 2003, BBC Radio broadcast its first programme entirely in Latin: readings from Pliny the Elder. The humorous book *X-treme Latin* (2004) by Henry Beard caters to baser interests, allowing readers to learn translations of contemporary phrases. These include *Lingua Latina – iurisperiti ea utuntur ut te defraudent* (Latin – lawyers use it to screw you) and *Estne cubiculum deliberationis instructum cistula potionum spirituosarum?* (Does the jury room have a minibar?).

The phenomenon of lawyers being criticised for their use of Latin is not a recent development. Cicero was berating lawyers for using outdated Latin in 63 BC. In his 'Pro L. Murena' he also attacks lawyers for thinking too much of themselves, and for their quibbling and verbosity. Speaking for Lucius Licinius Murena at his trial on a charge of electoral malpractice, Cicero chided the linguistic practices of earlier Roman lawyers as being 'long-winded' and 'filled to the brim with trickery and foolishness'. He said:

> As for myself, I have long found it extraordinary that so many of the finest legal brains should not yet have managed, even after so many years, to make up their minds as to whether one ought to say 'two days from now' or 'the day after tomorrow', 'judge' or 'arbitrator', 'case' or 'lawsuit'.[4]

The Civil Procedure Rules 1998 now insist that all the old esoteric or Latin phrases used by lawyers and judges are replaced with plain English equivalents. Thus, for example, a 'writ' is now a 'claim', a 'plaintiff' is now a 'claimant', guardian *ad litem* (guardian to the suit) is a 'litigator's friend', an *in camera* (in a vaulted room) hearing has become a 'private hearing', an *amicus curiae* (friend of the court) is now, simply, an 'advocate to the court', and an order of *certiorari* (to be made certain) is a 'quashing order'.

How have the lawyers coped with all this change? For many of the more seasoned practitioners the radical changes required in practice seem to have been a considerable challenge. Things did not get off to a good start. The morning the new rules came into effect in April 1999, one of the first barristers on his feet in the High Court was swiftly knocked back by the presiding judge. 'My Lord,' offered the experienced counsel, 'I appear for the plaintiff in this action.' The withering judicial riposte was instantaneous: 'No you don't, you appear for the claimant.'

Latin has been banned from the law courts before, only to be promptly reintroduced when lawyers could no longer tolerate the withdrawal symptoms. In 1731, Parliament passed an Act abolishing law-Latin in legal proceedings (written to come into effect two years later), which read:

> Whereas many and great mischiefs do frequently happen to the subject of this kingdom, from the proceedings in courts of justice being in an unknown language, those who are summoned and impleaded having no knowledge or understanding of what is alleged for or against them in the pleadings of their lawyers and attornies . . . To remedy these great mischiefs . . . be it enacted that from [25 March 1733] all writs . . . process . . . pleadings . . . indictments . . . judgments . . . shall be in the English tongue and language only.

Lawyers then faced the challenge of rendering certain Latin phrases into English; for example *nisi prius* (unless before), *quaere impedit* (wherefore he hinders) and *habeas corpus* (you [must] have the body) all caused great difficulty. According to the eighteenth-century legal writer Sir William Blackstone, these phrases were 'not capable of an English dress with any degree of seriousness'. So, in March 1733, a week before the first Act was due to come into effect, another Act was passed which once again permitted lawyers to attack and parry in Latin. It amended the first Act, to allow Latin to be used in technical terms, customary phrases and abbreviations.

A good case for the use of Latin in court has been made by the former judge John Gray, who wrote in 2002:

Latin usage is to be forbidden in the courts, ostensibly to make the law more comprehensible and less intimidating to lay people, ad captandum vulgus ('to win over the crowd'). Yet Botanists, and those concerned with fragrances derived from plants, revere it as an international language by which species are named and can be identified. Nobody there suggests change because the practice might be thought elitist and offend the average gardener's sensitivities. Entomologists (insects) and Ichthyologists (fish) too are happy to classify in Latin.[5]

There is, however, a good argument for court proceedings being as much in ordinary, plain English as possible. In court, the rights of citizens are at stake. These are, especially for the people concerned, matters of very great importance. In criminal cases, a defendant might be imprisoned, or lose his or her job following a conviction. In family cases, issues of the very greatest consequence, such as access to children, are determined. And in civil cases, the courts resolve issues such as bitter neighbour disputes, the life or death of companies, and compensation claims worth millions of pounds. Citizens of the twenty-first century expect these proceedings to be conducted in a way that they can understand. As much as possible, therefore, the legal arguments and the judgment in a case should be rendered in modern English.

Latin knowledge is still very useful for the interpretation of many old cases, in other words most of the law reports. Additionally, Latin appears in the judgments of some judges who continue to use such phraseology, albeit with polite recognition that such use is not the modern way. In a case in 2000, Vanessa Dawn Dimond was the innocent victim whose Suzuki Vitara car was damaged in an accident by Robert J. Lovell in an accident in Sheffield. She tried to claim back the cost of hiring a Ford Mondeo from him, while her car was being repaired. The cost of this hire was quite high. She lost her claim for various legal reasons. One question for the court was whether an agreement she had with her insurance company (to get a hire car, following any accident, without cost to herself when she hired it) could affect the liability of a third party like Mr Lovell. Lord Hoffmann characterised one of the arguments as being 'as one used to say, *res inter alios acta*' – shorthand for *res inter alios acta alteri nocere non debet*, which means 'a person ought not to be prejudiced by what has been agreed between other persons'.[6] In the event, he stated that such a rule was not to be strictly applied today in some circumstances, so that if someone agreed to provide a valuable service to you without cost following an accident, such a cost might be unrecoverable by you.

Here are some useful phrases. The translations are, where suitable, functional not literal.

a posteriori: in reasoning, this means proving the cause from the effect, for example seeing a watch and concluding there was a watchmaker, or, like Robinson Crusoe, seeing a footprint on a desert island and inferring the presence of another person. This is called inductive reasoning, and is to be contrasted with knowledge gained prior to experience (see *a priori*, below).

a priori: in reasoning, this means inferring effects from given causes, without investigation. *A priori* knowledge is derived prior to experience. This is known as deductive reasoning, and is often used in mathematics. It is to be contrasted with knowledge gained after experience (see *a posteriori*, above). *A priori* reasoning proceeds from theoretical deduction and not from observation or experience.

argumentum ad hominem: 'argument to the person' – an argument not in general or impersonal terms but directed at a particular person; an argument focused on the personal characteristics or situation of someone. Attacking a judgment for alleged incoherence might be proper, but trying to invalidate a judgment by alleging senility in the judge who delivered it would be *argumentum ad hominem*.

cessante ratione legis, cessat lex ipsa: 'when the reason for its existence ceases, the law itself ceases to exist'. This is truer of judge-made common law principles than of the contents of legislation.

damnum sine injuria esse potest: 'there can be damage [such as physical injury or financial loss] without injury [legal wrong]', i.e. not all hurt and harm is legally actionable. If you bruise someone in a rugby match or open a bakery near another bakery, there is normally no legal remedy for the people who have been hurt or suffered economic loss.

de minimis non curat lex: 'the law does not concern itself with the smallest, trivial matters'. You cannot take legal action for being heavily jostled in an unruly queue.

expressio unius est exclusio alterius: 'the expression of the one is the exclusion of the other'. Where land is conveyed by deed, and it is not clear whether certain parts should be included in the transfer, it is a question of fact whether particular parcels are covered by the deed. However, the express mention of certain property, for example 'quarries', may show that other property such as 'mines' was not intended to be transferred, on the principle *expressio unius est exclusio alterius*.

habeas corpus: 'you are to have the body'. Part of a longer phrase describing a claim by which the detainer of a person is required to produce 'the body' (i.e. the living person) to a court to justify the detention.

in pari delicto, potior est conditio defendentis (or *possidentis*): where both parties are equally at fault, the defendant (or the person in possession of disputed property) is in the stronger position.

quis custodiet ipsos custodes?: 'who shall guard the guards?', i.e. even guards and protectors can be deficient.

qui facit per alium facit per se: 'he who employs another person to do something, does it himself'.

suppressio veri, suggestio falsi: 'the deliberate suppression of truth implies something untrue'. This is the cold cost of being 'economical with the truth'.

PUNCTUATION

Lynne Truss's award-winning book *Eats, Shoots & Leaves: The Zero Tolerance Approach to Punctuation* presents a compelling case for accuracy in the art by telling the following joke. A panda walks into a café. He orders a sandwich, eats it, then draws a gun and fires two shots in the air. 'Why?' asks the confused waiter, as the panda moves towards the exit. The panda produces a badly punctuated wildlife manual and tosses it over his shoulder. 'I'm a panda,' he says, at the door. 'Look it up.' The waiter turns to the relevant entry and finds an explanation. 'Panda. Large black-and-white bear-like mammal, native to China. Eats, shoots and leaves.'

Punctuation is very important in law. Consider the difference between 'a woman, without her man, is nothing' and 'a woman: without her, man is nothing'. Truss also cites an example from a 1937 exam in which candidates were asked to punctuate the following sentence: 'Charles the First walked and talked half an hour after his head was cut off.' The answer: 'Charles the First walked and talked. Half an hour after, his head was cut off.'

Much can swing on a single punctuation mark. Take Sir Roger Casement. He was hanged by a comma. Casement was convicted in the First World War of conspiring with the Germans to further an Irish insurrection. The contentious punctuation mark appeared in some but not all versions of the law under which Casement was prosecuted: the Treason Act 1351. Ultimately the comma allowed the definition of a traitor to include someone whose treachery, like Casement's, was committed outside the realm in Germany. He made his nefarious plans with others while he was abroad. The relevant part of the Act translated from the Norman French said that a man was guilty if he was:

> adherent to the enemies of our Lord the King in the Realm giving them aid or comfort in his Realm or elsewhere . . .

There are different ways of reading this section of the Act. To be convicted, a defendant must have 'been adherent to', in other words 'helped', the enemies of the king. It did not matter whether the enemies were in the country or in another country. But what about the defendant – did it matter if he was outside the country when he gave his alleged help?

The prosecution relied on a version of the Act with commas in it. The relevant section was punctuated in this way:

> adherent to the enemies of our Lord the King in the Realm, *giving them aid or comfort in his Realm*, or elsewhere . . . [Emphasis added]

The prosecution argued that if the middle explanatory clause 'giving them aid and comfort in the realm' is treated as bracketed, and covered up for a moment, then the first bit of the sentence can be joined with the last bit to read, 'adherent to the enemies of our Lord the King in the Realm . . . or elsewhere'. That means it would be a crime to be adherent to the king's enemies either by doing the adhering at home in the realm, or by doing the adhering elsewhere, like Germany. In which case, Casement would be guilty.

Casement's barrister, A.M. Sullivan KC, argued that the Act applied only to stay-at-home traitors, not to his client. He said the court should not interpret the Act as the prosecution wanted it to, because there were no commas in the original law. He continued:

> [N]o inference can be drawn from punctuation. The whole matter should be determined without any theory as to punctuation . . . and in dealing with a penal statute crimes should not depend on the significance of breaks or commas. If a crime depended on a comma, the matter should be determined in favour of the accused and not of the Crown.[7]

He argued that the appearances of the phrase 'in the Realm' and 'in his Realm' were a clear indication that to be treason, an activity had to be done within the country. Moreover, the phrase 'or elsewhere' had to be interpreted as referring to the king's enemies, not to the alleged traitor. It was treason to help the king's enemies wherever they were, provided the help was rendered in the realm.

However, two of the five judges, Justices Darling and Atkin, went to the Public Record Office to check with a magnifying glass what was on the original Statute Roll and Parliamentary Roll. Mr Justice Darling reported, 'there is a mark which we looked at carefully with a magnifying glass.' Referring to such marks as they had spotted, Mr Justice Atkin said, 'I think they are really to represent commas.'[8]

Casement's appeal was rejected, and on 3 August 1916 he was hanged at Pentonville prison.

Historically, legal documents were written down only as evidence of what was said; they were not designed for studied interpretation. Punctuation, adapted from a Greek system, was used to assist in public readings, and so some documents were punctuated from very early history. Falsifying the meaning of a document by the artful insertion of squiggles and dots is relatively easy, but there was never an edict prohibiting punctuation in legal instruments. Nowadays, the use of punctuation in statutes can be considered in order to make sense of the law. As Lord Lowry once noted, 'Why should not literate people, such as judges, look at the punctuation in order to interpret the meaning of the legislation as accepted by Parliament?'[9]

LEGAL WORDS THAT HAVE BECOME COMMON

Law is a major part of social life, so many legal words and phrases, or phrases with legal references in them, have been absorbed into general language. Many common words such as 'culprit', 'international', and 'codify' all originated in legal writing. English is rich in legal expressions such as 'that story would be laughed out of court' and 'I hold no brief for the Football Association but . . .'

One word that occurs frequently in textbooks and case reports in all branches of English law is the word 'reasonable'. In fact, more cases have hinged upon the meaning of this word than any other. In an early Latin form, the word appears in the first great treatise on English law produced in 1189 and ascribed to Ranulf de Glanville, the chief justiciar of England. In answer to the question of when a mortgage debt should be paid in the absence of an express agreement, Glanville launched a thousand years of conjecture and courtroom quibbling by answering, *rationabile terminum*, 'a reasonable time'. In 1215, the Magna Carta spoke of *rationabile auxilium*, 'a reasonable aid', in an attempt to put a limit on the level of tax a king or lord might levy on the knights in order to defray the expenses of ransom (money demanded for hostages or prisoners of war), knighting his eldest son, and marrying off his eldest daughter. Defining what is meant by 'reasonable' has foxed the best legal practitioners and philosophers, and many today accept the scepticism of Lord Goddard, who said in 1952, 'I have never yet heard any court give a real definition of what is a "reasonable doubt".'[10] A very reasonable point.

The opposite phenomenon – common words that become legally recognised – is also a regular feature of linguistic development. Judges must ensure that the language recognised in the court is not a code that ossified centuries ago when the style of wigs that they wear were the fashion. In a case in 1857, Chief Justice Pollock stated, 'Judges are philologists of the highest order.'[11] (Philology is the science of language, especially in a comparative or historical setting.) In fact, Baron Martin once suggested that judges are bound to know 'the meaning of all words in the English language'.[12] Sometimes, though, even the best judges are challenged by today's rapidly developing vocabulary. In 2003, presiding in an intellectual property case about rap music, Mr Justice Lewison had to discern the meaning of phrases like 'mish mash man' and 'shizzle my nizzle'. Andrew Alcee, the writer of 'Burnin'', a track that was a hit for the concept group (a group with no fixed membership) Ant'ill Mob in 2001, claimed that lyrics 'laid over' the top of the Heartless Crew's remix of the song constituted 'derogatory treatment' of the copyright. Mr Alcee claimed that terms like 'shizzle my nizzle', 'mish mish man', and 'string dem up' referred to drugs and violence, and so 'distorted and mutilated' his original tune. The judge said the claim had led to the 'faintly surreal experience of three gentlemen in horsehair wigs [himself and the two barristers] examining the meaning of such phrases'. He admitted that even after playing the record at half speed and referring to the *Urban Dictionary* on the internet he was unable to be sure of the meaning of the slang. He concluded that the latter words 'for practical purposes were a foreign language'.[13] The claim failed.

NAMES

The law relating to proper names is vibrant. This is because, among other things, so much hinges on commercial property rights associated with names, and upon personal identity. The legal disputes are many and varied.

Can one charity, for example, take action against another if the newer one has adopted a very similar name? The courts have said there is such an action. The economic tort of 'passing off' (torts are civil wrongs other than breaches of contract) is intended to protect businesses with established reputations from having trade diverted from them by other businesses that have adopted misleadingly similar names. The tort was developed to cater to the needs of commercial concerns, but the courts have applied this law to charities. In one case, *British Diabetic Association v Diabetic Society Ltd and others* (1995), the British Diabetic Association won an injunction to stop a breakaway group from calling itself the Diabetic Society. The court held that the concept of trade for the purposes of this tort was to be seen as wider than in a tax or commercial setting. It did not matter that the newer title was used without an intention to deceive the public if in practice the public will in fact be misled. It was also no defence for the newer organisation to say the public would recognise the difference between the two organisations if the public paid very close attention to the details. The court took that principle from an earlier decision about a company selling lemon juice.

In the earlier case, *Reckitt and Colman Products Ltd v Borden Inc and others* (1990), the court had held that it was no defence for the newer organisation to say that purchasers of a product would not be misled if they were 'more careful, more literate or more perspicacious'. In this case, the claimants had sold their product (preserved lemon juice), known as Jif lemon, in plastic lemons since 1956, and its appearance and brand name were established in the public mind. Virtually no attention was paid by shoppers to the label. There was bound to be confusion in the mind of the public in respect of the defendant's lemon juice, also sold in plastic lemons, which was an imitation of the claimant's product. It was held that the imitators had acted fraudulently in selling their product.

Problems occur when companies want to register common words or names as intellectual property. When should one common surname be allowed to become a registered trademark? In *Nichols plc v Registrar of Trade Marks* (2005), the court was told that a company had applied to register the surname 'Nichols' as a UK trademark for vending machines, and food and drink typically dispensed through such machines. One of its main products was the soft drink called Vimto. The Registrar, whose decision was successfully appealed against in this case, applied the criteria that: (1) in judging the capacity of a surname to distinguish goods or services, consideration would be given to the commonness of the name, based on a specified number of times that it appeared in an appropriate telephone directory; and (2) consideration would be given to the number of undertakings engaged in the relevant trade.

The Registrar, having noted that 'Nichols', or phonetically similar names, appeared more than the specified number of times in the London telephone directory (483 against a maximum of 200), refused registration in respect of food and drink, but granted it in respect of vending machines, on the grounds that the size of the market in the first case was large, but in the second was more specialised.

The High Court referred to the Court of Justice of the European Communities for a preliminary ruling on the question of what criteria were applicable to the determination of whether a surname, and in particular a common one, was to be refused registration as a trademark, on the grounds that it was 'devoid of any distinctive character' in European law. The European Court of Justice ruled that the distinctive character of all marks was to be assessed in relation to the goods or services involved, and to the perception of the relevant consumers, with a specific assessment in each case. It ruled that a Registrar should not judge whether a name can be registered simply by looking at how numerically common it was.

Under English law, a commoner problem has concerned neologisms, that is made-up or newly coined words. A word can be registered as a trademark provided it satisfies certain conditions. It must be an invented word, and it must not indicate the character and quality of the goods to which it refers. In a case in 1946, about whether the word 'oomphies' could enjoy trademark registration in connection with footwear, Mr Justice Evershed, with perfect poise, noted that the word 'oomph' originated as a description of '. . . a cinema actress, Miss Ann Sheridan, and, as I understand it, after being particularly applied to her, it has achieved a significance'.[14] Nonetheless, it was an invented word, and although American slang signifying 'sex appeal', it did not refer to the character of the footwear in question, so it was a registrable trademark.

A business trading on the good name of another enterprise might be committing various torts, including that of 'passing off'. A Sheffield hair salon called British Hairways, which opened in 1990, and a shop called Herrods, which opened in London in 1994, did not impress British Airways or the owners of Harrods, and solicitors' letters were quickly fired off at both name adapters. The Business Names Act 1985 precludes registration of names that are already registered, and names that are 'offensive' or would amount to crimes. Odd nominal questions have arisen elsewhere. In 1962, an American court held that there had been no unlawful discrimination by a telephone company that had refused to put the name of a registered company in its telephone directory. Mr Robert A. Williams and his wife Mrs Fern G. Williams, who ran a trash haulage firm, had wanted their company to be placed first in the telephone directory. The name they tried to get entered, which was perhaps echoed in the sound they made when they heard the judge rule against them, was 'AAAAAAAAAAAAAAAAAAAAAAAA'.[15]

Cases from other jurisdictions have raised other points of legal interest. Rarely have legal arguments about the word 'virgin' been as consequential as those raised in a case in the United States Federal Court in New York in 2005. Sir Richard Branson's Virgin Group claimed that owners of websites such as the online cigar merchant virgincigar.com were committing 'cyberpiracy' by using the word 'virgin' in their domain names. Lawyers for the Virgin Group demanded that the companies named in the suit transfer their domain names (i.e. their 'www.' names) to its client, Sir Richard Branson's company. All the companies complied except the small New York clothing firm VirginThreads, operated from the home of Jason Yang, its sole proprietor. Yang fought the action as over 6,000 pages were linked to his website, and he needed the business (his total sales in 2004 amounted to $105,000, as opposed to Virgin's $8.1 billion). He said, 'Morally, I don't think it is right for me to give up my name.' Virgin, which sells clothes in the US, argued that consumers would think any product with the prefix 'virgin' was part of the Virgin Group. Additionally, under American law, owners have a duty to police their trademarks, and failure to do so can be construed as an abandonment of the mark. Mr Yang argued that 'virgin', unlike fabricated names such as Altria or Kodak, is too common an English word to be owned by a company. In the event, the matter was settled and the smaller company agreed to change its name.

To be trademarks, words must be distinctive. They cannot be descriptive, because this would unfairly circumscribe rival traders' abilities to market their products. Curiously, the European Court of Justice has ruled that 'Baby Dry' (for nappies) is a 'lexical invention' and should enjoy a community trademark, but that 'Doublemint' is too descriptive for the same privilege.[16]

A rose by any other name might smell just as sweet, but whether that is so of MPs is another matter, especially if one changes his name to Haddock. In 2002, the MP for Great Grimsby, formerly known as Austin Mitchell, temporarily changed his name, declaring this by deed poll, to Austin Haddock. He did this to promote the struggling fish industry in his constituency.

A surname in common law is simply the name by which someone is known. The use of surnames was introduced around the time of the Norman conquest in 1066 but was not commonly adopted until the late 1300s. As names could be arbitrarily assumed, there were no legal requirements as to how they should be changed, and, leaving aside children and companies, that is still the position today. As Lord Justice

Ormrod noted in a case in 1979, 'a surname in common law is simply the name by which a person is generally known, and the effect of a deed poll is merely evidential: it has no more effect than that.' In other words, showing that you have changed your name by deed poll provides some evidence that you have changed your name legally, but it can be contradicted by other evidence, for example if you continue to use another name for all formal purposes like filling in forms and documents.[17] The award for most unusual name-change must go to Michael Howard, who became overdrawn by £10 in 1995 and was charged £20 by his bank in Horsforth, Leeds. By deed poll he declared his new name to be 'Yorkshire Bank PLC Are Fascist Bastards'. He said, 'I have 69p left in my account and I want the bank to return it by cheque in my full new name.'[18] His wish, though, was not granted.

In 2004, a father from Zhengzhou, Henan province, in China, was refused official permission to name his son '@' after the keyboard character. Officials declined the application on the legal basis that all names must be capable of being translated into Mandarin.

PROFANE LANGUAGE

'To some this may appear to be a small matter, but to Mr Harry Hook it is very important' . . . so begins the celebrated judgment of Lord Denning in a case from 1976. Mr Hook, who had been a Barnsley market trader for six years, had his licence revoked by the local council after he had urinated in a side street on an evening when the toilet was shut. He had been confronted by an official. Denning explained:

> We are not told the words used by the security officer. I expect they were in language which street traders understand. Mr Hook made an appropriate reply. Again, we are not told the actual words, but it is not difficult to guess. I expect it was an emphatic version of 'You be off'.[19]

Judges, of course, sometimes cannot avoid repeating the vulgar words of litigants or witnesses in order to have points clarified. 'You don't accept the bit about "get out of the room and take the fucking money"?' Mr Justice McCombe, for example, enquired of a High Court witness in a case in 2002. The swearing is often an integral part of statements that have potential legal significance. Sometimes the profanities are drearily mundane, for example 'We are the Preston hooligans. We want to kick your fucking heads in', which was considered in a case about whether a young man called John Joseph Cawley was guilty of a public order offence at the Shay Football Stadium in Halifax in 1975. He was eventually convicted.[20]

However, sometimes there is evidence of some verbal flourish. A libel case, involving the former Liverpool goalkeeper Bruce Grobbelaar, was the setting for a profusion of imprecations ricocheting off the court walls, from the direct 'there's fuck all chance of winning Newcastle' to, in literary terms, the rather arch use of hyperbaton in the phrase 'one hundred and twenty-five fucking thousand pounds cash'.[21] Those statements, and others, were legally relevant to whether the goalkeeper had accepted money to fix games. Mr Grobbelaar eventually won a libel action against a paper that had made such an accusation, but the House of Lords reduced his damages from £85,000 to £1.[22]

One case in which the precise connotations of swear words was judicially examined was *Snook v Mannion* (1982). The Divisional Court held that the words 'fuck off', when said to police officers by a man on his front driveway, were not clear enough to indicate that the man wanted to revoke their implied licence to be there.

Quite what words would have been clear enough to revoke the officers' implied licence to be on the driveway was not explained in any great detail by Mr Justice Forbes. This is curious. Someone who steadfastly remained somewhere, having been told what the officers were told, might be opening themselves to an enquiry from their aggressor such as 'What part of "fuck off" do you not understand?' However, the court's unusual interpretation of language might be explicable when the wider story of the case is taken into account.

On 17 April 1981, Brian Snook had been out drinking when he drove his Ford Cortina home near Lydney in Gloucestershire. He drove in an erratic manner and reached speeds of 55 mph in a built-up area. Two policemen followed him home in a police car. Mr Snook drove up his front driveway, got out of the car, and then threw his keys into a flowerbed. The officers walked on to his drive and told him they suspected him of driving while under the influence of alcohol. They requested a breath sample. He declined, saying he was on his own drive. He was eventually arrested and convicted for drink-driving. The court decided that police officers, like other citizens, had an implied licence to be on someone's driveway between the front gate and the front door if they thought they had legitimate business with the occupier. In this case, the words 'fuck off', uttered by a man who had been drinking, were not 'a sufficiently express rebuttal' of the implied licence the police officers had to be on the drive.

Finally, on this theme, there are occasions when bad language can be used by a lawyer with an ulterior motive. Sir Robert Megarry has recounted an instructional account from the memories of W.A. Fearnley-Whittingstall QC.[23] In the early 1930s, a barrister who was opening a prosecution for housebreaking was plagued by a fidgety juror. The trouble lay in the juror's mackintosh. He began by keeping it on, then, he took it off and sat on it, then, finding this uncomfortable, he put it on the edge of the jury box; next he put it on the floor under his seat, and finally he picked it up and put it on his lap. This done, he embarked on a discussion with his neighbour in conversational tones, possibly about the lack of amenities in the jury box. At this time the prosecuting barrister had been trying to open the case, and had reached the point when the householder had left his dinner to go to his study and there encountered the accused.

Although the barrister had looked hard and often at the juror, the juror had continued his fidgeting, unconcerned and perhaps oblivious of the unrest he was creating. His conversation with his neighbour proved to be the last straw. The barrister paused, looked straight at the juror and said, with great emphasis, 'Keep still, or I will knock your fucking block off.'

For a few seconds there was a deadly hush in court. The judge was bereft of words. The barrister then continued, imperturbably, 'Those, members of the jury, were the words the accused uttered to the householder when he entered his study.'

CONCISENESS

'Succinct' is not always the first word people would choose when describing lawyers. In 2001, a Practice Direction for the civil courts aimed to cut down the number of case citations lawyers make in their arguments.[24] Now only relevant and useful citations are permitted. This rule was designed to produce shorter cases and briefer law reports. Law reports of over 50 pages are not uncommon today, and some from earlier times are notably more lengthy. One House of Lords' decision, *R v Millis* (1844), for example, offers 120 pages summarising lawyers' arguments, followed by over 200 pages of judgments from the Law Lords, on the law concerning the validity of Presbyterian marriages. Not all law reports are that long. Glasses should be raised to the leading judge in *Hall v Hall* (1788), and to its court reporter. The entire report runs simply: 'Reprizal was said by Lord Thurlow C. to be a common drawback.'

Sometimes a case can be neatly encapsulated in a short but intriguing report title. One to raise an eyebrow is the 1836 case reported under the exquisite heading *The King v Forty-Nine Casks of Brandy*. This dispute between the king and the estate of William Bankes, owner of coastal land including Corfe Castle, concerned who had the best title to casks that had washed ashore near Poole in Dorset. The court divided the casks between the disputants. It is not recorded how they celebrated their gains.

In 2005, a controversial service for literature students was launched, aiming to deliver potted versions of major works, including *Bleak House*, in a few lines of mobile text message. The summary of *Romeo and Juliet* begins 'FeudTween2hses – Montague&CapuletRomeoMfalls_<3w/_JulietC@marrySecretly' (A feud between two houses – Montague and Capulet. Romeo Montague falls in love with Juliet Capulet and they marry secretly). Although concision is not always seen as a typical lawyerly characteristic, much legal work involves great expertise in the art of precis. Law has long enjoyed a sophisticated system of concision in 'headnotes' above law reports. Thus a 93-page law report for *A and others v Secretary of State for the Home Department* (2005) appears with a trenchant one-page synopsis of its judicial reasoning. A decision made by Mr Justice Parke in 1830 is succinctly headnoted as 'Possession in Scotland evidence of stealing in England'.

According to Cicero, *legem brevem esse oportet* ('a law should be brief'). Those who have drafted the Companies Act 2006 would not accept Cicero's dictum as a universal truth. The Act runs to 1,300 sections and is the longest piece of legislation ever drafted. But shorter legislation can be just as intricate. The Civil Jurisdiction and Judgments Act 1982, which facilitates a person suing in one European Community country for alleged wrongs done in another, is a shorter Act, but it drew some memorable criticism in Parliament because of its intellectually challenging intricacy. It was described by Lord Foot as being a body of law that 'gives to the word "complexity" a new dimension'. Speaking of the draft legislation in 1981, Lord Hailsham, the Lord Chancellor, said, 'There is nothing whatever I can do to make my speech short, and those who expect to find it of throbbing human interest will, I fear, be wholly disappointed. The road lies uphill all the way.'[25]

ARCANE LEGAL WORDS AND PHRASES

In *Gulliver's Travels*, Jonathan Swift wrote about lawyers who had 'a peculiar Cant and Jargon of their own, that no other Mortal can understand'. Today, a fair part of legal language is still just as esoteric. Some mysterious words are explained below.

chose in action (noun, pronounced 'shows in action'): a legal right to procure a sum of money owed. A cheque is such a financial entitlement. There is a popular myth that a cheque can be written on anything and still be valid. The origin of this myth might be an A.P. Herbert story, 'Uncommon Law', published in 1935 and dramatised on television in June 1967. In this story, a fictitious character called Albert Haddock wrote a cheque for £57 to the Inland Revenue on the side of a white cow, and led the cow to the tax offices. Missing the fact that this story was merely a joke, an American newspaper, the *Memphis Press-Scimitar*, published the case of 'the negotiable cow' as true. Since then, this myth has often been repeated.

deed poll: a legal document made by one person, or several, simply expressing a common intention. Contrast an indenture, which is a document made by two or more people agreeing to do something or create obligations. Historically, deeds were short, so two or more copies were written on one piece of parchment. Some words (such as the word cirographum, 'handwriting') were written in between the copies. A wavy or indented line was cut through the dividing words. This might afterwards show that the severed deed tallied with the other part or parts. By contrast with those sorts of document, a simple declaration (for example if a person declared an intention to change his name from Smithie to Smith) that did not need to match with another undertaking was simply cut evenly from the rest of the parchment, as when a coupon is torn across a dotted line.

The section was thus cut, or 'polled', and the deed became known as a deed poll.

defalcation (noun): misappropriation of money, or the amount misappropriated. In 1988, the Privy Council dismissed an appeal by Chan Man-sin against his conviction in Hong Kong for theft. While an accountant, Chan had forged cheques for $HK4.8m on company accounts, depositing them in his accounts. He was charged with theft when his defalcations were discovered.

engross (verb): this does not mean to participate regularly in negotiations during sumptuous legal luncheons and dinners, but to prepare a final copy of a deed or contract with all the formal clauses included, prior to its execution (i.e. signing) by the parties.

hearsay: the evidence of someone other than the person who is testifying in court, or statements in documents offered to prove the truth of what is asserted in court. If, for example, you did not see a man in a red shirt run out of the bank holding a briefcase, but you heard an office colleague who was looking out of an office window across the street from the bank say, 'I think I know that man in a red shirt who has just run out of the bank holding a briefcase', then the only evidence that a man in a red shirt ran out of the bank holding a briefcase is hearsay evidence. You are not a direct witness, but you can report what a witness is supposed to have seen and said. Although there are exceptions to it, the general rule is that hearsay is inadmissible evidence. In an episode of *The Simpsons*, the judge rebukes the hapless lawyer Lionel Hutz: 'Mr Hutz, we've been here for four hours. Do you have any evidence at all?' To which Hutz optimistically replies, 'Well, your Honour. We've plenty of hearsay and conjecture. Those are kinds of evidence.'

laches (pronounced 'lay-cheese'): an unconscionable delay. The doctrine of laches bars an action if it is stale. Negligence or unreasonable delay in asserting a right will defeat its enforcement. In a dispute between family members about a family business, the Court of Appeal in 2000 rejected a claim by a son where the relevant events involving his father and brothers had occurred between 19 and 37 years prior to the commencement of proceedings.

misfeasance (noun): an old term meaning the unlawful performance of a lawful act. For the tort of 'misfeasance in a public office' it is not necessary to prove malice. In a case in 1984, the Ministry of Agriculture banned the importation of French turkeys in order to protect British producers. The Court of Appeal ruled that it did not matter that the Ministry had not acted to harm French interests but merely to protect those in Britain. It was enough that an official knew he was acting beyond his powers, and that his action would financially injure others.

recuse (verb): to refuse. To reject a judge in a particular case as unsuitable through having a real or apparent interest in the case. Often used in the reflexive form 'he recused himself'. This is an old civil and canon law term. In 1999, at Winchester Crown Court, Judge Patrick Hooton, who had participated in pheasant shoots, recused himself from presiding in a case involving an animal rights protester. The Court of Appeal has said that recusal should not be based on 'the religion, ethnic or national origin, gender, age, class, means or sexual orientation of the judge'.

time immemorial: time beyond legal memory. Not how long a late-afternoon land law lecture seems to have lasted to its wearied listeners, but the formal beginning of English law, which commenced on 3 September 1189 – the accession of Richard I. Today, an ancient custom can have the force of law, like a right over land, if it can be shown to have existed since 'time immemorial'. The Statute of Westminster in 1275 fixed 1189 as the earliest date from which evidence in land disputes could be considered, because then, in 1275, a living man might be able to testify about what his father had told him existed in 1189.

voire dire (noun): a preliminary examination by the judge of a court witness in which he is required 'to speak the truth' in answer to questions put to him. If he appears incompetent, for example not of sound mind, he can be rejected as a witness. The word 'verdict' has a similar etymology. Kings in England spoke French for centuries after the Norman conquest in 1066, and more than 10,000 French words were absorbed into the language, including many legal words used at court.

The writer Flann O'Brien said, 'I suppose that so long as there are people in the world, they will publish dictionaries defining what is unknown in terms of something equally unknown.' There are, however, several good legal dictionaries to assist with the reading of the law. *The Oxford Dictionary of Law*, 7th edition, edited by Elizabeth A. Martin and Jonathan Law, and the *Collins Dictionary of Law*, 2nd edition, by W. J. Stewart and Robert Burgess, are both very helpful texts.

The language of the law is important in any general language, but especially so in English. As one prominent English and American practitioner has noted, although English is a relatively young language, it is more widely used than any language ever has been, and 'the English-speaking trial is recognisably the same animal, from the Antipodes to Alberta.'[26] So, a good knowledge of English and an appreciation of the language of English law affords an understanding of a phenomenon that has spread over much of the world.

FURTHER READING

Louis Blom-Cooper, ed., *The Law as Literature*, London: Bodley Head, 1961.

Keith Evans, *The Language of Advocacy*, Oxford: Oxford University Press, 1998.

John Gray, *Lawyers' Latin*, London: Hale, 2002.

David Mellinkoff, *The Language of the Law*, Toronto: Little Brown and Co., 1963.

William Twining and David Meirs, *How To Do Things With Rules*, 5th edition, London: Butterworths, 2010.

This final chapter aims to encourage further exploration of legal themes. There are many varieties of legal food for thought, and something, therefore, appealing to almost every taste. Many people who study law develop specialist areas of interest or expertise. Choosing such specialist interests is best done after developing a wide knowledge of the field in general.

It is sometimes said that ignorance of the law is no defence. There is some judicial authority for this. Chief Justice Ellenborough, for example, said in one case in 1802, 'Every man must be taken to be cognisant of the law; otherwise there is no saying to what extent the excuse of ignorance might not be carried. It would be urged in almost every case.'[1] That judicial opinion, however, has often been repudiated in other courts. In 1846, for example, Mr Justice Maule said, 'There is no presumption in this country that every person knows the law; it would be contrary to common sense and reason if it were so.'[2] The idea that lawyers or judges should be legally omniscient has been even more indignantly denied: 'God forbid that it should be imagined that an attorney, or a counsel or even a judge is bound to know all the law.'[3]

The English lawyer and politician, Sir Henry Finch, once noted that 'Sparks of all Sciences in the world are raked up in the ashes of the law.'[4] The following examples, taken from literature, cases, lawyers, websites, venues and films, are designed to ignite further interest in the pursuit of knowledge. To give the encouragement some focus, the knowledge celebrated here has a legal theme.

TEN LEGAL LITERARY CLASSICS

Students wishing to excel at law should read widely. The more styles, forms and epochs of literature you read, the better. Law and literature are importantly related subjects. Justice Frankfurter, the esteemed American judge, once replied to a young person who asked him about a legal career by saying:

> The best way to prepare for the law is to come to the study of the law as a well-read person. Thus alone can one acquire the capacity to use the English language on paper and in speech and with the

habits of clear thinking which only a true liberal education can give. No less important for a lawyer is the cultivation of the imaginative faculties by reading poetry, seeing great paintings, in the original or in easily available reproductions, and listening to great music. Stock your mind with the deposit of much good reading, and widen and deepen your feelings by experiencing vicariously as much as possible the wonderful mysteries of the universe, and forget all about your future career.[5]

It is undoubtedly good to enrich yourself with literature from eclectic sources. Here, keeping within a boundary of books with legal themes, are ten classic texts.

Bleak House (1853), by Charles Dickens

An inspirational and devastatingly funny tour of the law and the legal system. This panoramic epic tale concerns the interminable Court of Chancery case of *Jarndyce v Jarndyce*, and how it affects all involved in it: 'This scarecrow of a suit has, in the course of time, become so complicated that no man alive knows what it means. The parties to it understand it least . . . no two Chancery lawyers can talk about it for five minutes without coming to a total disagreement as to all the premises.' It is a magnificent story of timelessly comic characters and wonderful plot intrigue. It is also one of the most enjoyable engagements with legal system critique and socio-legal studies in the library.

Cannibalism and the Common Law (1984), by A.W.B. Simpson

In 1884, Captain Thomas Dudley and Edwin Stephens were convicted of the murder of a cabin boy, Richard Parker. Following the capsizing of their yacht *Mignonette*, the boy was killed on a dinghy 1,600 miles from the coast after 20 days adrift. They ate his liver and drank his blood to survive, and were rescued four days later. Their defence of 'necessity' was rejected, although their death sentences were later commuted to sentences of prison with hard labour. This book is a superbly detailed and vivid account of the events, their wider background, and the legal and philosophical reasoning that came to bear on the case.

The First Rumpole Omnibus (1983), by John Mortimer

In the barrister Horace Rumpole, Sir John Mortimer QC created a ubiquitously adored character who occupies a part of the national consciousness. Rumpole's dicta include 'Never plead guilty!' and 'A person who is tired of crime is tired of life'. He is enthusiastic about wine and Wordsworth, works well for his clients, has an endearing joie de vivre, and is not worried about career advancement.

The Merchant of Venice (1600), by William Shakespeare

The questions of justice, legal technique and jurisprudence that are raised in this play are numerous, and of great social significance. In Act IV, Scene i, a gripping trial scene, Portia says:

> The quality of mercy is not strain'd,
> It droppeth as the gentle rain from heaven
> Upon the place beneath: It is twice blest;
> It blesseth him that gives and him that takes.

This is one of many points that have resonated through centuries of legal debate. Another matter often discussed is whether rules should be bent to produce justice. In a tenancy agreement case in 1976, Lord Justice Lawton declined to bend the rules in the 1968 Rent Act, concluding:

> I could only do so by stretching the law. Adapting Shakespeare's words, I might be doing a great right but I would be doing a little wrong and as Portia said: 'Twill be recorded for a precedent, And many an error by the same example will rush into the state. It cannot be.' I would dismiss the appeal.[6]

The Old Munster Circuit (1939), by Maurice Healy

A charming unstructured anthology of humorous legal stories from Ireland. Maurice Healy KC was a prominent lawyer with a rich cornucopia of anecdotes. The stories include instances of judicial severity such as that of Lord Justice Holmes, who sentenced an old man from a farming community to 15 years. The convict cried for mercy, saying he would not live to finish the sentence. 'Well,' said the judge, 'try to do as much of it as you can!' The contribution of litigants is also well documented, such as the defendant in a case tried by Chief Baron Palles, concerning the allegedly unfair sale of a horse. Examining the ethics of horse-dealing, the baron at one point barked at the defendant, 'That's not what you told [the purchaser] at the Bandon Fair.' 'Oh no, but I'm on me oath now,' came the reply, which won him the case.

Orley Farm (1862), by Anthony Trollope

This novel revolves around a case of forgery, and the emotions, guilt and pathos of its main character, Lady Mason. The story concerns her involvement in the drawing up of a codicil to her husband's will. The account of the legal action is carefully interwoven with dramas of marriage and love. Although it contains some legal errors, the book is highly engaging in the way it critically exposes aspects of the morality and work of nineteenth-century law and lawyers. It is a marvellous study of the subtleties of language and the use of rhetoric. Trollope, whose father was a chancery barrister, creates a wonderfully vivid picture of the barrister Mr Chaffanbrass, who could 'maintain his opinion, unshaken, against all the judges in the land'.

The Trial (1925), by Franz Kafka

In a letter, Kafka once wrote that 'I think you should only read those books which bite and sting you.' Decidedly, this brilliant book does not induce in most readers a state of blissful Nirvana. It is a terrifying nightmare of what can happen in excessively bureaucratic regimes and totalitarian states. Kafka, who had studied law, wrote it in 1914 while he was an official in the Workmen's Accident Insurance Institute in Prague. In the book, Joseph K., a bank officer is shocked to find himself suddenly arrested for an unspecified crime, and must defend himself against a charge about which he can get no information. After being arrested he is released but required to report regularly to the court. The development of his plight is agonising, and the story is a very stimulating introduction to many aspects of legal theory and philosophy.

To Kill A Mockingbird (1960), by Harper Lee

A tense and exquisitely well-told story about adult attitudes to race and class in the deep south of America in the 1930s. At the heart of the story, which is told through the eyes of a child, is the struggle of a heroic lawyer, Atticus Finch, with the bitter prejudice around him. The drama features the case of a black man charged with the rape of a white girl. The narrative is by turns philosophical, exuberant, humorous and exciting, and contains many memorable passages. Much of the story is tantalisingly unpredictable. As Calpurnia, one character in the story, notes, 'First thing you learn when you're in a lawin' family is that there ain't any definite answers to anything.'

Uncommon Law: being 66 Misleading Cases (1969), by A.P. Herbert

This very amusing collection of concocted cases contains episodes and lines that have become part of legal legend. Many of the cases involve the fictional veteran litigant Albert Haddock. The wit and humour of the barrister Sir Alan Herbert (who was the MP for Oxford University for 15 years) is very warm. The stories include lines from lawyers, judges and witnesses such as 'A high-brow is the kind of person who looks at a sausage and thinks of Picasso' and 'People must not do things for fun. We are not here for fun. There is no reference to fun in any Act of Parliament.'

The Winslow Boy (1946), by Terence Rattigan

Set just before the First World War, this play revolves around a father's attempts to have his young son, who has been charged with petty theft, exonerated. The action moves from letters in the newspapers, to questions in the House of Commons, and then to trial. Rattigan's writing is exciting, and his characters are realistically drawn. The drama explores many parts of the relationship between truth, justice and social attitudes.

TEN REMARKABLE WITNESSES

The volumes of law reports are encyclopaedic in their coverage of human life and all its interests and activities. Cases cover an astonishing array of aspects of commerce, business, sport, art, science, technology, human relations, history, geography, theology, war, politics, delinquency, medicine, transport and much else. Their range can be exemplified in many ways. Here, for example, is a collection of cases involving unusual witnesses. Most people who give evidence in law courts are ordinary people. But sometimes testimony comes from some extraordinary sources.

There are various pleasures for a barrister to have in London on a December morning, but among them is certainly not to be in court cross-examining a witness whose work experience includes having been Chief Justice, and then Lord High Chancellor for 25 years. That, though, was what Sir John Campbell had to do when **Lord Eldon** was summoned as a witness in a case in 1833.[7] John Dicas, a lawyer who had been imprisoned for contempt in another case, called Lord Eldon to support his claim that such a jailing was not permitted. Eldon testified about the proper Chancery practice and was then cross-examined – circumstances which discouraged lines from counsel such as 'In truth, your knowledge of court procedure is really at the lower end of the scale, isn't it?'

The novelist **Anthony Trollope** was once called as a post office supervisor to give expert evidence at a post office robbery trial before Baron Bramwell in 1857. Leaving the witness box, he was brought back by the overly conscientious barrister A.G. Codd. Trollope was asked to confirm that he was also an author. 'What was the last book you wrote?' Codd asked. Trollope replied, 'Barchester Towers'. 'Well then,' asked Codd, 'was there a word of truth in that book from beginning to end?' A perplexed Trollope said his book was fiction. Codd asked the jury if they would dare convict his client, the defendant, on the evidence of someone who had written a book without a word of truth in it. They did.

In November 1878, the artist **James Whistler** sued John Ruskin, Slade Professor of Fine Art at Oxford, for libel. Ruskin had been rude about a Whistler painting. In the case, Whistler (who won) was not intimidated by Sir John Holker, who appeared for Ruskin. Questioned incredulously whether he asked two hundred guineas 'for the labour of two days', Whistler replied, 'No, I ask it for the knowledge of a life-time.' Later asked, 'Do you think you could make me see the beauty of that picture?', Whistler let silence hang long before saying, 'I fear it would be as hopeless as for a musician to pour his notes into the ear of a deaf man.'

On Tuesday, 2 June 1891, **HRH the Prince of Wales** entered the witness box in the High Court to give evidence in a case of slander brought by Sir William Gordon-Cumming. The Prince, who had been called by the plaintiff, was examined and cross-examined about his role in a game of cards, in Tranby Croft near Doncaster. In the game – baccarat – the plaintiff had won £100 but was accused of cheating. The Prince, who had sat on a special seat next to the Lord Chief Justice during the case, gave clear evidence, but not enough to save Sir William. After a seven-day trial, the jury found for the defendants in 10 minutes.

On Friday, 28 October 1960, the novelist **E.M. Forster** went into the witness box at the Old Bailey to give evidence for the defence at the trial of Penguin Books arising from the publication of D.H. Lawrence's *Lady Chatterley's Lover*. He said he knew Lawrence quite well and kept in touch with him. He placed Lawrence 'enormously high' in contemporary literature, describing him as the 'greatest imaginative novelist' of his generation. The jury, who also heard Cecil Day Lewis defend the book, acquitted Penguin Books, and the novel sold three million copies in a year.

In an obscenity trial in 1971, concerning the satirical magazine *OZ*, **John Peel**, the radio presenter, was called to testify about the quality of music reviews in the paper. In cross-examination he was abruptly asked why he had broadcast that he once had venereal disease. He explained that a BBC programme to encourage check-ups needed volunteers to speak about their experiences. He wanted to dispel shame and encourage participation. He said, 'I wouldn't be surprised to find that quite a few people in this courtroom had had . . . venereal disease whether they would admit it or not.' The barrister suddenly got very angry, saying, 'Which part of the court had you in mind?' Mr Peel coolly replied, 'All parts of the court.' The judge then said, 'Let's go on to another topic.'

In 1993, in Court 39 in the Royal Courts of Justice, the singer **George Michael** gave evidence in a commercial contract case. Mr Michael was later judicially praised for being intelligent, articulate and honest in his testimony. Answering the question of what he had earned, he passed a note to the judge and said, 'I think you might be a little shocked.' Cross-examined about his artistic style, Mr Michael spoke to an enrapt audience about a pelvic wiggle he performed in the video for the single 'I Want Your Sex'. He revealed, though, that the close-up shot was of a stand-in who was better suited to such an exposure.

In 1994, the actress **Gillian Taylforth**, famous for playing Kathy Beale in 'EastEnders', sued the *Sun* for libel. The newspaper had claimed she performed oral sex on her fiancé in a car on a sliproad to the A1. One day, the court moved to a car park to watch reconstructions of the event in a Range Rover, with and without a seat belt being worn. However, Miss Taylforth had been filmed at a party demonstrating her technique with a sausage, and the tape was sent to George Carman QC, who dramatically presented it as evidence midway through the trial. Mr Carman later said, 'That was crucial because she was a very good witness; butter wouldn't melt in her mouth.'

In 2003, the actress **Catherine Zeta-Jones** and her husband, Michael Douglas, sued *Hello!* magazine for publishing unauthorised photographs of their wedding. James Price QC, representing *Hello!*, asked her what aspects of her wedding she had wanted to 'keep secret away from the prying eyes of the world', as she was pictured in *OK!* magazine embracing her husband. To laughter in court, she replied, 'There is embracing and there is embracing. They are two very different things.' When Mr Price declared that he had not been offered £1 million for pictures of his wedding, the actress looked him up and down carefully before replying, 'I can understand that.'

In 2005, in Dublin Circuit Civil Court, **Bono**, the lead singer of U2, gave lively testimony. At issue was the ownership of items, including a Stetson hat, worn by Bono on U2's 'Joshua Tree' tour in 1987. The band's former stylist claimed the items were given to her as gifts. Bono produced laughter in court when, reflecting on the band's attempts to improve its image, said, 'In a way it was the last thing we always thought about, as might be obvious looking at the earlier photos.'

TEN GREAT LAWYERS

Among the great lawyers whose work all those who study law, or like to read about it, should know are the following doyens of the legal profession.

Marcus Tullius Cicero (106–43 BC)

Cicero was a lawyer widely respected for his philosophical writing, understanding of Greek philosophy, and the structure that his analyses gave to Roman law. He viewed justice as the highest human virtue, and his work is a cornucopia of percipient observations about law. He was eventually murdered as an opponent of Octavian.

Domitius Ulpianus (c. AD 170–228)

An outstanding jurist and prolific writer whose influence upon the theory and practice of law has been extensive. He forged the systematisation of rules and the exposition of legal principles in a way that has since shaped the law of over 60 countries. When the Emperor Justinian published the unprecedented *Digest of Roman Law* in AD 533, one-third of it was extracts from the work of Ulpianus. He sat as a judge in York.

Sir Thomas More (1478–1535)

More was the son of a judge. He became a barrister of Lincoln's Inn in 1501, Speaker of the House of Commons in 1523, and Lord Chancellor in 1529. He was a very successful commercial lawyer and legal writer and was perhaps best known for writing *Utopia* (a word based on two Greek words – ou, 'not', and topos, 'place', meaning 'nowhere'), a marvellous book depicting a society that rules itself by reason, and in which there are no lawyers!

Louis Dembitz Brandeis (1856–1941)

Brandeis was deeply concerned with issues of social justice, and the originator of what became a ubiquitous form of legal argument, the 'Brandeis Brief'. In a US Supreme Court case in 1907 about a state statute, Brandeis, who later became a Supreme Court judge, innovated a form of legislative interpretation by introducing social study reports to assist the court in construing the law.

Clarence Darrow (1857–1938)

Darrow was a celebrated American defence lawyer and formidable orator, committed to defending freedom of expression and opposing the death penalty. He defended war protesters charged with having violated sedition laws, and in 1925 defended John Scopes, a high-school teacher who had broken state law by presenting the Darwinian theory of evolution. In 1926 he won an acquittal for a black family, that of Dr Ossian Sweet, who had resisted a savage racist mob trying to expel them from a white district in Detroit.

Mohandas Karamchand Gandhi (1869–1948)

This world-famous advocate of non-violent social reform qualified as a barrister and joined the Inner Temple, London. His practice flowered in South Africa and he became more socially focused after he was asked to take off his turban in court.

He refused. He was later imprisoned in South Africa and India for his activities. A superb exponent of the arts of negotiation and mediation.

William Henry Thompson (1885–1947)

Thompson was a solicitor from Preston, Lancashire, who qualified in 1908, was imprisoned as a conscientious objector, and became the country's leading expert on working people's compensation. A supporter of the suffragettes and co-founder of the National Council for Civil Liberties, he established a law firm in 1921 to act for workers. Today, Thompsons is the largest personal injury and employment rights firm in the UK, with 50,000 cases being run at any time.

Lord Denning of Whitchurch (1899–1999)

A man of monumental influence on the development of English law, both in its substance and style. His time at Oxford as a mathematical scholar was followed by legal study, and then a highly successful career as a barrister. During his 40 years as a judge he reformed many areas of English law, including the law of contract, of unmarried partners, and of judicial review. Not, though, an unblemished record of greatness, as his views on racial issues were somewhat contentious.

Nelson Mandela (1918–)

A Nobel Peace Prize-winner and former president of South Africa, Mandela has helped shape modern history. He was the only black student in his law faculty. He set up his own practice in 1952 and acted for clients who were victims of the apartheid system. He insisted on using the 'whites only' entrance to courts, and campaigned relentlessly for an end to apartheid. He also successfully resisted an attempt by the Transvaal Law Society to have him struck off the rolls of attorneys.

Lord Woolf (1933–)

Lord Woolf has given shape and colour to British law and the legal system on a grand scale. He has with great distinction held office as Master of the Rolls, Lord Chief Justice and a Lord of Appeal. He has been an immensely influential judge across the whole canvas of law and the legal system. He has delivered many volumes of judgments that have changed and clarified law (often followed all over the Commonwealth), and has changed prison policy, completely redesigned the civil justice process (the Woolf Reforms), and presided over major criminal justice reform. In his support of the independence of the judiciary in the UK and other countries, he has acted with incalculable energy.

TEN GREAT PLACES TO EXPERIENCE LAW LIVE

Law is debated, dissected, legislated, argued, judged, applied and appealed at various venues. Here are some good places to visit. You should always contact the place in advance to check it will be open when you plan to go. Court addresses and details are available via the website <http://www.justice.gov.uk/about/hmc>.

Your Local Coroner's Court

A coroner, a senior lawyer or doctor, must hold an inquest if someone dies a violent or unnatural death, or dies suddenly while in prison or in other specified circumstances. Coroners can also hold inquests if, after a post-mortem examination, the cause of death remains unknown. The coroner's court establishes how, when and where the death occurred. A coroner may sit alone or with a jury of between seven and 11 people. Your local authority will have details of when and where the court sits. In Scotland, sudden death investigations are carried out by procurators fiscal.

Your Local County Court

There are 228 county courts handling claims in contract and in tort (and 179 of these also deal with family issues). Cases ranging from defamation to divorce are handled here, but most claims concern the recovery and collection of debt. The next most common types of claims relate to recovery of land and personal injury.

The Court of Appeal

The Court of Appeal normally sits at the Royal Courts of Justice in London. It deals with appeals in criminal cases from the Crown Court and civil cases from the High

Court, tribunals, and, in certain cases, county courts. These hearings deal with subtle points of law, which are argued by advocates. For further information about the Court of Appeal, go to <http://www.justice.gov.uk/courts/rcj-rolls-building/court-of-appeal. This site contains contact details for the civil and criminal divisions.

The Crown Court

The Crown Court sits at about 90 venues in England and Wales, within six regions called circuits, and these are presided over by High Court judges, circuit judges and part-time recorders. The court usually sits with a jury and hears serious criminal cases. It is the stage of the classic English law trial, of which the central London court, the Old Bailey, is best known. In Scotland, the High Court of Justiciary sits with a jury of 15, and the sheriff courts also deal with some serious cases.

Employment Tribunals

Employment tribunals are judicial bodies established to resolve disputes between employers and employees over employment rights. The jurisdiction includes unfair dismissal, redundancy payments and discrimination. They are like courts but not as formal, for example wigs and gowns are not worn. As Mr Justice Jackson has said, 'The principle of open justice applies to employment tribunals with just as much force as it applies to court proceedings.' For further information, and to check on local offices, visit the website <http://www.employmenttribunals. gov.uk>.

The High Court

Generally, the most difficult and complicated civil trials are heard at first instance in the High Court, either at the Royal Courts of Justice in London or at High Court centres in England and Wales. The High Court is made up of three divisions: Chancery, Family and Queen's Bench. For a description of the work they do, see Chapter 2.

The House of Commons

The factory of British law. It is most instructive to witness parliamentary debate in the chamber, and also to go to the Select Committees. These committees scrutinise government and its policy proposals, and conduct in-depth inquiries on topical issues. As part of the inquiry process, committees take evidence from a wide range of experts, including academics, special interest groups, civil servants and others, as well as government ministers. You can simply queue for public entry to Parliament on an afternoon when it is sitting, but it is better to obtain tickets in advance from your MP. For daily and weekly information about what is on, consult <http://www.parliament.uk>.

The Supreme Court

The Supreme Court, situated in central London, is the final court of appeal in the UK for civil cases. It hears appeals in criminal cases from England, Wales and Northern Ireland. It hears cases of the greatest public or constitutional importance affecting the whole population. Members of the public are welcome to observe cases but space in the public galleries is limited, which may mean you have to wait before gaining access to the courtroom. Normally you should be able to observe a case at some point during your visit. The court can offer tours of the building for groups of eight or more but these need to be booked in advance. The court is open to the public, Monday to Friday, 10 a.m. to 4.30 p.m. with the courts in session Mondays (11 a.m. to 4.30 p.m.) and Tuesday to Thursdays (10.30 a.m. to 4.30 p.m.). The court does not sit on Fridays. Before a visit, check the latest information at: <http://www. supremecourt.gov.uk/visiting/index.html>.

Local Government Planning

At local planning committee meetings, usually held in a large meeting room in the evening, local residents' and businesses' proposals for new buildings, parts of buildings, houses, shops, car parks, etc. are heard. Lawyers often appear for interested parties. The best way to get details of your local council meetings is to contact your local council. A good directory is at <http://www.direct.gov.uk/en/DL1/Directories/Localcouncils/index.htm>.

Your Local Magistrates' Court

Magistrates' courts are usually made up of three people from the local community who have no professional legal qualifications. They are known as lay magistrates or justices of the peace (JPs). The magistrates receive training to give them sufficient knowledge of the law and of the nature and purpose of sentencing. A court clerk advises them on law and procedure. In some areas, a paid professional district judge sits alone instead of the JPs. Magistrates' courts deal with about 98 per cent of criminal cases. In Scotland, the district courts have a similar jurisdiction.

TEN GREAT FILMS FOR THOSE INTERESTED IN LAW

The portrayal of law in films has a long history. Films with legal themes have been made since the 1930s. An early example is *Counsellor at Law* (1933), in which the stresses and challenges of a city law practice are shown in a fraught human drama. Through ambition and conscientious work, lawyer George Simon (John Barrymore), from a poor immigrant background, establishes a successful law practice. The film captures the pressure of the work and the ethical dilemmas in which the lawyer is placed.

It is important to have a good knowledge of popular films about law, if only to be able to highlight in debates and discussions anything you think is contentious about them. Law and the legal system are major political subjects now, like the health system and the education system. Public opinion about law and the legal system matters today in a way that it did not 50 years ago.

What one American lawyer has observed about the United States is true for most developed countries:

> Lawyers have a great many varied images of themselves and of their enterprise, and like the blind man and the elephant, the image of the profession depends upon whether you are grasping the trunk or the tail. Lawyers live and work in a world of law, courtrooms, conferences and libraries, but the vast majority of America's non-lawyers do not learn about the law in the bright light of a line-up, from the jury box, or even standing before a judge. The average American's most continuous association with legal institutions is in the world of television and film.[8]

Here are some classic films that, in various ways, stimulate thought about legally important themes. Your interest, though, should be in new films as much as these productions.

Adam's Rib (1949)

This battle-of-the-sexes comedy was very advanced for its time. The story is of a happily married couple of lawyers (Katharine Hepburn and Spencer Tracy) whose marriage becomes strained when they serve as advocates on opposite sides of the same headline-making attempted-murder trial. The trial concerns a woman who had shot her husband for having an adulterous relationship. Tracy prosecutes and Hepburn defends. Historically, a man who attacked his wife in an act of adultery was afforded a defence unavailable to a wife who attacked her husband similarly *in flagrante delicto*. In what was a distinctly radical presentation in 1949, the film contains several expositions of the need for legal equality between the sexes. Hepburn's character, Amanda Bonner, a clever Yale-educated lawyer, uses in her arguments both wide social points and technically adept legal points. She delivers many trenchant speeches and sharp lines ('We don't want advantages, and we don't want prejudices!'). The story was inspired by the real legal case of a husband–wife lawyer team (William and Dorothy Whitney) who, after the divorce proceedings for actors Raymond Massey and Adrianne Allen, divorced – and married their respective clients.

Witness for the Prosecution (1957)

A convalescent and cantankerous London barrister, Sir Wilfrid Robarts (Charles Laughton), returns to practice after suffering a heart attack and is supposed to be undertaking only civil cases of a simple kind. But the curious case of Leonard Stephen Vole (Tyrone Power), a charmer accused of murdering a rich middle-aged widow whose money he inherits, proves irresistible for Sir Wilfrid. Especially when he meets the accused's wife, the remarkable Christine Vole (Marlene Dietrich). Christine is to appear as a witness – not for the defence, but for the prosecution. Francis Compton gives an excellent performance as the judge. Also of note is designer Alexander Trauner's wonderful recreation of the Old Bailey. The film, directed by Billy Wilder, was an adaptation of the Agatha Christie play. It is a masterpiece of plot intrigue, thrilling suspense and dry wit. At the close of this film, a narrator implores the audience not to divulge the ending. The concluding twist is marvellous, and the narrator's request is respected in this summary!

12 Angry Men (1958)

In Manhattan's Court of General Sessions, a juror with doubts in a murder trial gradually manages to convince the others that the case is not as obviously clear as it first appears. An 18-year-old Puerto Rican or Hispanic American (his racial background is never specified) is accused of stabbing his father to death. If found guilty, he will be executed. In the jury room 11 of the jurors quickly vote 'guilty'. Henry Fonda, playing Mr Davis, enters a 'not guilty' vote to necessitate some deliberation. All but three minutes of this classic 96-minute film was shot inside the spartanly furnished 16-by-24-foot jury room. It is a magnificently suspenseful film that builds its drama not on action but on the nature of truth, the impediment of prejudice, the power of reason, and the importance of evidence. The acting and direction are superlatively executed. As one of the original film posters noted, 'It explodes like 12 sticks of dynamite.'

Compulsion (1959)

The film is set in 1920s Chicago. Two law students kidnap and murder a boy in an act of wanton depravity. This was based on a real case (*Illinois v Nathan Leopold and Richard Loeb*). The film includes a powerful concluding argument from the lawyer for the defendants, Jonathan Wilk (Orson Welles). The character was modelled on the famous lawyer Clarence Darrow. The eloquent speech, commonly regarded as the longest true monologue on film, is a case against the death penalty. It is not a contrived argument to raise doubts about their guilt; Wilk concedes their guilt. It is simply a potent plea against the state's being able to execute two youths, notwithstanding the heinous nature of their crime. Whatever your view on capital punishment, this is a thought-provoking film.

Inherit the Wind (1960)

This is a drama of the real-life 1925 trial in Dayton, Tennessee, known as the 'Scopes Monkey Trial'. In this Stanley Kramer film, a teacher, B.T. Cates, is arrested for teaching Darwin's theories of evolution. Famous lawyer Henry Drummond (Spencer Tracy) is the defence lawyer, and the fundamentalist, Matthew Brady, is the prosecutor. In the real case, Clarence Darrow defended and William Jennings Bryan prosecuted. The film is electrifyingly stimulating in the way it explores the 'evolution versus creationism' debate in the context of some legal rules of evidence.

The film reflects the events following the enactment by the Tennessee legislature of an Act making it illegal for any publicly funded institution to teach 'the theory that denies the story of the divine creation of man as taught in the Bible, and to teach instead that man has descended from a lower order of animals'. John Scopes was a biology teacher who set himself up to be prosecuted to highlight the contentious law. William Jennings Bryan was a famous orator, fundamentalist Christian and thrice-defeated candidate for the American presidency. He volunteered to prosecute. Darrow was an agnostic, liberal and famed criminal lawyer. He accepted the case to defend Scopes on behalf of the Civil Liberties Union. The issue at the heart of this dispute is encapsulated in this exchange from the case in which, remarkably, William Jennings Bryan also took the stand as a witness:

> Darrow: Have you ever investigated to find out how long man has been on the earth?

> Bryan: I have never found it necessary.

Victim (1961)

Dirk Bogarde plays Melville Farr, a prominent barrister about to 'take silk' (become a QC). He manages to track down a person who is blackmailing him. Mr Farr is homosexual, and the film was made at a time when homosexuality between consenting adults was still a crime. This film is not argumentative, but it presented a clear case for the anachronistic law to be changed. It was the first film in English to use the word 'homosexual'. The dramatic intrigue takes place around a murder mystery. The film is tautly suspenseful and has a thoughtful script. It includes exchanges such as this:

> Detective Inspector Harris: I can see you're a true puritan, Bridie. Eh?

> Bridie: There's nothing wrong with that, Sir.

> Detective Inspector Harris: Of course not. There was a time when that was against the law, you know.

QB VII (1974)

Dr Adam Kelno (Anthony Hopkins) arrives in England after the Second World War. He has come from a concentration camp in Nazi Europe, and faces war crime charges in England. When a witness is unable to identify Kelno as one of the doctors who castrated him in the concentration camp, the doctor is released. He goes to Arabia, where he works for years improving public health. He returns to England and is knighted. Twenty years later, a book is published by Abe Cady (Ben Gazzara) which names him as a willing participant in horrific Nazi medical experiments on Jews in the camps. Kelno sues for defamation. The film's title refers to the courtroom in which the trial was held: Queen's Bench, courtroom VII. Based on the Leon Uris book, this five-hour film was fairly described as 'stunning' in *The Times*. It is based upon a real case against Uris following the publication of *Exodus*. The film's legal drama twists and turns right to the end.

Class Action (1991)

Jedediah Tucker Ward (Gene Hackman) is a San Francisco attorney who specialises in representing people of modest means in battles against mighty opponents. In this story, he acts for a client who is suing a car company, having been badly burned in an accident that seems to be the result of a negligently designed vehicle. Ward discovers that the lawyer defending the car company is his estranged daughter Maggie (Mary Elizabeth Mastrantonio), who specialises in corporate law and works for an old, traditional law firm. The film weaves legal themes with social, political and familial ones.

Let Him Have It (1991)

This is a film about a miscarriage of justice – the notorious case of Derek William Bentley. At the Central Criminal Court on 11 December 1952, he was convicted of the murder of PC Sidney Miles. Mr Bentley did not actually shoot the officer. The gun was fired by his 16-year-old accomplice, Chris Craig, in a failed burglary attempt, but Mr Bentley was convicted under the principles of 'joint enterprise', even though he was being held by a police officer, under arrest, metres away from where his accomplice fired the pistol. Referring to the gun his friend was holding, Derek Bentley is alleged to have said, 'Let him have it, Chris' – an ambiguous phrase, as it could mean either 'relinquish the weapon to the officer' or 'fire on him'. Despite a plea by the jury for clemency, Mr Bentley was hanged on 28 January 1953.

The trial was seen as unfair in a number of respects. For example, although 18, Bentley had a mental age of 11, but this was information kept secret from the jury. Additionally, the judge's summing-up to the jury was astonishingly biased in favour of the police. He repeatedly implied that Bentley was guilty as charged, although this was for the jury to decide. After decades of campaigning by Bentley's family, and over six years after the film was released, in August 1998, on a momentous day in legal history, the Court of Appeal cleared Bentley of the murder for which he had been hanged 45 years earlier. In giving judgment, the Lord Chief Justice Lord Bingham said, ' . . . the summing-up in this case was such as to deny the appellant that fair trial which is the birthright of every British citizen.'

My Cousin Vinny (1992)

While on a driving trip during a break, two students from New York University are wrongly accused of murder in rural Alabama. The lawyer they choose is one of their cousins, Vincent Gambini (Joe Pesci). Mr Gambini is a streetwise lawyer who used to be a cab driver. He became a lawyer after running rings around a prosecutor when prosecuted for a traffic offence, and impressing the judge so much he told Gambini he should go to law school. To the boys' shock, it turns out, however, that this is their cousin's first murder trial, that it took six times for him to pass his Bar exams, and he is not accustomed to Southern legal rules or court manners. He is assisted by his razor-sharp fiancée Mona Lisa Vito (Marisa Tomei), though their views don't always elide.

> VINNY GAMBINI: Your Honor, may I have permission to treat Ms Vito as a hostile witness?
>
> MONA LISA VITO: You think I'm hostile now, wait 'til you see me tonight.
>
> JUDGE CHAMBERLAIN HALLER: Do you two know each other?
>
> VINNY GAMBINI: Yeah, she's my fiancée.
>
> JUDGE CHAMBERLAIN HALLER: Well, that would certainly explain the hostility.

The relationship between street sense and legal formality, and the clashes with a stern judge and the prosecutors, generate an acute and humorous take on the law.

TEN CLASSIC LAW SCHOOL WITTICISMS

Wit has always been a feature of legal education – here are ten exemplars:

In an American law lecture in the 1920s, the lecturer asked Smith, a student, to argue an answer to a legal scenario outlined to the class.

STUDENT: Well, sir, I could probably argue that either way.

LECTURER: [Thunders] That's no good. In law greater certainty is required.

STUDENT: Well, I'm not sure.

LECTURER   You're in shallow water, and sinking. You'll never succeed in law. I must ask you to leave the class.
[The student walked to door and said something as he left.]

LECTURER: What did you say?

STUDENT: I said you can go to Hell!

LECTURER: Come back Mr Smith, I think you might make a good lawyer after all.

★ ★ ★

A barrister was once seen coming out of a law school where he did part-time teaching in London. He was striding towards the courts carrying a very large stack of law books. Passing by, a student quipped, 'I thought you carried all that information in your head?', to which the scholarly barrister replied: 'I do; these are for the judge.'

★ ★ ★

A prominent high school headmaster wrote to the Vice Chancellor of a university saying that the school was going to have an event and wanted a distinguished academic as a guest speaker. The headmaster said his school would be especially interested in a speaker from the Faculty of Law, but 'we don't want anyone lower than a dean'. The Vice Chancellor replied saying 'Don't worry, you will be okay, we have no one around here lower than a dean.'

★ ★ ★

The life of law academics is now exceptionally busy and demanding but this was not always the case. For decades in the twentieth century it was a regret of law school deans that law lecturers did not like to be timetabled to teach on a Wednesday, because it would 'spoil two weekends'.

* * *

In the early twentieth century, at the end of a lecture in Harvard Law School, a student asked Professor Edward Warren a question about a particularly knotty legal problem. Warren replied: 'Well, if you want to know what the law was, go and see Dean Pound. If you want to know what the law ought to be, go and see Professor Ames. If you want to know what it's going to be, ask Professor Beale. But if you want to know what the law is, young man, then sit down.'

* * *

This legal problem was written on the cloakroom wall in an American law school. 'You are an attorney in a local practice and an elderly client pays you your $300 fee for drafting her will but she mistakenly pays you $500. Ethical dilemma: Do you tell your partner?'

* * *

In America, the lawyer Thurman Arnold (1891–1969) was once asked by the Attorney General whether he had taken a course in ethics while at Harvard. Thurman said he had not. The Attorney-General replied, 'Well, if in the course of your practice you become involved in difficult and protracted litigation . . . and it becomes apparent that somebody has got to go to jail, be sure that it's your client.'

* * *

A law tutor at an ancient English university college was once taken to hospital very ill. He needed an operation. When he was recovering in hospital he was given a telegram by the nurse. He was very weak so she read it aloud. It was from his college. 'Your colleagues send you very best wishes for your recovery. This motion was passed this morning at a meeting of the Senior Common Room by a majority of 13–12 with six abstentions.'

* * *

Thomas Ebenezer Webb, a distinguished scholar, and brilliant teacher (and later a judge in Ireland), was exasperated by the idea that youth necessarily entailed irresponsibility. In a case where his client's liquor licence application was opposed by the police on the grounds of the applicant's youth, Webb replied, 'Alexander the Great at the age of 22 had . . . brought the entire Persian Empire under his sway . . . At 23 Descartes evolved a new system of philosophy. At 24 Pitt was Prime Minister of Great Britain . . . and at 25 Napoleon Bonaparte saved the Republic. Is it now to be judged that at 25 my client, Peter Mulligan, is too young to manage a public house in Capel Street?'

* * *

In 1916, Sir Roger Casement had been convicted of treason and sentenced to death. His appeal had failed. He had one last hope – an appeal to the Lords – but only if it could be shown that 'a point of general public importance' was at stake. There was just such a point of importance according to Sir William Holdsworth, author of a voluminous and classic history of English law. When Casement's defence team put this to the prosecutor, the Attorney-General Frederick Edwin Smith KC MP, he rejected the argument with the withering rider, 'I am well acquainted with the legal attainments of Sir William Holdsworth. He was, after all, runner up to me in the Vinerian prize when we were at Oxford.'

TEN CLASSIC JUDGMENT OPENINGS

As in literature, the opening to a judgment can be attention-grabbing. Here are ten classic cases, including exemplars from Lord Denning, who once said: 'I start my judgment with a prologue – as the chorus does in one of Shakespeare's plays – to introduce the story . . .'

R v Barnsley Metropolitan Borough Council, ex parte Hook (1976)

'To some this may appear to be a small matter, but to Mr Harry Hook it is very important.'

One evening, after Barnsley market had closed, Harry Hook, a trader, urinated in a side street because the toilets were closed. Only council officers saw him. They shouted at him. He shouted back. Denning said 'We are not told the actual words, but it is not difficult to guess. I expect it was an emphatic version of "You be off".' Mr Hook lost his trader's licence. Overturning that ban, Denning ruled that the council committee that heard Mr Hook's case had unfairly excluded him from the meeting at key points.

Kieran Sutton v Kay Hutchinson (2005)

'The appellant is a lap dancer. I would not, of course, begin to know exactly what that involves.'

That opening line of Lord Justice Ward is amusingly arch. The case concerned a rich businessman who successfully sued an escort for £73,000 he had given her as loans. Lord Justice Ward noted, 'He, being a rich businessman, sought, no doubt, to enliven his lonely evenings in London by seeking entertainment at the Spearmint Rhino club in Tottenham Court Road'. The court noted he invited a dancer to dinner but 'It was not exactly the traditional boy meets girl, "Let's have dinner, darling" kind of invitation.'

Beswick v Beswick (1966)

'Old Peter Beswick was a coal merchant in Eccles, Lancashire.'

Another Denning opening. Mr Beswick was over 70, and made an agreement transferring his business to his nephew in exchange for a weekly payment as a consultant at £6.10s a week and then £5 a week for his wife, Ruth, after he died. Ruth, though, was later given only one payment, and sued for the rest. She won and the House of Lords confirmed her victory.

Palm Developments Ltd v Secretary of State for Communities and Local Government (2009)

'What is a tree?'

In this case, a property development company wanted to clear land in a young patch of woodland in North Halling in Kent, but was prevented by a tree preservation order. The Town and Country Planning Act 1990, however, gave no definition of 'tree'. After much analysis, Mr Justice Cranston concluded that 'there are no limitations in terms of size for what is to be treated as a tree. In other words, saplings are trees.'

Cummings v Granger (1976)

'This is the case of the barmaid who was badly bitten by a big dog. It was a guard dog, an Alsatian about two years old. It kept guard over a yard next to the Maypole public house in East London.'

Another dramatic opening from Denning. Sandra Cummings suffered severe facial injuries when the Alsatian attacked her in the yard. She lost her claim, as she was a trespasser and had voluntarily accepted the risk.

R (Mondelly) v The Commissioner of the Police for the Metropolis (2006)

' "Just a spliff, man", responded Mr Mondelly, when he was arrested by two police officers at his home at 9.30 p.m. on 16 February 2005.'

So begins the judgment of Lord Justice Moses in a case concerned with whether it was unlawful to caution a person caught in possession of cannabis. Police investigating a burglary in Hackney had gone to the wrong address, but smelt cannabis there and had eventually cautioned Mondelly. The High Court held the caution was lawful.

Hinz v Berry (1970)

'It happened on April 19, 1964. It was bluebell time in Kent.'

Lord Justice Denning memorably began a dreadfully shocking case with this arresting line. Mrs and Mrs Hinz were going on a picnic with their eight children. They had stopped their van, and Mrs Hinz had gone to pick bluebells with one of her daughters when a car ran into her family on the other side of the road, and she suffered severe nervous shock. Denning upheld an award of high damages.

Miller v Jackson (1977)

'In summertime village cricket is the delight of everyone. Nearly every village has its own cricket field where the young men play and the old men watch.'

Lord Justice Denning's florid opening in a case in which Mr and Mrs Jackson had sued the Lintz Cricket Club, in Burnopfield, County Durham, after cricket balls kept hitting their house. The couple won damages for negligence but did not get an injunction for nuisance.

Lloyds Bank Ltd v Bundy (1974)

'Broadchalke is one of the most pleasing villages in England. Old Herbert Bundy was a farmer there. His home was at Yew Tree Farm. It went back for 300 years.'

Thus began Lord Denning in a case in which a bank tried to get possession of the farmer's Wiltshire home. The farmer won, because he had been pressured to sign a document without having had independent advice.

Sidcup Building Estates Ltd v Sidery (1936)

'It really comes to this, that if this case were different from what it is he might succeed, but as this case is what it is this appeal must be dismissed.'

The first and last line of Lord Chief Justice Hewart's 'Alice in Wonderland' judgment in a case involving a vehicle offence for which a company was prosecuted.

TEN CLASSIC LEGAL MISTAKES

Although the law spends a lot of time focusing on the difference between right and wrong, it is not a machine that itself always operates perfectly. Lawyers and judges have made some odd errors – here are ten remarkable ones.

In 1602, the advocate **Thomas Harris** rose to his feet in a case and gave a forceful argument for the defendant. It was flawless. The only problem was that Harris had been engaged as lawyer for the plaintiff. The same mistake was made by John Dunning in 1776 but when his junior counsel whispered in his ear that he seemed to be arguing for the wrong side, the quick-witted Dunning confidently told the court that he had just summed up the case against his client and would now proceed to refute it.

Colin Blackburn was called to the Bar in 1838 but made slow progress. He had not taken silk in 1859 when he was suddenly elevated to become a judge of the Queen's Bench. It is commonly thought that the judicial status he won was really intended for a namesake QC and the promotion was a case of mistaken identity. Sir Colin, however, soon proved himself to be a most learned judge and by 1867 he was appointed one of the first Lords of Appeal in Ordinary.

Occasionally a court makes a decision having overlooked law that was binding on it – a decision **per incuriam** – Latin for 'through an error'. In 2002, in a case where an 'intentionally homeless' claimant challenged a council's refusal to provide her with accommodation, the Court of Appeal ruled that a 2001 precedent was wrong because it had ignored relevant law: section 122 Immigration and Asylum Act 1999, and section 17A Children Act 1989.

In 1999, at Cardiff crown court, **Alan Rashid** was mistakenly sentenced to two years in prison because a juror coughed just as the jury foreman said the 'not' in 'Not Guilty'. Judge Gibbon, thinking that Mr Rashid had been found guilty on the charge of making a threat to kill, jailed him for two years. The puzzled jurors assumed that Mr Rashid was being sentenced for other offences of which they were unaware, until, on the way out of the building, one juror asked an usher why Mr Rashid had been imprisoned after being found 'not guilty', and the truth was revealed.

In the trial In Alice's Adventures in Wonderland, when the King calls for a verdict, the Queen of Hearts says 'No, no! Sentence first – verdict afterwards'. Outside of Wonderland, though, things of equal oddity have happened. Frequently hearing long-winded arguments can provoke judicial impatience. In 1970 in Sheffield, a rather distracted **Mr Justice Howard** sentenced a young man to 14 years before the court had been told the facts of the case.

The aphorism *in vino veritas* has no applicability in a court. In 1981, the Supreme Court of Indiana suspended an attorney, **Douglas D. Seely, Jr.**, for 90 days for being drunk in court. The report notes that during an armed robbery trial in which he acted for the defendant 'he staggered when walking before the jury and he fell asleep several times during the course of the morning proceedings'. He then failed to return to court after lunch and was discovered comatose in his car outside the court.

In 1965, speaking about the way a judge should make decisions, Lord Justice Diplock said 'he must not spin a coin'. **Judge James Michael Shull** did not agree. He declared to litigants that he would settle their child visitation dispute by flipping a coin. He was removed from office in 2007 by the Virginia Supreme Court. Shull admitted tossing a coin to determine which parent should have a child at Christmas. He said he was trying to encourage the parents to decide the issue themselves.

Magistrate Hector Graham was sitting at Luton Magistrates' Court just before Christmas in 2000. A downcast convicted man stood before the bench about to be sentenced for a property crime when the courtroom suddenly rang out to the tune 'Santa Claus is Coming to Town'. Mr Graham opened his jacket in a panic and agitatedly began fiddling with his musical novelty Santa Claus tie. The magistrate's tie then burst into 'We Wish You a Merry Christmas' before stopping, at which point the defendant was jailed for four months.

Judges should be able to act with reasonable expedition. As Hamlet notes in his famous soliloquy, among the things that make life intolerable is 'the law's delay'. In *Collis v Nott*, a case about a surety who had paid off a bond, **Lord Eldon** heard the arguments in 1817. Seven years later, pressed for his judgment by exasperated litigants it became evident that he had completely forgotten the case and it had to be argued again from scratch.

Sir John Mortimer recounted an event of forgetfulness and mishearing. At the end of a long trial in London involving scores of witnesses, the judge arrived in court on Monday morning and announced some bad news. He said, in his refined English accent, he had composed his 40-page summing-up over the weekend but had left it at his cottage in Devon and so would have to adjourn the case for a day. 'Fax it up, my Lord!' one helpful barrister suggested, jumping to his feet, to which the judge replied 'Yes, I'm afraid it does rather.'

TEN REMARKABLE PIECES OF EVIDENCE

Evidence used in court is usually documentary but remarkable exhibits also feature in some cases, and sometimes, if an object cannot be brought into court, the court will go to the thing in question.

A Deadly Bath

On 12 July 1912, at a house in Herne Bay, Kent, Bessie Munday, 35, drowned in a bath. At the Old Bailey, George Joseph Smith was prosecuted for her murder. During the trial, the bath was brought into the court and used for demonstrations about how she might have been killed. The defence said she might have had an epileptic fit and drowned but Smith had two other 'wives' (he was a serial bigamist), both of whom had drowned in baths. He was convicted and hanged in 1915.

A Subliminal Image

In 1985, the television satire programme *Spitting Image* broadcast a subliminal message advertising the sexual prowess of its makers. Norris McWhirter complained. Later, the programme broadcast an image of Mr McWhirter's head superimposed on the body of a naked woman. His young nephew spotted the image by accident when freeze-framing a video. The image, lasting 0.24 of a second, was shown to magistrates, who issued a summons against the Independent Broadcasting Authority (IBA). The summons was later ruled to be invalid as it was not based on any known offence.

Platform 13, Euston Station

On 8 June 1954, Edith Hare went to Euston station to see her husband off to Chester. She was holding their baby and waving goodbye when she was struck by an open door as the train was pulling away. Throwing her baby to safety, she was knocked between the platform and the train. Her action for compensation succeeded. To ensure the judgment took in all the evidence, Lord Chief Justice Goddard made a special visit to platform 13.

A Virile Member

A Miss Grimbaldeston had sought to end her marriage to a Mr Anderson on the basis of nullity through impotence. In 1778, the case went on appeal to the Arches Court at Canterbury. Inspectors had to assess the husband's condition. The examination conducted 'behind the scenes' showed that Mr Anderson's manhood (known in old reports as a 'virile member') was judged to be 'soft and short', but the judge, Dr Calvert, noted that such flaccidity 'does not always continue' and the marriage should run for three months before the court's judgment could be conclusive.

The Haystack and the Bale

The old law of deodand (a gift to God) required that whatever item was the 'immediate occasion' of the death of any person, including things like weapons or even cartwheels, was forfeit to the Crown so that it could be sold and the proceeds put to pious uses. Blackstone likened it to the Mosaical law: 'if an ox gore a man that he die, the ox shall be stoned'. In 1535, a jury in Nottinghamshire considered the death of Anthony Wylde, who had been suffocated in the fall of an enormous haystack. However, the jurors, most of whom would have been farmers, decided that the thing to blame and to be forfeit, was merely a small bale.

A Little Spanish Town

In 1963, the copyright owners of the song 'In a Little Spanish Town' sued the owners of the song 'Why' for breach of copyright. Both songs were played to the Court of Appeal, and it rejected the claim. Lord Justice Willmer said while it was important to consider the manuscript of music, similarity had to be determined 'by the ear as well as by the eye'. He said 'the effect on the ear was one of noticeable similarity' but there was insufficient evidence of copying. Music to the ears of the defendant.

The Hailsham Confession Tape

In 1998, Simon Davey was prosecuted for burglary when, fuelled by 'eight to ten' pints, he broke into Hailsham police station in East Sussex one night to report himself for having used a taxi without the means to pay. When a tape of the confession he made to police was played at his trial, it produced uncontrollable laughter from the jury and court officers. The judge, who also manifested amusement, ordered the tape to be stopped and directed the jury to find Mr Davey not guilty.

The Palm Court Hotel, Malta

In 1998, three families sued a travel company for an allegedly disastrous holiday involving dirty rooms, cockroaches, a filthy swimming pool, and chaotic dining facilities. To assist him in his decision, District Judge Anthony Cleary went to experience the facilities at the Palm Court Hotel. Immersing himself in the evidence, he even took a dip in the pool. He was not convinced by the complaints. He awarded minimal damages and said that the scales of justice 'come down with a pretty hefty thump' on the defendant's side.

The Yo-Yo Cheerio 99 Advert

In 1932, the *Evening Standard* published a comical advert for a yo-yo. It suggested the 'devil on a string' was so occupying that it could become addictive. It told the story of an upright man, Mr Blennerhassett, who worked in Throgmorton Street, bought two for his children but got hooked and 'taken away' to rehab. Mr William Lewis Blennerhassett, a distinguished member of the Stock Exchange, and who worked in Throgmorton Street, sued for defamation. He was shown to be different in key respects from the man in the advert, and was asked by counsel if he had a sense of humour. He did not reply. He lost.

Miss Lillian Pelkey's Petticoat

In Los Angeles, before the Second World War, George W Hazeltine, 86, lay ill in hospital. He wanted to make a new will and leave $10,000 to his nurses, Miss Pelkey, and Madeline Higgins. There being no paper to hand, Miss Pelkey pulled up her dress, placed a board under her petticoat, and the will was pencilled on her undergarment. The document was eventually admitted to probate, but the nurses were prevented from benefiting from the will because they were attesting witnesses of it.

Glossary of Terms[1]

A

A *posteriori* – in the context of reasoning, proving the cause from the effect, e.g. seeing a watch and concluding there was a watchmaker, or, like Robinson Crusoe, seeing a footprint on a desert island and inferring the presence of another person. This is inductive reasoning.

A *priori* – in the context of reasoning, inferring effect from given causes, without investigation. *A priori* knowledge is derived prior to experience. This is known as deductive reasoning.

Act – A law made in Parliament, also called a statute. An Act sets out legal rules, and has normally been passed by both Houses of Parliament in the form of a Bill and agreed to by the Crown.

Adjournment – A temporary postponement of legal proceedings.

ADR – Alternative Dispute Resolution. Methods of resolving disputes which do not involve the normal trial process.

Advocate – A lawyer who speaks for a client in a court of law.

Aggravating – Factors making a situation worse. For example, burglary is aggravated in the eyes of a court if the burglar is armed, or injures someone while committing the offence.

Alibi – (Latin for elsewhere) A defence that someone accused of a crime was not there at the time and could not have committed the offence.

Appeal – A formal request to a higher court that the verdict or ruling or sentence of a court be changed.

B

Bail – Release of a defendant from custody until their next appearance in court. This can be subject to security being given and/or compliance with certain conditions, such as a curfew.

BAILII – The British and Irish Legal Information Institute, which provides free access to the British and Irish primary legal materials on the internet, including a wide variety of court judgments.

The Bar – Barristers are 'called to the Bar' when they have finished their training, and as a result are then allowed to represent clients. The Bar is also a collective term for all barristers, represented by the General Council of the Bar.

Barrister – A barrister is a legal practitioner in England, Wales and Northern Ireland. The name comes from the process of being called to the Bar after being trained. Barristers represent individuals in court, and provide them with specialist legal advice. Barristers must usually be instructed (hired) through a solicitor, but a change to the rules in 2004 means that members of the public may now approach a barrister directly in certain circumstances.

The Bench – Judges or magistrates sitting in court are collectively known as 'the Bench'.

Bill – A draft of a proposed law presented to Parliament. Once agreed by Parliament and given Royal Assent by the ruling monarch, Bills become law and are known as Acts. The parts of a Bill are called clauses; these become sections once a Bill becomes an Act.

Binding/bound over – Being placed under a legal obligation, for example being 'bound over' to keep the peace. Failure to observe a binding order may result in a penalty.

C

Cadit quaestio – 'the question falls' – the question is at an end. There will be no further discussion or argument.

CAFCASS – The Children and Family Court Advisory and Support Service. CAFCASS looks after the interests of children involved in proceedings in the family courts in England and Wales and works with children and their families to advise the courts on children's best interests in family cases, be that in divorce and separation, adoption, or child care and supervision proceedings.

Case law – The body of law created by judges' decisions on individual cases.

Cessante ratione legis, cessat lex ipsa – when the reason for its existence ceases, the law itself ceases to exist. Truer of common law than of legislation.

Circuit judge – A judge who normally sits in the county court and/or Crown Court.

Civil court – A court that deals with matters concerning private rights and not offences against the state.

Chambers – This has two meanings: a private room or courtroom from which the public are excluded, in which a judge may conduct certain sorts of hearings, for example family cases; or offices used by a barrister.

Compensation – A sum of money paid to make amends for loss, damage, hardship, inconvenience or personal injury caused by another.

Contempt of court – An offence that can lead to a fine and even imprisonment because of a lack of respect or obedience by an individual in a court of law. You are also in contempt of court if you disobey an injunction or court order.

Constitutional Reform Act – The Constitutional Reform Act 2005 reformed the office of Lord Chancellor, established the Lord Chief Justice as head of the judiciary of England and Wales and President of the Courts of England and Wales, and created the Supreme Court of the United Kingdom. In addition the Act also made provision for the creation of a Judicial Appointments Commission, an Office of Judicial Complaints, and a Judicial Appointments and Conduct Ombudsman.

Counsel – A barrister.

The Crown – The institution of the monarchy, or the historical power of the monarchy, usually exercised today through government and courts. It is the Crown that brings all criminal cases to court, via the Crown Prosecution Service.

Crown Court – The Crown Court deals with all crime committed for trial by magistrates' courts. Cases for trial are heard before a judge and jury. The Crown Court also acts as an appeal court for cases heard and dealt with by magistrates.

Cui bono? – 'to whom good?' In other words, who stands to gain? Used by the ancient Roman lawyer Cicero. In trying to solve a mystery or crime it is often useful to look for someone who would stand to gain by the event.

Culpability – Blame.

Curfew – A legal order confining someone to their home, sometimes for set times of the day.

Custodial sentence – Where an offender is confined to a prison or young offenders' institution for a set period of time.

D

Damnum sine injuria esse potest – there can be damage (such as physical injury or financial loss) without there being a legal wrong.

DCA – The Department for Constitutional Affairs, which, before the Ministry of Justice, was formerly responsible for running the courts and improving the justice system, human rights and information rights law, and law and policy on running elections and modernising the constitution. The Ministry of Justice was established on 9 May 2007 and is now responsible for policy on the overall criminal, civil, family and administrative justice system, including sentencing policy, as well as the courts, tribunals, legal aid and constitutional reform.

Defendant – A person who appears in court because they are being sued, standing trial or appearing for sentence.

De minimis non curat lex – the law does not concern itself with the smallest, trivial matters.

Disclosure – A three-tiered system in criminal proceedings which ensures vital information on both sides of a court case can be seen by all parties:

- Primary disclosure is the duty of the prosecutor to disclose material to the defence which undermines the case against the accused. Primary disclosure is triggered where the accused faces trial in a magistrates' court and pleads not guilty, or the case is transferred for trial by jury;
- A defence statement sets out the general nature of the defence, indicating matters on which the accused takes issues with the prosecution and why. A defence statement is compulsory for an accused facing trial by jury, and is optional for an accused facing a summary trial;
- Secondary disclosure takes place as soon as possible after receiving a defence statement, and provides details of any information which had not previously been disclosed and which might reasonably be expected to assist the accused's defence as set out in the defence statement.

In civil proceedings, all relevant documents have to be disclosed unless they are governed by privilege (see below).

District Judge (Magistrate) – Known as stipendiary magistrates before 2000, District Judges are full-time members of the judiciary and deal with a broad range of cases appearing before magistrates' courts – especially the lengthier and more complex criminal cases and care cases relating to children. They may sit with lay magistrates or alone.

District Judges – Formerly known as County Court Registrars, District Judges sit in the county courts or district registries in a specific region. Much of the work of

District Judges is in chambers, and they have the power to try actions in a county court below a specified financial limit which is reviewed from time to time. Cases above that limit are generally heard by a Circuit Judge. District Judges also act as arbitrators in the county courts, hear matrimonial cases and deal with nearly all the preliminary stages in civil and family proceedings and pre-trial reviews. Some also determine cases involving children.

Draft Bill – An early version of a proposed Bill before it is introduced into Parliament.

E

Easement – An easement is a right that the owner of one piece of land has over another piece of land. One piece of land has the benefit and the other has the burden of the rights. In some cases, both pieces of land have benefits and burdens. An easement attaches to the land itself and is not a personal right. Therefore the benefit and burden of the easement remain on the affected land upon change of ownership. Common examples of easements are rights of way over shared access ways/drive ways and rights to run service pipes and cables.

Embezzlement – Dishonestly appropriating another's assets for one's own use.

F

Feme sole – (pronounced femm soul) a single woman, including those who have been married.

Feme covert – (pronounced femm cuvert) a married woman (from the Latin *femina viro co-operta*).

Fraud – An act or instance of deception.

G

Gavel – A small mallet used to signal for attention. One of the most famous symbols of the judiciary, but ironically, they are not and never have been used in English or Welsh courtrooms.

H

Hearing – Proceedings held before a court.

High Court – A civil court consisting of three divisions: the Queen's Bench, which deals with civil disputes including breach of contract, personal injuries, commercial and building cases, libel or slander; Family, which is concerned with matrimonial matters and proceedings relating to children or adults who cannot make decisions for themselves; and Chancery, which deals with property matters including fraud and bankruptcy.

Home Office – The government department responsible for internal affairs, including crime, in England and Wales.

I

In pari delicto, potior est conditio defendentis (or possidentis) – where both parties are equally at fault, the defendant (or the person in possession of disputed property) is in the stronger position.

Independence of the judiciary – Public confidence in the judiciary requires that judges decide cases according to law and not according to bribery, threats or political pressure. Various rules promote free and fearless judging – judicial salaries are not annually approved by Parliament, and judges can't be sued for any judicial utterances.

J

JCO – The Judicial Communications Office, which exists to enhance public confidence in the judiciary for England and Wales, advises members of the judiciary on media matters and helps them communicate with each other.

Judiciary – Collective term for the 43,000 judges, magistrates and tribunal members who deal with legal matters in England and Wales.

JP – Justice of the Peace. The official title of a magistrate.

L

Law Commission – Independent body set up by Parliament to review and recommend reform of the law in England and Wales.

Law Lord – The unofficial title of the former Lords of Appeal in Ordinary (now Justices of the Supreme Court) who delivered opinions in the House of Lords, the highest court for England and Wales before October 2009.

Lawyer – General term for someone practising law, such as a solicitor or barrister.

Lord Chief Justice – Head of the judiciary of England and Wales and President of the Courts of England and Wales.

M

Magistrate – Magistrates are members of the public who voluntarily give up their time to act as lay judges in magistrates' courts. They need have no formal legal qualifications, although they are trained in court procedures.

Magistrates' court – The magistrates' courts are a key part of the criminal justice system – virtually all criminal cases start in a magistrates' court and over 95 per cent of cases are also completed there. In addition, magistrates' courts deal with many civil cases, mostly family matters. Cases in the magistrates' courts are usually heard by panels of three magistrates (Justices of the Peace), of which there are around 28,000 in England and Wales.

Margin of appreciation – The term 'margin of appreciation' refers to the 'room for manoeuvre', or leeway, given to countries under the European Convention on Human Rights to meet their obligations. In *Klass v Germany* (1978), the Court granted German authorities a measure of discretion in preparing a system of secret surveillance in the fight against terrorism, which was necessary in a democratic society in the interests of national security and crime prevention. However, in *D.H. v the Czech Republic* (2007), the Court held that the margin of appreciation could not serve to justify racial or ethnic segregation in education.

Mediation – Process taking place outside a court to resolve a dispute.

Misfeasance – an old term meaning the unlawful performance of a lawful act. As opposed to malfeasance (certain sorts of intrinsically unlawful conduct), or nonfeasance (an omission to do something that should by law be done).

Mitigating – Arguments made on behalf of a defendant who has admitted or been found guilty of an offence, in order to excuse or partly excuse the offence committed and attempt to minimize the sentence.

MoJ – The Ministry of Justice was established on 9 May 2007. It has responsibility for the courts, sentencing, prisons, rehabilitation plus former DCA policies like voting, Crown dependencies, human rights, tribunals and freedom of information.

O

Open court – The vast majority of hearings in England and Wales are held in open court, with members of the public free to enter the courtroom and observe proceedings. Some sensitive cases, such as family matters, may be held 'in camera', which means 'in the chamber' or in private, although the Latin tag should not, since the Civil Procedures Rules 1998, be used in new cases.

P

Parliamentary sovereignty – The highest power in British democracy is that of the electorate – expressed through its representatives in Parliament. This is the supreme (or 'sovereign') power. Legislation can be used to make any imaginable law. In 1917, Lord Justice Scrutton contemplated that a statute could make 'two plus two equal to five'. Some economists, though, have been doing that for a while.

Plea and case management hearings – A preliminary hearing, before a judge at a Crown Court, where the accused may indicate whether or not they plan to plead guilty and have the chance to argue that there is insufficient evidence for the case to go before a jury. Directions are also given on matters such as what evidence will be admitted.

Preferment – Advancing to a higher rank; another term for promotion.

Pre-trial hearing – A short court hearing at which a judge considers how ready all parties in a case may be for the trial and fixes a timetable where necessary.

Privilege – The right of a party to refuse to disclose a document or produce a document or to refuse to answer questions on the ground of some special interest recognised by law.

Probate – The legal recognition of the validity of a will.

Prosecution – The conduct of criminal proceedings against a person.

Pupillage – Pupillage is the final stage of training to be a barrister. It usually takes a year to complete, with the year divided into two six-month periods spent working in a set of chambers.

Q

QC – Barristers and solicitors with sufficient experience and knowledge can apply to become Queen's Counsel. QCs undertake work of an important nature and are referred to as 'silks', a name derived from the black court gown that is worn. QCs will be known as King's Counsel if a king assumes the throne.

Qui facit per alium facit per se – he who employs another person to do something, does it himself.

Quis custodiet ipsos custodes? – Who shall guard the guards? I.e. even guards and protectors can be deficient.

R

Recorder – A Recordership appointment, which carries almost the same powers as a Circuit Judge, is made by the Queen, and lasts for five years. Recorders generally sit for between four and six weeks a year, and normally spend the rest of the time in private practice as barristers or solicitors.

Rule of law – This is a defining characteristic of civilised democracies. Famously articulated by the Victorian jurist A.V. Dicey, the principle means that everyone, however powerful, must obey the democratically passed law, and no one is above the law. The rules are more important than important people. We are ruled by the rules, not by rulers.

S

Separation of powers – Rooted in ideas of Aristotle, and popularised by the French writer Montesquieu, this precept notes that there are three types of governmental function: legislative, executive and judicial. If more than one of those is given to one person or agency it is a threat to the freedom of citizens. Not rigidly applicable in the UK as, for example, the law lords are judicial but can legislate.

Statutory law – A law that has been passed by an Act of Parliament.

Summary trial – Trial taking place in a magistrates' court.

Suppressio veri, suggestio falsi – the deliberate suppression of truth implies something untrue. The cold cost of being 'economical with the truth'.

Supreme Court – The Supreme Court was created under the terms of the Constitutional Reform Act 2005, and completes the separation of the UK's legal and judicial systems. Justices of the Supreme Court will no longer be able to sit or vote in the House of Lords. Slightly confusingly, the High Court and Court of Appeal were, prior to 2009, referred to as the Supreme Court – today they are called the 'Senior Courts of England and Wales'.

Suspended sentence – A custodial sentence, but one which will not result in time spent in custody unless another offence is committed within a specified period.

T

Time immemorial – time beyond legal memory. For legal purposes this is taken to be from the accession of Richard I, September 3rd, 1189. In English law a custom can today be obligatory on those within its scope if its practice can be shown to have existed since time immemorial. The choice of 1189 as the starting point for legal memory was made by the Statute of Westminster in 1275, which fixed that date as the earliest in respect of which actions about certain land ownership disputes could be brought.

Tort – A civil wrong committed against a person for which compensation may be sought through a civil court, e.g. cases of personal injury, negligent driving and libel.

Tribunal – Tribunals are an important part of the judicial system, but function outside of courtrooms. There are nearly 100 different tribunals in England and Wales, each dedicated to a specific area – from pensions appeals to asylum and VAT matters. It is an extremely diverse system – the largest tribunal takes over 230,000 cases a year (Employment Tribunal), while some rarely sit. Some are based on a presidential structure, while some are regional; some panels are legally qualified, some are not. Some tribunals are very formal, with legal representation common, but many are not.

U

Uphold/upheld – Where an appeal against a judicial decision ends with the original ruling being maintained.

W

Ward of court – A minor (under 18) who is the subject of a wardship order. The order ensures that the court has custody, with day-to-day care carried out by an individual(s) or local authority. As long as the minor remains a ward of court, all decisions regarding the minor's upbringing must be approved by the court, e.g. transfer to a different school, or medical treatment.

Wardship – A High Court action making a minor a ward of court.

Y

YJB – The Youth Justice Board for England and Wales oversees the youth justice system and works to prevent offending and reoffending by children and young people under the age of 18, to ensure that custody for them is safe and secure, and to address the causes of their offending behaviour.

Notes

1 The importance of Law

1 A.V. Dicey, *Lectures on the Relation Between Law and Public Opinion in England During the Nineteenth Century* (1905; Honolulu: University Press of the Pacific, 2001), p. 14.

2 Seinfeld, 'The Visa', episode 56 (1993) <seinfeldscripts.com/TheVisa.html> (accessed 2 August 2010).

3 Denning LJ, *Packer v Packer* [1954] P 15 at 22.

4 *Boston Globe*, 10 June 1993.

5 Thomas Aquinas, *Summa Theologiae* (1266–73), 95.

6 Denis Lloyd, *The Idea of Law* (Harmondsworth: Penguin, 1964), p. 24.

7 Sir Patrick Devlin, *The Enforcement of Morals* (Oxford: Oxford University Press, 1965), pp. 13–14.

8 Sir Thomas More, *Utopia* (1516, trans. Paul Turner, London: Penguin Books, 1961), p. 106.

9 Frederick Engels, *The Condition of the Working Class in England* (1845; London: Panther, 1969), p. 306.

10 A.W.B. Simpson, *Invitation to Law* (Oxford: Blackwell, 1988), p. 9.

11 A.V. Dicey, *Introduction to the Study of the Law of the Constitution* (1885; London: Macmillan, 1893), p. 183.

12 *Gouriet v Union of Post Office Workers* [1977] QB 729 (CA), 761–2; [1977] 3 All ER 70 (HL).

13 *Guardian*, 22 November 2002.

14 E.P. Thompson, *Whigs and Hunters: The Origin of the Black Act* (Harmondsworth: Penguin, 1975), p. 266.

15 Harper Lee, *To Kill a Mockingbird* (1960; London: Arrow Books, 1997), p. 226.

16 Anatole France, *Le Lys Rouge* (1894; Paris: Calmann-Levy, 1923), p. 113.

17 Emile Durkheim, *The Division of Labour in Society* (1893; Basingstoke: Macmillan, 1984), pp. 63 and 58.

18 Lewis Carroll, *Through the Looking-Glass – And What Alice Found There* (1871; London: Macmillan, 1996), p. 124.

19 Arthur Symonds, *The Mechanics of Law Making* (1835), cited in R.E. Megarry, *A Second Miscellany at Law* (London: Stevens, 1973), p. 289.

20 *The Philadelphia Inquirer*, 27 April 2003.

21 *The Times*, 8 July 1997.

22 1,244,120 according the American Bar Association, National Lawyer Population by State, 2012.

23 Charles Hamson, *The Law: Its Study and Comparison, An Inaugural Lecture* (Cambridge: Cambridge University Press, 1955), p. 11.

24 Michael Furmston, 'Ignorance of the Law', *Legal Studies* 1 (1981), 37.

25 2 *Coke's Reports*, parts III–IV, pp. xiv–xviii (Butterworth edn 1826).

26 (1607) 12 Co. Rep. 63.

27 Dicey, *Lectures on the Relation Between Law and Public Opinion*, p. 44.

28 *The Work of the Health and Safety Commission and Executive*, House of Commons, Work and Pensions Committee, Fourth Report of Session 2003–4, Vol III, Written Evidence, House of Commons, 14 July 2004, Ev 219, para. 16; Dr. Jukka Takala, Introductory Report: Decent Work – Safe Work (International Labour Organisation, 2005), p. 5. <http://www.ilo.org> (accessed 15 August 2013).

29 'New Bill to Enable Delivery of Swift and Efficient Regulatory Reform to Cut Red Tape' Jim Murphy. Cabinet Office News Release, 12 January 2006. London: Cabinet Office Press Office.

30 *R v Cotswold Geotechnical Holdings Ltd*, Court of Appeal (Criminal Division) [2011] EWCA Crim 1337.

31 *British Safety* https://www.britsafe.org/news/lion-steel-fined-%C2%A3480000-third-corporate-manslaughter-case.

32 At the time there had been only two convictions, not three. The MP did not cite her source for the annual deaths data. The HSE figures for the last four years have been lower. Even on the lower figure of 150 deaths a year, though, many prosecutions could be brought.

33 Gary Slapper, *Blood in The Bank* (Ashgate, 1999).

34 *Hutton v West Cork Railway Company* (1883) 23 Ch D 654 at 672.

35 'UK internet use doubles in six years', *Financial Times*, 28 February 2013.

2 Judges

1 *Allen v Jackson* (1875) 1 Ch D. 399 at 405.

2 Lord Reid, 'The Judge as Law Maker', *Journal of the Society of Public Teachers of Law* 22 (1972).

3 A.V. Dicey *Lectures on the Relation Between Law and Public Opinion in England During the Nineteenth Century* (1905; Honolulu: University Press of the Pacific, 2001), p. 486.

4 All data from Judicial Statistics, Judiciary of England and Wales, Annual Diversity Statistics, 2009.

5 *Guardian*, 19 December 2000.

6 *St Edmundsbury and Ipswich Diocesan Board of Finance v Clark* [1973] 2 All ER 1155.

7 *Kempster v Deacon* (1696) 1 Ld Raym 76, 2 Salk 663, 91 ER 947.

8 'Would Your Honour Like to Try the Holiday?', *The Times*, 1 September 1998.

9 Hansard (NS), vol. 9, col. 745 (1823), cited in R.E. Megarry, *A Second Miscellany-at-Law* (London: Stevens, 1973), p. 5.

10 *New York Times*, 3 April 1988, p. 24.

11 *Guardian*, 2 November 2002.

12 *Re A (children) (conjoined twins: surgical separation)* [2000] 4 All ER 961.

13 *R v R (Rape: marital exemption)* [1991] 4 All ER 481.

14 Ibid, p. 483.

15 *C v Director of Public Prosecutions* [1995] 2 All ER 43.

16 Ibid, p. 64.

17 *Pepper (Inspector of Taxes) v Hart* [1993] 1 All ER 42 at p. 49.

18 *R v Clegg* [1995] 1 All ER 334 at p. 346.

19 Judicial Studies Board, *Strategy* 2007–11, p. 1. Online. Available: <http://www. jsboard. co.uk/aboutus/jsbstrategy.htm> (accessed 28 July 2010).

20 'Shooting judge drops animal-rights trial', *The Times* (early edition), 6 August 1999.

21 *Dimes v Grand Junction Canal Proprietors* (1852) 3 HL Cas 759 at 793.

22 *In Re Pinochet No 2* [1999] 1 All ER 577.

23 *R v Bow Street Metropolitan Stipendiary Magistrate ex parte Pinochet Ugarte* [1999] 1 All ER 577 at 598–9.

24 *Locabail (UK) Ltd. v Bayfield Properties Ltd* [2000] 1 All ER 65 at 77.

25 *Sir Alexander Morrison & Anr v AWG Group Ltd & Anr* [2006] EWCA Civ 6, 3.

26 *Cottle v Cottle* [1939] 2 All ER 535.

27 The source for this and other data used here is <www.judiciary.gov.uk>.

28 *The Times*, 10 June 2000.

29 *Ex p. Hall, re Wood* (1883) 23 Ch D 644 at 653.

30 26 June 1997, Smith Bernal Transcript Report No. 9605492/W4, pp. 8–9.

31 <http://www.dca.gov.uk/magist/recruit/magrecruit.htm> (accessed 28 July 2010).

32 Quoted by Trevor Grove, *The Magistrate's Tale* (London: Bloomsbury, 2002), p. 242.

3 Lawyers

1 *The Times*, 18 October 2005.

2 Cited in Sadakat Kadri, *The Trial: A History from Socrates to O.J. Simpson* (London: HarperCollins, 2005), p. 82.

3 A.W.B. Simpson, *Invitation to Law* (Oxford: Blackwell, 1988), pp. 13–14.

4 The Law Society, *Annual Statistical Report*, 2009.

5 Cited in R.G. Hamilton, *All Jangle and Riot* (Abingdon: Professional Books, 1986), p. 19.

6 Brian Abel-Smith and Robert Stevens, *Lawyers and the Courts* (London: Heinemann, 1967), p. 24.

7 Cited ibid, p. 455.

8 Quoted ibid.

9 J.H. Baker, *The Legal Profession and Common Law* (London: The Hambledon Press, 1986), p. 143.

10 Cited in Abel-Smith and Stevens, *Lawyers and the Courts*, p. 227.

11 *Law Society Gazette*, 2 July 2009.

12 *The Times*, 12 July 1999.

13 *The Times*, 8 October 2009.

14 *The Gazette*, 23 and 30 January 2003.

15 *Tito and others v Waddell and others (No 2); Tito and others v Attorney-General* [1977] 3 All ER 129.

16 All statistics from the Bar Council; see <http://www.barcouncil.org.uk/about/statistics> (accessed 2 August 2010).

17 Bar Council, July 2013, Press Release.

18 *McKenzie v McKenzie* [1971] Ch 33, [1970] 3 All ER 1034.

19 *R v Leicester City Justices, ex parte Barrow and another* [1991] 3 All ER 935.

20 *R v Bow County Court, ex parte Pelling* QBD 26 January 2000, CO/539/98, Transcript: Smith Bernal.

21 *Rondel v Worsley* [1969] 1 AC 191, [1967] 3 All ER 993.

22 *Arthur JS Hall and Co v Simons and Other Appeals* [2000] 3 All ER 673 at 689.

23 [2000] 3 All ER 673 at 703.

24 *R v Clinton* [1993] 2 All ER 998.

25 [2000] 3 All ER 673 at 683–4.

26 J.S. Mill, 'The Subjection of Women' (1869), Ch. 2, para. 2.

4 Cases and the Courts

1 *Willis v Baddeley* [1892] 2 QB 324 at 326.

2 *Lynch v Director of Public Prosecutions for Northern Ireland* [1975] 1 All ER 913 at 939.

3 *Duport Steel v Sirs* [1980] 1 All ER 529 at 551.

4 Archbold: *Criminal Pleading, Evidence and Practice* (London: Sweet & Maxwell, 2009), 19–1, p. 1898.

5 *Re A (children) (conjoined twins: surgical separation)* [2000] 4 All ER 961 at 1024.

6 A.W.B. Simpson, *Invitation to Law* (Oxford: Blackwell, 1988), p. 66.

7 Quoted in L. Blom-Cooper (ed.), *The Law as Literature* (London: Bodley Head, 1961), p. 229.
8 *Froom v Butcher* [1975] 3 All ER 520 at 522.
9 *Practice Note (Judicial Precedent)* [1966] 3 All ER 77.
10 See *Austin v Mayor and Burgesses of the London Borough of Southwark* [2010] UKSC 28 Lord Hope, paras 24–25.
11 *Midland Bank Trust Co v Hett, Stubbs & Kemp* [1979] Ch 384.
12 *R v Lambeth London Borough Council, ex parte W* [2003] UKHL 57, [2002] EWCA Civ 613.
13 'Statistics on deaths reported to coroners, England and Wales, 2011', Ministry of Justice Statistics Bulletin, 17 May 2012.

5 Case Technique

1 *Kleinwort Benson Ltd v Lincoln City Council* [1998] 4 All ER 513 at 537.
2 *R v Governor of Brockhill Prison (ex parte Evans)* [2000] 4 All ER 15.
3 *Alcock v Chief Constable of South Yorkshire Police* [1991] 4 All ER 907 at 913.
4 *McFarlane v EE Caledonia Ltd* [1994] 2 All ER 1 CA at 14.
5 *Oliver v City of Raleigh* (1937) 193 SE 853 at 857.
6 Lord Denning, *The Discipline of Law* (London: Butterworths, 1979), p. 287.
7 Frances Gibb, Lecture, 16 March 2006, Queen Mary's College, University of London.
8 Cited in Edward Grierson, *Confessions of a County Court Magistrate* (London: Victor Gollancz, 1972), p. 16.
9 *Emmens v Pottle* (1885) 16 QBD 354 at 357.

6 Interpreting Acts of Parliament

1 *Metropolitan Railway Co v Fowler* [1892] 1 QB 165 at 183.
2 *Taff Vale Railway Co v Cardiff Railway Co* [1917] 1 Ch 299 at 317.
3 R.E. Megarry, *A New Miscellany-at-Law* (Oxford: Hart Publishing, 2005), p. 183.
4 Ibid.
5 *Re Castioni* [1891] 1 QB 149 at 167.
6 *Keown v Coventry Healthcare NHS Trust* [2006] EWCA Civ 39 CA (Civ Div).
7 *Duport Steel v Sirs* [1980] 1 All ER 529 at 541.
8 *Sweet v Parsley* (1970) [1969] 1 All ER 347 at 349.
9 Ibid at 356.
10 *Director of Public Prosecutions v Schildkamp* [1969] 3 All ER 1640 at 1641.
11 *Gibson v Ryan* [1967] 3 All ER 184 at 186.
12 *R v Inhabitants of Sedgley* (1831) 2 B & Ad 65 at 73.
13 *Re Smith's estate* (1887) 34 ChD 589 at 595.
14 *R v Minister of Health, ex parte Villie*rs [Divisional Court] [1936] 2 KB 29.

15 *R v A sub nom R v Y* [2001] UKHL 25, para 1.
16 *Compania Maritima San Basilio SA v Oceanus Mutual Underwriting Association (Bermuda) Ltd* [1977] QB 49 at 68.
17 *The Leeds Teaching Hospitals NHS Trust v Mr and Mrs A and others* [2003] EWCA 259 (QB), para 20.
18 Ibid, para 22.
19 *M v the Netherlands* (1993) 74 D&R 120, para 1.
20 *The Leeds Teaching Hospitals NHS Trust v Mr and Mrs A and others* [2003] EWCA 259 (QB), para 54.
21 *Seaford Court Estates v Asher* [1949] 2 All ER 155 at 164.

7 Types of Law

1 YB 48 Edw III H., p. 11.
2 Oliver Wendell Holmes, *The Common Law* (1881; Cambridge, Mass., Harvard University Press, 2009), p. 1.
3 A.W. Bradley and K.D. Ewing, *Constitutional and Administrative Law*, 13th edn (Harlow: Pearson, 2003), p. 3.
4 Ibid, p. 4.
5 'Our New Constitution', *Law Quarterly Review* 120 (2004), p. 243.
6 Bradley and Ewing, *Constitutional and Administrative Law*, p. 631.
7 Glanville Williams, *Textbook of Criminal Law* (London: Stevens, 1983), p. 27.
8 *Proprietary Articles Trade Association v Att-Gen for Canada* [1931] AC 310 at 324.
9 Williams, *Textbook of Criminal Law*, p. 29.
10 Emile Durkheim, *The Division of Labour in Society* (1893; Basingstoke: Macmillan, 1984), p. 61.
11 Sir Carleton Allen, *Legal Duties and Other Essays in Jurisprudence* (Oxford, Clarendon Press, 1931), pp. 233–4, quoted in J.C. Smith and B. Hogan, *Criminal Law* (London: Butterworths, 1992), p. 16.
12 J. Edwards, *The Law Officers of the Crown* (London: Sweet & Maxwell, 1964), p. 338.
13 Leon Radzinowicz, *A History of English Criminal Law*, Vol. 2 (London: Stevens, 1956), p. 208.
14 Cited in K.W. Lidstone, R. Hogg, F. Sutcliffe, *Prosecutions by Private Individuals and Non-Police Agencies* (London: HMSO, 1980), p. 2.
15 *Gouriet v Union of Post Office Workers* [1977] 3 All ER 70 (HL) at 97 and 79 respectively.
16 William Blackstone, *Commentaries on the Laws of England*, 4 vols. (1765–9), IV; ed. Wayne Morrison (London: Cavendish Publishing, 2001), pp. 5–6.
17 Jeremy Bentham, *The Theory of Legislation* (1864) London: William Stevens, p. 55.

18 Ewan McKendrick, *Contract Law* (Basingstoke: Macmillan, 2003), p. 1.
19 B.S. Markesinis and S.F. Deakin, *Tort Law* (Oxford: Clarendon Press, 1999), p. 36.
20 See Chapter 4.
21 Co. Litt. 272b. This is the commentary of Sir Edward Coke (pronounced 'Cook') on the fifteenth-century judge Sir Thomas Littleton.
22 *Re Golay's Will Trust* [1965] 1WLR 969 at 972.
23 Kevin Gray and Susan Francis Gray, *Land Law* (London: Butterworths, 2001), p. 1.
24 Kate Green and Joe Cursley, *Land Law* (Basingstoke: Palgrave, 2001), p. 7.
25 P.M. Bromley, *Family Law* (London: Butterworths, 1976), p. 1.
26 Rambert De Mello (ed.), *Human Rights Act 1998* (Bristol: Jordan Publishing, 2000), p. 119.
27 Ibid.

8 The Jury

1 Sir Patrick Devlin, *Trial By Jury*, The Hamlyn Trust (London: Stevens, 1956), p. 164.
2 William Blackstone, *Commentaries on the Laws of England*, 4 vols. (1765–9); ed. Wayne Morrison (London, Cavendish Publishing, 2001), IV, p. 350.
3 Alexis de Tocqueville, *Democracy in America*, ed. Alfred A. Knopf (New York: Random House, 1835), p. 284.
4 <http://www.alanmacfarlane.com/law/audiovisual.html> (accessed 30 July 2013).
5 Aristotle, *Politics*, 1268b, 8–11.
6 M.N. Hansen, *The Athenian Democracy in the Age of Demosthenes* (London: Bristol Classical Press, 1999), p. 18. I am very grateful to Dr Peter Haarer of Corpus Christi College, Oxford, for his explanations and thoughts, on which I rely here, and his kind help with the literature.
7 <http://www.justice.gov.uk/publications/are-juries-fair.htm> (accessed 30 July 2013).
8 *The Times*, 1 April 2010.
9 This was held in *Williams v Beesley* [1973] 3 All ER 144, HL – although on its particular facts there was not even any question of integrity or honour. The House of Lords ruled that it was acceptable for a trial of civil negligence against a solicitor to be held without a jury because the particular facts of the case did not involve any allegations which if true were capable of impugning the honour or integrity of the solicitor.
10 *Ward v James* [1966] 1 QB 273, [1965] 1 All ER 563, CA.
11 *Sims v William Howard & Son Ltd* [1964] 1 All ER 918, at 921.
12 See Blackstone, *Commentaries*, III, p. 379, and IV, p. 350.

13 See 3 Geo. II, c. 25 (Juries) (1729), s. 11.

14 By the Criminal Justice Act 1972, s. 64(2), Sch. 6, Pt I.

15 County Courts Act 1984, s. 67.

16 Juries Act 1974, s. 16(1).

17 *Practice Direction (criminal: consolidated)* [2002] 3 All ER 904, 46.1.

18 *Re Wright, Lambert v Woodham* [1936] 1 All ER 877 at 879, CA.

19 *R v Watson* [1988] 1 All ER 897 at 903, CA.

20 *R v Buono* (1992) 95 Cr App Rep 338, CA. See also *Morrison v Chief Constable of West Midlands Police* [2003] All ER (D) 220 (Feb), CA: simply reminding the jury of the general expense of trials by jury did not automatically constitute misdirection by the judge.

21 The Rt Hon. Lord Justice Auld, *Review of the Criminal Courts of England and Wales* (London: The Stationery Office, 2001).

22 *Practice Direction (Crown Court: Jury Service)* [2005] 1 WLR 1361 (substituting new paragraphs IV.42.1 to IV.42.3 of Practice Direction (criminal: consolidated) [2002] 3 All ER 904, 42.1).

23 *Daily Telegraph*, 17 June 2004.

24 *Independent*, 14 June 2004.

25 Report of the Departmental Committee on Jury Service, Cmnd 2627, 1965.

26 *Attorney-General v Associated Newspapers Ltd & Ors* [1994] 1 All ER 556.

27 *Ellis v Deheer* [1922] All ER Rep 451 at 454.

28 *Journal (Newcastle)*, 9 July 1998.

29 *The Times*, 31 July 1996.

30 *Observer*, 28 May 2006.

31 Penny Darbyshire, 'The Lamp That Shows That Freedom Lives – Is It Worth the Candle?' [1991] Crim LR 740 at 745.

32 David Rose, *In the Name of the Law* (London: Jonathan Cape, 1996).

33 *Bushel's Case* (1670) Vaugh 135, Freem KB 1; (1670) 1 Mod Rep 119, 86 ER 777.

34 *Bushel's Case* (1670) Freem 5.

35 *Guardian*, 12 February 1987.

36 *Independent*, 23 May 1992.

37 *Wetherall v Harrison* [1976] QB 773.

38 Stephen Adler, *The Jury: Disorder in the Court* (New York: Main Street Books, 1995).

39 *Guardian*, 31 January 1998.

40 *Independent*, 20 April 1999.

41 *Independent*, 6 August 1999.

42 *The Times*, 9 November 1993.

43 Blackstone, *Commentaries*, IV, p. 350.

44 Trevor Grove, *The Juryman's Tale* (London: Bloomsbury, 1998), p. 207.

45 *R v Nurlon Abdroikov and others* [2005] EWCA Crim 1986.
46 Ibid, para 30.
47 *Mortimer's Miscellany*, Redgrave Theatre, Clifton, Bristol, 17 September 2005.
48 Blackstone, Commentaries, IV, p. 350.
49 Grove, *The Juryman's Tale*, p. 12.

9 Language and Law

1 F. Pollock and F.W. Maitland, *History of English Law*, 2nd edn, Vol. 1 (Cambridge: Cambridge University Press, 1968), p. 87.
2 *Dano Ltd v Earl Cadogan and Others* [2003] *The Times*, 14 March, LTL 19/5/2003, *The Times*, 2 June 2003 (CA).
3 *Ballard v North British Railway Co* [1923] SC (HL) 43 at 56.
4 Cicero, *Defence Speeches*, trans. D.H. Berry (Oxford: Oxford University Press, 2000), pp. 77–8.
5 John Gray, *Lawyers' Latin: A Vade-Mecum* (London, Robert Hale, 2002), p. 14.
6 *Dimond v Lovell* [2000] 2 All ER 897 at 906.
7 *R v Casement* [1917] 86 LJKB (n. s.) 482 at 486.
8 Ibid.
9 *Hanlon v The Law Society* [1980] 2 All ER 199 at 221.
10 *R v Summers* [1952] 1 All ER 1059 at 1060.
11 *Ex parte Davis* (1857) 5 WR 522 at 523.
12 *Hills v London Gaslight Co* (1857) 27 LJ Ex 60 at 63.
13 *Confetti Records (a Firm) and Others v Warner Music UK Ltd (trading as East West Records)* [2003] EWCh 1274, *The Times*, 12 June 2003.
14 *Re La Marquise Footwear's Application* [1946] 2 All ER 497 at 498.
15 *AAAAAAAAAAAAAAAAAAAAAAAA Inc v SW Bell Tel. Co* [1962] OK 163, 373 P.2d 31.
16 *Procter & Gamble v OHIM* (C383/99 P) [2002] Ch 82; *OHIM v Wm Wrigley Jr Co* (C19/01 P) [2004] 1WLR 1728.
17 *D v B (otherwise D) (child: surname)* [1979] 1 All ER 92 at 97.
18 *Daily Mail*, 30 January 1995.
19 *R v Barnsley Metropolitan Borough Council ex p Hook* [1976] 3 All ER 452 at 454.
20 *Cawley v Frost* [1976] 3 All ER 743.
21 *Grobbelaar v News Group Newspapers Ltd and another* [2001] 2 All ER 437 at 447, 453.
22 *Grobbelaar v News Group Newspapers Ltd and another* [2002] 4 All ER 732.
23 R.E. Megarry, *A New Miscellany-at-Law* (Oxford: Hart Publishing, 2005), p. 115.
24 *Practice Direction (Citation of Authorities)* [2001] 1 WLR 1001.
25 Hansard, HL, 3 December 1981, Vol. 425 col. 1126.

26 Keith Evans, *The Language of Advocacy* (Oxford: Oxford University Press, 1998), p. ix.

10 Miscellany

1 *Bilbie v Lumley* (1802) 2 East 469 at 472.
2 *Martindale v Falkner* (1846) 2 CB 706 at 719.
3 Chief Justice Abbott in *Montriou v Jeffreys* (1825) 2 C & P 113 at 116.
4 *Nomotexnia, (Law, or a Discourse thereof in Four Books)* English version, 1627, London, p. 6
5 Felix Frankfurter, *Of Law and Men* (New York: Archon Books, 1965), pp. 103–4, cited in Michael Furmston, 'Ignorance of the Law', *Legal Studies*, 1 (1981), 49.
6 *Farrell and another v Alexander* [1976] 1 All ER 129 at 143.
7 *Dicas v Lord Brougham and Vaux* (1833) 6 C & P 249.
8 Rennard Strickland, 'The Cinematic Lawyer: The Magic Mirror and the Silver Screen', *Oklahoma City University Law Review*, 22: 1 (1997) 13.

Glossary

1 I am pleased to acknowledge the Glossary of the Judiciary of England and Wales for many of the entries here.

Bibliography

Abel-Smith, Brian, and Robert Stevens, *Lawyers and the Courts* (London: Heinemann, 1967)

Adler, Stephen, *The Jury: Disorder in the Court* (New York: Main Street Books, 1995)

Allen, Sir Carleton Kemp, *Law in the Making*, 7th edn (Oxford: The Clarendon Press, 1964)

Aquinas, Thomas, *Summa Theologiae* (1266–73); see *Selected Writings*, ed. Ralph McInerny (Harmondsworth: Penguin, 1999)

Archbold: *Criminal Pleading Evidence and Practice* (London: Sweet & Maxwell, 2006)

Aristotle, *Politics* (2009 edn, Oxford: Oxford University Press), 1268b, 8–11

Auld, The Rt Hon. Lord Justice, *Review of the Criminal Courts of England and Wales* (London: The Stationery Office, 2001)

Baker, J.H., *The Legal Profession and Common Law* (London: The Hambledon Press, 1986)

Bentham, Jeremy, *An Introduction to the Principles and Morals of Legislation* (1780; ed. J.H. Burns and H.L.A. Hart, New York: Oceana, 1970)

——, *The Theory of Legislation* (1864) London: William Stevens

Blackstone, William, *Commentaries on the Laws of England*, 4 vols. (1765–9); ed. Wayne Morrison (London: Cavendish Publishing, 2001)

Bogdanor, Vernon, 'Our New Constitution' 120 *Law Quarterly Review*, 120 (2004), 242

Bogdanor, Vernon (ed.), *The British Constitution in the Twentieth Century* (Oxford: Oxford University Press, 2005)

Bradley, A.W., and K.D. Ewing, *Constitutional and Administrative Law*, 13th edn (Harlow: Pearson, 2003)

Bromley, P.M., *Family Law* (London: Butterworths, 1976)

Carroll, Lewis, *Through the Looking Glass – And What Alice Found There* (1871; London: Macmillan, 1996)

Cicero, *Defence Speeches*, trans. D.H. Berry (Oxford: Oxford University Press, 2000)

Darbyshire, Penny, 'The Lamp That Shows That Freedom Lives – Is It Worth the Candle?' [1991] Crim LR 740

De Mello, Rambert (ed.), *Human Rights Act 1998* (Bristol: Jordan Publishing, 2000)

Denning, Lord, *The Discipline of Law* (London: Butterworths, 1979)

——, *The Due Process of Law* (London: Butterworths, 1980)

——, *The Closing Chapter* (London: Butterworths, 1983)

——, *Landmarks in the Law* (London: Butterworths, 1984)

Devlin, Sir Patrick, *Trial By Jury* (The Hamlyn Trust, London: Stevens, 1956)

——, *The Enforcement of Morals* (Oxford: Oxford University Press, 1965)

Dicey, A.V., *Introduction to the Study of the Law of the Constitution* (1885; London: Macmillan, 1893)

——, *Lectures on the Relation between Law and Public Opinion in England during the Nineteenth Century* (1905; Honolulu, Hawaii: University Press of the Pacific, 2001)

Durkheim, Emile, *The Division of Labour in Society* (1893; Basingstoke: Macmillan, 1984)

Edwards, J., *The Law Officers of the Crown* (London: Sweet & Maxwell, 1964)

Engels, Frederick, *The Condition of the Working Class in England* (1845; London: Panther, 1969)

Evans, Keith, *The Language of Advocacy* (Oxford: Oxford University Press, 1998)

France, Anatole, *Le Lys Rouge* (1894; Paris: Calmann-Levy, 1923)

Frankfurter, Felix, *Of Law and Men: (Papers of Addresses of Felix Frankfurter, 1939–1956)* (New York: Archon Books, 1965)

Furmston, Michael, 'Ignorance of the Law', *Legal Studies*, Vol. 1 (1981), 36–55

Gower, L.C.B., 'English Legal Training', *Modern Law Review*, 13:2

Gray, John, *Lawyers' Latin: A Vade-Mecum* (London: Robert Hale, 2002)

Gray, Kevin, and Susan Francis Gray, *Land Law* (London: Butterworths, 2001)

Green, Kate, and Joe Cursley, *Land Law* (Basingstoke: Palgrave, 2001)

Grierson, Edward, *Confessions of a County Court Magistrate* (London: Victor Gollancz, 1972)

Griffith, J.A.G., *The Politics of the Judiciary*, 5th edn (London: Fontana Press, 1997)

Grove, Trevor, *The Juryman's Tale* (London: Bloomsbury, 1998)

——, *The Magistrate's Tale* (London: Bloomsbury, 2002)

Hamilton, R.G., *All Jangle and Riot* (Abingdon: Professional Books, 1986)

Hamson, Charles, *The Law: Its Study and Comparison, An Inaugural Lecture* (Cambridge: Cambridge University Press, 1955)

Hansen, M.N., *The Athenian Democracy in the Age of Demosthenes* (London: Bristol Classical Press, 1999)

Harris, Brian, *Injustice: State Trials from Socrates to Nuremberg* (Stroud: Sutton Publishing, 2006)

Hart, H.L.A., *The Concept of Law* (Oxford: Clarendon Press, 1961)

Helmholz, R.H., *The Oxford History of the Laws of England*, Vol. 1 (Oxford: Oxford University Press, 2005)

Herbert, A.P., *Uncommon Law* (1935; Thirsk: House of Stratus, 2001)

Judicial Studies Board, 'Strategy 2007–11', (www.judiciary.gov.uk)

Lee, Harper, *To Kill a Mockingbird* (1960; London: Arrow Books, 1997)

Lacey, Nichola, *A Life of H L A Hart* (Oxford: Oxford University Press, 2004)

Lidstone, K.W., R. Hogg, and F. Sutcliffe, *Prosecutions by Private Individuals and Non-Police Agencies* (London: HMSO, 1980)

Lloyd, Denis, *The Idea of Law* (Harmondsworth: Penguin, 1964)

McKendrick, Ewan, *Contract Law* (Basingstoke: Macmillan, 2003)

Maine, Henry, *Ancient Law* (1861; London: John Murray, 1905)

Malleson, K., *The New Judiciary – The Effect of Expansion and Activism* (Aldershot: Ashgate, 1999)

Markesinis, B.S., and S.F. Deakin, *Tort Law* (Oxford: Clarendon Press, 1999)

Matthews, Paul, and John Foreman (eds.), *Jervis on Coroners* (London: Sweet & Maxwell, 1993)

Megarry, R.E., *A New Miscellany-at-Law* (Oxford: Hart Publishing, 2005)

——, R.E., *A Second Miscellany-at-Law* (London: Stevens, 1973)

More, Sir Thomas, *Utopia* (1516; trans. Paul Turner, London: Penguin, 1961)

Norrie, A., *Crime, Reason and History* (London: Butterworths, 1993)

Oliver, Dawn, and Gavin Drewry (eds.), *The Law and Parliament* (London: Butterworths, 1998)

Parris, Matthew, and Phil Mason, *Read My Lips* (Harmondsworth: Penguin, 1997)

Pollock, F., and F.W. Maitland, *History of English Law*, 2nd edn, Vol.1 (Cambridge: Cambridge University Press, 1968)

Radzinowicz, Leon, *A History of English Criminal Law*, Vols. I, II (London: Stevens, 1956)

Reid, Lord, 'The Judge as Law Maker', *Journal of the Society of Public Teachers of Law*, 22 (1972)

Rose, David, *In the Name of the Law* (London: Jonathan Cape, 1996)

Sampson, Anthony, *The Anatomy of Britain* (London: Hodder and Stoughton, 1962)

Sanders, A., 'Criminal Justice: The Development of Criminal Justice Research in Britain', in P. Thomas (ed.), *Socio-Legal Studies* (Aldershot: Dartmouth, 1997), pp. 185–205

Sharpe, J.A., *Crime in Early Modern Britain 1550–1750* (London: Longman, 1984)

Shetreet, Shimon, *Judges on Trial: A Study of the Appointment and Accountability of the English Judiciary* (Amsterdam: North-Holland Publishing Company, 1976)

Sigler, J.A., 'Public Prosecutions in England and Wales', *Criminal Law Review* (1974), 642–51

Simpson, A.W.B., *Invitation to Law* (Oxford: Blackwell, 1988)

——, *Leading Cases in the Common Law* (Oxford: Clarendon Press, 1995)

Smith, J.C., and B. Hogan, *Criminal Law* (London: Butterworths, 1992)

Stafford, R.J., *Private Prosecutions* (London: Shaw & Sons, 1989)

Stein, P., *Legal Institutions* (London: Butterworths, 1984)

——, *Roman Law in European History* (Cambridge: Cambridge University Press, 1999)

Strickland, Rennard, 'The Cinematic Lawyer: The Magic Mirror and the Silver Screen', *Oklahoma City University Law Review*, 22: 1 (1997) 13

Symonds, Arthur (ed.), *The Mechanics of Law Making* (1835; Cambridge: Chadwyck-Healey in association with the British Library and Avero Publications, 1989)

Thompson, E.P., *Whigs and Hunters: The Origin of the Black Act* (Harmondsworth: Penguin, 1975)

de Tocqueville, Alexis, *Democracy in America*, ed. Alfred A. Knopf (New York: Random House, 1835), p. 284

Truss, Lynne, *Eats, Shoots & Leaves* (London: Profile Books, 2003)

Wendell Holmes, Oliver, *The Common Law* (1881; Cambridge, Mass.: Harvard University Press, 2009)

Williams, Glanville, *Textbook of Criminal Law* (London: Stevens, 1983)

Woolf, Lord, *The Pursuit of Justice* (Oxford: Oxford University Press, 2008)

Table of Cases

A (children) (conjoined twins: surgical separation), Re [2000] 4 All ER 961   **89, 275, 276**
A and others v Secretary of State for the Home Department [2004] UKHL 56   **227**
AAAAAAAAAAAAAAAAAAAAAAAAA Inc v SW Bell Tel. Co [1962] OK 163,
   373 P.2d 31   **281**
Adler v George [1964] 2 QB 7   **135**
Alcock v Chief Constable of South Yorkshire Police [1992] 1 AC 310;
   [1991] 4 All ER 907   **117–19, 120, 277**
Allen v Jackson (1875) 1 Ch D. 399   **274**
Associated Provincial Picture Houses Ltd v Wednesbury Corporation [1948]
   1 KB 223   **87**
Atkinson & Anor v Seghal [2003] EWCA Civ 697   **123–4**
Attorney-General v Associated Newspapers Ltd & Ors [1994] 1 All ER 556   **124, 280**
Austin v Mayor and Burgesses of the London Borough of Southwark [2010]
   UKSC 28   **277**
AXA General Insurance Ltd v The Lord Advocate [2011] UKSC 46   **129**

B (Children), Re [2005] EWCA Civ 643   **181–2**
Ballard v North British Railway Co [1923] SC (HL) 43   **281**
Barber v Somerset County Council [2004] UKHL 13   **175–6**
Barnett v Chelsea & Kensington Hospital Management Committee [1968]
   1 All ER 1068   **110–11**
Bellinger v Bellinger [2003] UKHL 21   **145–6**
Beswick v Beswick [1967] UKHL 2   **253**
Bilbie v Lumley (1802) 2 East 469   **281**
Bradford v Robinson Rentals Ltd [1967] All ER 267   **114, 115**
Brannan v Peek [1948] 1 KB 68   **131**
British Diabetic Association v Diabetic Society Ltd and others [1995]
   4 All ER 812   **221**
Bruce v Hamilton (1599) (Court of Session, unreported)   **15, 45**
Burmah Oil Company Ltd v Lord Advocate [1965] AC 75   **137**
Bushel's Case (1670) 124 ER 1006; (1670) Vaugh 135, Freem KB 1; (1670)
   1 Mod Rep 119, 86 ER 777   **84, 199–200, 280**

C v Director of Public Prosecutions [1995] 2 All ER 43   **275**
Carlill v Carbolic Smoke Ball Company [1892] EWCA Civ 1; [1893] 1 QB 256   **85**
Case of Prohibitions (1607) 12 Co. Rep. 63   **16, 45, 84**
Castioni, Re [1891] 1 QB 149   **277**
Cawley v Frost [1976] 3 All ER 743   **281**
Central London Property Trust Ltd v High Trees House Ltd [1947] KB 130   **86, 161**
Chelsea Yacht & Boat Co v Pope [2000] 1 WLR 1941   **179–80**
Collis v Nott (1823) Hansard (NS), vol. 9, col. 745   **30, 257**
Compania Maritima San Basilio SA v Oceanus Mutual Underwriting
   Association (Bermuda) Ltd [1977] QB 49   **278**
Confetti Records (a Firm) and Others v Warner Music UK Ltd (trading as
   East West Records) [2003] EWCh 1274   **281**
Cooper and others v Shield [1971] 2 All ER 917   **131**

Corkery v Carpenter [1951] 1 KB 102 135–6
Cottle v Cottle [1939] 2 All ER 535 51, 275
Cummings v Granger [1977] QB 397 253–4

D v B (otherwise D) (child: surname) [1979] 1 All ER 92 281
Dano Ltd v Earl Cadogan and Others [2003] The Times, 14 March, LTL 19/5/2003,
  The Times, 2 June 2003 (CA) 281
Davis, Ex parte (1857) 5 WR 522 281
Dicas v Lord Brougham and Vaux (1833) 6 C & P 249 281
Dimes v Grand Junction Canal Proprietors (1852) 3 HL Cas 759 47, 275
Dimond v Lovell [2000] 2 All ER 897 281
Director of Public Prosecutions v Schildkamp [1971] AC 1; [1969]
  3 All ER 1640 138–9, 277
Donoghue v Stevenson [1931] UKHL 3 85, 175
Duport Steel v Sirs [1980] 1 All ER 529 83, 276, 277
DWR Cymru Cyf v Edgar (2004) All ER(D) 05 (Nov) 174

Elitestone Ltd v Morris [1997] 1 WLR 687 179
Elkins v Cartlidge [1947] 1 All ER 829 131
Ellis v Deheer [1922] All ER Rep 451 280
Emmens v Pottle (1885) 16 QBD 354 277
England v Cowley (1873) LR 8 Exch 126 115–16
Entores Ltd v Miles Far East Corporation [1955] 2 QB 327 173

Fardon v Harcourt-Rivington [1932] All ER Rep 81; (1932) 146 LT 391 108–9, 110
Farrell and another v Alexander [1976] 1 All ER 129 281
Fisher v Bell [1961] 1 QB 394 134
Fitzpatrick v Sterling Housing Association Ltd [1998] 1 FLR 6 145
Froom v Butcher [1975] 3 All ER 520 277

Ghaidan v Godin-Mendoza [2004] UKHL 30 38, 120, 145
Gibson v Ryan [1968] 1 QB 250; [1967] 3 All ER 184 140, 277
Golay's Will Trusts, Re [1965] 1 WLR 969 177–8, 279
Gouriet v Union of Post Office Workers [1978] AC 435; [1977] QB 729
  (CA), 761–2; [1977] 3 All ER 70 (HL) 170, 273, 278
Grobbelaar v News Group Newspapers Ltd and another
  [2001] 2 All ER 437; [2002] 4 All ER 732 281
Guinness Trust (London Fund) v Green [1955] 1 WLR 872 212

H v Ministry of Defence [1991] 2 All ER 834 189
Hall, ex p, re Wood (1883) 23 Ch D 644 275
Hall (Arthur JS) and Co v Simons and Other Appeals [2000] 3 All ER 673 276
Hall v Hall (1788) 226
Hanlon v The Law Society [1980] 2 All ER 199 281
Heydon's Case (1584) 76 ER 637 135
Hills v London Gaslight Co (1857) 27 LJ Ex 60 281
Hinz v Berry [1970] 2 QB 40 254
Hirst (John) v UK (No.2) (2004) 38 EHRR 40 97, 165–6
HL v UK 45508/99 (2004) ECHR 471 88
Holmes v Checkland (1987) 169
Hutton v West Cork Railway Company (1883) 23 Ch D 654 274

Kempster v Deacon (1696) 1 Ld Raym 76, 2 Salk 663, 91 ER 947   275
Keown v Coventry Healthcare NHS Trust [2006] EWCA Civ 39   **132–3, 277**
Kirk v Colwyn (1958)   51
Kleinwort Benson Ltd v Lincoln City Council [1998] 4 All ER 513   **112–13, 277**

La Marquise Footwear's Application, Re [1946] 2 All ER 497   281
Leach v R [1912] AC 305   136
Leeds Teaching Hospitals NHS Trust v Mr A, Mrs A and Others [2003]
    EWCA 259   **150–5, 278**
Lewis (David) v Director of Public Prosecutions [2004] EWHC 3081 (Admin)   131
Liquidators of BCCI v Bank of England (2004)   72
Locabail (UK) Ltd v Bayfield Properties Ltd [2000] 1 All ER 65   **49, 50, 275**
Lynch v Director of Public Prosecutions for Northern Ireland [1975] 1 All ER 913   **83, 276**

M v Netherlands (1993) 74 D&R 120   **154, 278**
McFarlane v E E Caledonia Ltd [1994] 2 All ER 1; [1994] 2 All ER 1 CA   **119, 277**
McKenzie v McKenzie [1971] Ch 33; [1970] 3 All ER 1034   **72, 276**
Mareva Compania Naviera SA v International Bulkcarriers SA [1975]
    2 Lloyd's Rep 509   162
Martindale v Falkner (1846) 2 CB 706   281
Metropolitan Railway Co v Fowler [1892] 1 QB 165   277
Midland Bank Trust Co v Hett, Stubbs & Kemp [1979] Ch 384   277
Miller v Jackson [1977] QB 966   **107, 254**
Milroy v Lord [1862] EWHC J78   84
Montriou v Jeffreys (1825) 2 C & P 113   **124, 281**
Morrison (Sir Alexander) & Anr v AWG Group Ltd & Anr [2006] EWCA Civ 6   275
Morrison v Chief Constable of West Midlands Police [2003]
    All ER (D) 220 (Feb), CA   280
Moy v Pettman Smith (a firm) (2005) UKHL 7   80

Nichols plc v Registrar of Trademarks [2004] ECR I-8499   **221–2**

Oakley v Lyster [1931] 1 KB 148   116
OHIM v Wm Wrigley Jr Co (C19/01 P) [2004] 1WLR 1728   281
Oliver v City of Raleigh (1937) 193 SE 853   277

Packer v Packer [1954] P 15   273
Palm Developments Limited v Secretary of State for Communities and
    Local Government [2009] EWHC 220 (Admin)   253
Pengelley v Bell Punch Co. Ltd [1964] 1 WLR 691   **141–2**
Pepper (Inspector of Taxes) v Hart [1993] AC 593; [1993] 1 All ER 42   **146, 152, 275**
Phonographic Performance Ltd v South Tyneside Metropolitan Borough
    Council [2001] 1 WLR 400   141
Pinochet No 2, In Re [1999] 1 All ER 577   **47, 275**
Polemis & Furniss, Withy & Co Ltd, Re [1921] 3 KB 560   107
Powell v Kempton Park Racecourse [1899] AC 143   **140–1**
Proctor & Gamble v OHIM (C383/99 P) [2002] Ch 82   281

R (Mondelly) v Commissioner of Police of the Metropolis [2006]
    EWHC 2370 (Admin)   254
R v A sub nom R v Y [2001] UKHL 25   **129, 143, 278**

R v Barnsley Metropolitan Borough Council ex p Hook [1976]
3 All ER 452 — 252, 281
R v Bow County Court, ex parte Pelling QBD 26 January 2000,
CO/539/98 — 276
R v Bow Street Metropolitan Stipendiary Magistrate ex parte
Pinochet Urgarte [1999] 1 All ER 577 — 48, 107, 275
R v Buono (1992) 95 Cr App Rep 338, CA — 280
R v Casement [1917] 86 LJKB (n. s.) 482 — 281
R v Clegg [1995] 1 All ER 334 — 275
R v Clinton [1993] 2 All ER 998 — 276
R v Cotswold Geotechnical Holdings Ltd, Court of Appeal (Criminal Division)
[2011] EWCA Crim 1337 — 274
R v Forty-Nine Casks of Brandy (1836) 3 HAGG 257 — 227
R v Fricker [1999] EWCA Crim 1773 — 202–3
R v Governor of Brockhill Prison (ex parte Evans) [2000] 4 All ER 15 — 277
R v Inhabitants of Sedgely (1831) 2 B & Ad 65 — 142, 277
R v Lambeth London Borough Council, ex parte W [2003] UKHL 57;
[2002] EWCA Civ 613 — 96, 277
R v Leicester City Justices, ex parte Barrow and another [1991] 3 All ER 935 — 276
R v Millis (1844) 10 Cl. & F. 534 — 226
R v Minister of Health, ex parte Villiers [Divisional Court] [1936] 2 KB 29 — 277
R v Nurlon Abdroikov and others [2005] EWCA Crim 1986 — 281
R v R (Rape: marital exemption) [1991] 4 All ER 481 — 92, 275
R v Summers [1952] 1 All ER 1059 — 281
R v Sussex Justices ex parte McCarthy [1924] 1 KB 256; [1923] All ER 233 — 47
R v Thomas Guy Moringiello 26 June 1997, Smith Bernal Transcript
Report No. 9605492/W4 — 51
R v Watson [1988] 1 All ER 897; [1988] QB 690 — 192, 280
R v Wood (1832) 3 B. & Ad. 657 — 169
Reckitt & Colman Products Ltd v Borden Inc [1990] 1 WLR 491 — 221
Rondel v Worsley [1969] 1 AC 191; [1967] 3 All ER 993 — 276

St Edmundsbury and Ipswich Diocesan Board of Finance v Clark [1973]
2 All ER 1155 — 275
Salomon v A Salomon & Co Ltd [1897] AC 22 — 85
Seaford Court Estates v Asher [1949] 2 All ER 155 — 278
Shaw, Lord — 212
Sims v William Howard and Son Ltd [1964] 2 QB 409; [1964] 1 All ER 918 — 189, 279
Smith's estate, Re (1887) 34 ChD 589 — 277
Snook v Mannion [1982] Crim LR 601 — 225
Sutton (Kieran) v Kay Hutchinson [2005] EWCA Civ 1773 — 252–3
Sweet v Parsley [1970] AC 132; [1969] 1 All ER 347 — 137, 277

Taff Vale Railway Co v Cardiff Railway Co [1917] 1 Ch 299 — 277
Tito and others v Waddell and others (No 2); Tito and others v
Attorney-General [1977] 3 All ER 129 — 276
Tremain v Pike [1969] 1 WLR 1556 — 114–15

U (Mrs) v Centre for Reproductive Medicine [2002] EWCA Civ 565 — 153

Van Duyn v Home Office [1975] Ch. 358 — 87–8

W (Children), Re [2010] UKSC 12   **92**
Ward v James [1966] 1 QB 273; [1965] 1 All ER 563, CA   **279**
Wetherall v Harrison [1976] QB 773   **280**
White (Henry) and others v Chief Constable of South Yorkshire and
    others [1999] 2 AC 455   **119–20**
White v White and Motor Insurance Bureau [2001] UKHL 9   **147–9**
Williams v Beesley [1973] 3 All ER 144   **279**
Willis v Baddeley [1892] 2 QB 324   **83, 276**
Woolmington v Director of Public Prosecutions [1935] AC 462   **86**
Wright, Lambert v Woodham, Re [1936] 1 All ER 877   **280**

Yemshaw v London Borough of Hounslow [2011] UKSC 3   **120**
Young v Bristol Aeroplane Co Ltd [1944] KB 718 CA   **95, 97**

Table of Legislation

Access to Justice Act 1999 — **34, 65, 67**
Act of Settlement 1701 — **52**

Betting Act 1853 — **140**
Bill of Rights 1689 — **39**
  Art 9 — **40**
Brighton Corporation Act 1931 — **129–30**
Business Names Act 1985 — **222**

Children Act 1989
  s 17A — **256**
Civil Jurisdiction and Judgments Act 1982 — **227**
Companies Act 1948
  s 332(3) — **139**
Companies Act 2006 — **227**
Constitutional Reform Act 2005 — **30**
Contempt of Court Act 1981 — **195, 197**
  s 8 — **194, 196**
Copyright, Designs and Patents Act 1988
  s 67 — **141**
Coroners Act 1988 — **190**
Coroners and Justice Act 2009 — **101**
Corporate Manslaughter and Corporate Homicide Act 2007 — **21, 22, 23, 24**
County Courts Act 1984
  s 67 — **280**
Courts and Legal Services Act 1990 — **34, 65, 67, 69, 73**
Crime and Disorder Act 1998
  s 34 — **40**
Criminal Evidence Act 1898 — **136**
Criminal Justice Act 1972
  s 64(2) — **280**
  Sch. 6
    Pt I — **280**
Criminal Justice Act 2003 — **186, 187, 195, 207**
  s 321 — **192**
Criminal Law Act 1967
  s 3 — **199**

Dangerous Dogs Act 1991
  s 3(1) — **8**
Dangerous Drugs Act 1965
  s 5(b) — **137**

European Communities Act 1972 — **96, 149**

Factories Act 1961 — **142**
  s 28 — **141**

Forfeiture Act 1870   **165**
Freedom of Information Act 2000   **12, 164**

Genocide Act 1969   **199**

Housing Act 1925   **142**
Human Fertilisation and Embryology Act 1990   **151, 152, 153**
     Preamble   **151**
     s 28   **152, 153**
     s 28(2)   **154**
     s 28(3)   **154, 155**
     s 28(3)(a)   **154**
Human Rights Act 1998   **28, 37, 38, 103, 106, 129, 131, 143, 146, 149, 164**
     s 2   **96**
     s 3   **37, 103, 143, 145, 166**
     s 4   **37, 155**

Immigration and Asylum Act 1999
     s 122   **96, 256**

Judicature Acts 1873–75   **161**
Juries Act 1825
     s 26   **191**
Juries Act 1974   **186**
     s 16(1)   **280**
     s 17   **191**

Law of Property Act 1925   **100**
Legal Aid, Sentencing and Punishment of Offenders Act 2012   **81**
Licensing Act 1872
     s 12   **135**
Limited Liability Partnership Act 2000   **69**
London Open Spaces Act 1893   **142**

Matrimonial Causes Act 1973
     s 11(c)   **37, 146**
Mental Capacity Act 2005   **99**
Mental Health Discrimination Act 2013   **186**
Municipal Corporations Act 1835   **56**

Occupiers' Liability Act 1984
     s 1(1)(a)   **132**
Official Secrets Act 1920
     s 3   **135**

Parliament Act 1911   **129**
Poor Relief Act 1601   **142**
Prosecution of Offences Act 1985   **170**
     s 24   **169**
Public Order Act 1936   **131**

Rent Act 1968	**233**
Rent Act 1977	**38, 145**
Sched 1	
para 2	**145**
Restriction of Offensive Weapons Act 1959	**134**
Salmon and Freshwater Fisheries (Protection) (Scotland) Act 1951	
s 7	**140**
s 7(1)	**140**
s 10	**140**
Sex Disqualification (Removal) Act 1919	**56, 191**
Solicitors Act 1974	**75**
Statute of Gloucester (1278)	**91**
Statute of Westminster 1275	**230**
Street Betting Act 1906	**131**
Supreme Court Act 1981	**29**
s 69	**188**
Surrogacy Arrangements Act 1985	**151**
Town and Country Planning Act 1990	**253**
Treason Act 1351	**217–18**
Treasure Act 1996	**100**
Tribunals and Enforcement Act 2007	**33**
War Damage Act 1965	**137**
Wild Mammals (Protection) Act 1996	**129**
Youth Justice and Criminal Evidence Act 1999	
s 41	**143, 144**
s 41(3)(b)–(c)	**144**

SECONDARY LEGISLATION

Civil Procedure Rules 1998	**107, 172, 213**
Teachers (Compensation) (Advanced Further Education)	
Regulations 1983 (SI1983/856)	**130**

EUROPEAN CONVENTIONS

European Convention on Human Rights and Freedoms	**38, 102–3, 143, 145**
Art 6	**49, 144**
Art 8	**37, 38, 145, 154**
Art 8(1)	**155**
Art 12	**37**
Art 14	**106**
First Protocol	
Art 1–Art 2	**106**
Art 3	**106, 165, 166**
Sixth Protocol	
Art 1–Art 2	**106**

Index

abortion 18
accessible law 12–15
accidents 19–20
Acts of Parliament *see* statutes
Adam's Rib (film) 245
Administrative Court 98; Judge in Charge 32
administrative law 164–6
Alcee, Andrew 220
Alfred the Great, King 62
All England Law Reports (All ER) 123
Allen, Carleton 168
ambulance-chasing 64
Amnesty International 47
Anne, Princess 8
appointment of judges 28, 33–5, 36
Aquinas, Thomas 4
Aristotle 185
Arnold, Thurman 251
artificial reproduction 150–5
Asquith, Lord 92
assembly: freedom of 105
association: freedom of 105
asylum seekers 37
Atkin, Lord 167
Attard, Gracie and Rosie 36
AWG 51

Bacon, Francis 52
Bar Council 74, 75
Bar Professional Training Course (BPTC) 73–4
Bar Standards Board 74–5
Barrington, Jonah 52
barristers 61, 62, 63, 72–3; chambers 76–7;
        fusion of professions 65–6, 67; legal
        claims against 78; Queen's Counsel (QC) 74,
        75–6; rights of audience 65, 67, 68;
        ten classic legal mistakes 255–7; training
        and organisation 73–5
barristers' clerks 76
Bellinger, Elizabeth Ann 37
Berlusconi, Silvio 9
Berry, Steven 22
bias: judges 46–51
Bierce, Ambrose 21
binding over 55
Birkenhead, Lord 15

Blackburn, Colin 255–6
Blackstone, William 158, 170–1, 183, 206, 208–9,
        214, 258
Blake, Peter 187
Blom-Cooper, Louis 206
Blunkett, David 38
Bogdanor, Vernon 163–4
Bolingbroke, Henry 163
Bonaccorsi, Paolo 75
Bono 238
Boswell, James 44
Bowen, Lord 54
Bradley, A. W. 164
Brandeis, Louis Dembitz 3, 239
bribery 52
Buller, Francis 29
Burrell, Paul 36
Butler-Sloss, Elizabeth 150–1, 153–4, 155

Cameron, Glen 187
Campbell, Bruce 52
Campbell, Lord 47
capitalism 11
Carman, George 237
Carroll, Lewis 12
Casement, Roger 217–19, 252
cases: case law 83–8, 117–20; dissenting
        judgments 120–1; law online 124–5;
        law reporting 121–4; news reporting
        125–6; *obiter dicta* 109–12; *ratio decidendi*
        108–9, 113; ten classic judgment openings
        252–5; ten classic legal mistakes 255–7;
        titles 107–8; *see also* precedent
chambers 76–7
Chancery Division 32, 97, 98, 189
Charles Dickens: *Bleak House* 232
Chief Coroner 101
children: *doli incapax* 39–40; rights 18
Choate, Joseph 59
chose in action 228
Cicero, Marcus Tullio 3, 13, 213, 227, 238
Circuit Judges 32, 52
civil law 166, 171–2; contract law 172–4;
        family law 180–2; juries in civil cases 188;
        land law 178–80; tort law 174–6, 221;
        trusts law 176–8

civil (code) law systems 83, 159, 172
Clark, Andrew 59
Clark, Keith 70
Clarke, Charles 38
Class Action (film) 248
clear law 12–15
Cleary, Anthony 259
Clegg, Lee 41
Clifford Chance 70
Clinton, Bill 18
Codd, A. G. 236
codification of law 83, 159, 172
Cohn, Roy M. 36
Coke, Edward 15, 16, 76, 89, 177
collateral attacks 78, 79
common law 60, 88–9, 158–9, 162;
    development of 89–91, 159–60;
    presumption against Parliament
    changing the law 136
Companies Court 98–9
Compulsion (film) 246
conjoined twins 36, 89
conscience: freedom of 105
constitutional law 163–4
contempt of court 194, 195
contracts 35, 172–4
contributory negligence 93
copyright 259
Coroners' Courts 100–2, 190, 241
corporate manslaughter 19–24
corporate social responsibility 24
corruption 52
Cotswold Geotechnical Holdings 22
Cottenham, Lord 47
Counsellor at Law (film) 244
County Courts 99–100, 241; juries 189–90
Court of Appeal 95–6, 241–2
Court of Protection 99
courts 29, 30–2, 60, 90; administration of 41–3;
    fair hearing right 49, 104; hierarchy of 92–3;
    ten classic judgment openings 252–5;
    ten great places to experience law live
    241–4; *see also* individual courts
Cranston, Mr Justice 253
crime 167, 168; criminal law 11, 166, 167–71;
    juries in criminal cases 187–8, 192, 194–208;
    presumption against imposing criminal
    liability without fault 136–7; prosecution of
    offences 168–70
criminal damage 197, 198–9
cross-examination 72–3

Crown Court 29, 99, 183, 242
Crown Prosecution Service 170

Darbyshire, Penny 198
Darrow, Clarence 3, 239
Darwin, Charles 9
Davey, Simon 259
death: coroners and 100–2
declarations of incompatibility with HRA
    37–8, 106
deed poll 228
defalcation 228
democracy: law and 24–5
Denning, Lord 2–3, 8, 30, 43, 93, 155, 162, 173,
    224, 240, 252, 253, 254, 255
deodand 258–9
Devlin, Lord 199
Devlin, Patrick 5, 183
Dicas, John 236
Dicey, A. V. 1, 8, 17, 27–8
Dimond, Vanessa Dawn 215
Diogenes 3
Diplock, Lord 134, 256
Director of Public Prosecutions 170
disability 17, 57
discrimination 17; right not to be discriminated
    against 106
dismissal of judges 51–3
dissenting judgments 120–1
distinguishing precedent 113–16
District Judges 32
District Judges (Magistrates' Courts) 53, 55
Divisional Courts 96–7; *see also* individual
    divisions
DNA 18
doli incapax 39–40
Douglas, Michael 238
Dunning, John 255
Durkheim, Emile 11, 168
Dyson, Lord 193

education 14
Edward III, King 55
Edward VII, King (*formerly* Prince of Wales)
    236–7
ejusdem generis 140–1
Eldon, Lord 30, 236
elections: voting rights of prisoners 165–6
Ellenborough, Chief Justice 231
Employment Tribunals 242
Engels, Friedrich 6

engross 228
equality 10–11
equity 159, 160–2
Esher, Lord 83
Etherton, Mr Justice 212
ethnic minorities: barristers 74, 76; lawyers 66, 67; magistrates 57
European Court of Human Rights 101–2
European Union: interpretation of statutes and EU law 146–50
Evans, Glanville 19
Evans-Lombe, Mr Justice 51
Evershed, Mr Justice 222
evidence: hearsay 228–9; ten remarkable pieces of evidence 257–60
Ewing, K. D. 164
excommunication 20
expressio unius est exclusio alterius 142
expression: freedom of 105
Eyre, Edward 8–9

fair hearing right 49, 104
Falconer, Lord 57
Family Division 96, 189; President 32, 33
family law 180–2
family life: right to respect for 105, 154–5
Faulks, Esman 196
fees and charges 13, 64–5
feudalism 11
films: ten great films for those interested in law 244–9
Finch, Henry 231
Finnemore, Mr Justice 30
Foot, Lord 227
forced labour: prohibition of 104
Ford, Malcolm 3
Forster, E. M. 237
France, Anatole 11
Frankfurter, Mr Justice 231–2
freezing injunctions 162
Fuller, Thomas 8
Furmston, Michael 14

Gandhi, Mohandas Karamchand 3, 239–40
Gardiner, Lord 94
Gascoigne, William 45
generalia specialibus non derogant 142
genocide 199
Germany 10
Gibb, Frances 125, 126
Glanville, Ranulf de 219–20

Goddard, Lord 258
golden rule of statutory interpretation 134–5
Gordon, William 8
Gordon-Cumming, William 236
Graefe, Juergen 64
Graham, Hector 257
Gray, John 214–15
Griffith, J. A. C. 48
Griffiths, Lord 40
Grimes, Richard 23–4
Grobbelaar, Bruce 225
gross negligence: manslaughter and 19
Guatemala 46

habeas corpus 98
Hailsham, Lord 227
Hamson, Charles 14
Handelsman, J. B. 10
Hansard 40, 146
Hare, Edith 258
Harman, Lord 44
Harris, Thomas 255
Hastings, Patrick 72
Hazeltine, George W. 260
heads of state 10
Health and Safety Executive (HSE) 22, 23
Healy, Maurice: *The Old Munster Circuit* 233–4
hearsay 228–9
Henry II, King 90
Henry VIII, King 170
Herald of Free Enterprise disaster 20
Herbert, A. P. 228; *Uncommon Law: Being 66 Misleading Cases* 235
Hewart, Lord 255
Hibberd, Barry 187
High Court 29, 97–9, 242; Chancellor 32, 33; judges 32, 34–5; *see also* individual divisions
Hoffmann, Lord 47–8, 78–9
Holdsworth, William 252
Holker, John 236
homosexual people 18; succession to tenancies 38, 145
Hook, Harry 224, 252
Hooton, Patrick 46
House of Commons 242–3
House of Lords 39, 41; Appellate Committee 30–1, 40; precedent and 94
Howard, Michael 38
Hughes, Thomas 9

Human Genetics Commission 18
human rights issues 103, 154–5; declarations of
   incompatibility with HRA 37–8, 106;
   European Court of Human Rights 101–2;
   interpretation of statutes and 143–6; rights
   established under HRA 103–6

impartiality of judges 46–51
importance of law 1–4
impotence 258
Inches, Cyrus 59
Incorporated Council of Law Reporting 122
independence of judiciary 45–6
Indonesia 46
industrial accidents 19
Inherit the Wind (film) 246–7
Innocent IV, Pope 20
Institute of Legal Executives (ILEX) 62, 71
Internet 17, 25; law online 124–5
interpretation of statutes: dangers 131–3;
      ejusdem generis 140–1; European context
      146–50; *expressio unius est exclusio alterius*
      142; *generalia specialibus non derogant* 142;
      golden rule 134–5; human rights and 143–6;
      justice/truth and 150–6; literal rule 134;
      mischief rule 135–6; *noscitur a sociis* 141–2;
      other words in same Act 140; presumption
      against imposing criminal liability without
      fault 136–7; presumption against Parliament
      changing the law 136; presumption against
      retrospective operation 137–8; punctuation,
      cross-headings and side-notes 138–9;
      purposive approach 146–50; rules 133–8
Iraq 7

James VI of Scotland and I of England, King 15,
   16, 45
JMW Farms 22
judges 27–8, 183; administration of the courts and
      41–3; appointment 28, 33–5, 36; battle of the
      law-makers 37–41; case law and 83–8,
      117–20; communication with the public 43;
      impartiality 46–51; independence 45–6;
      judicial animation of the law 35–6; as jurors
      192–3; profile of judiciary 28–30; removal
      from office 51–3; retirement 29–30; role
      28–9, 38, 188; ten classic legal mistakes
      255–7; training 43–4; types of 30–2
Judicial Appointments Commission (JAC) 33
judicial review 164–5
Judicial Studies Board (JSB) 43–4

juries 183–5, 208–9; Coroners' Courts 101, 190;
      examples 194–208; judges as jurors 192–3;
      law of 185–6; majority verdicts 191–2;
      numbers of jurors 190–1, 193; when juries
      are used 186–91

Kafka, Franz: *The Trial* 234
Keith, Lord 39, 118–19
Kilmuir, Lord 43
Kronlid, Lotta 197

laches 229
land law 178–80
language, legal 12–13, 211–12; arcane legal words
      and phrases 227–30; conciseness 226–7;
      Latin 213–17; legal words that have become
      common 219–20; names 220–4; profane
      language 224–6; punctuation 217–19
Latimer, Hugh 52
Latin language 213–17
law online 124–5
law reporting 121–4
Law Society 65, 68, 75
Lawrence, D. H. 237
lawyers 59–61; fees and charges 13, 64–5; legal
      claims against 77–80; legal executives 61–2,
      71; new forms of organisation 69–70;
      numbers of 13–14, 61, 66–7, 73; other help
      in the courtroom 77; public image of 3, 13,
      59, 80–1; ten classic law school witticisms
      249–52; ten classic legal mistakes 255–7;
      ten great lawyers 238–41; *see also*
      barristers; solicitors
Lee, Harper 10; *To Kill a Mockingbird* 234–5
legal executives 61–2, 71
Legal Practice Course (LPC) 68
legal profession *see* barristers; lawyers; solicitors
Let Him Have It (film) 248–9
Lewison, Mr Justice 220
libel 225
liberty: right to 104
life: right to 104
life-support machines 18
Lilley, Peter 37
limited liability partnership (LLP) 69–70
Lion Steel Ltd 22
literal rule of statutory interpretation 134
literary classics 231–2; *Bleak House* (Charles
      Dickens) 232; *Cannibalism and the
      Common Law* (A. W. B. Simpson) 232;
      First Rumpole Omnibus (John Mortimer) 233;

To Kill a Mockingbird (Harper Lee) 234–5; *Merchant of Venice* (William Shakespeare) 233; *The Old Munster Circuit* (Maurice Healy) 233–4; *Orley Farm* (Anthony Trollope) 234; *The Trial* (Franz Kafka) 234; *Uncommon Law: Being 66 Misleading Cases* (A. P. Herbert) 235; *The Winslow Boy* (Terence Rattigan) 235
litigant in person 77
Lloyd, Denis 4–5
Lloyd of Berwick, Lord 41
local government planning committees 243
Lord Chancellor 33
Lord Chief Justice 32, 33
Lowry, Lord 40

Macclesfield, Lord 52
Macfarlane, Alan 184
Mackay, Lord 43
McKenzie friend 77
Macmillan, Lord 175
McWhirter, Norris 258
magistrates 53–5, 183; popular justice and 55–7
Magistrates' Courts 93, 100, 243–4
Mandela, Nelson 3, 240
manslaughter: corporate 19–24
Mareva injunctions 162
Marlow, Tony 37
marriage: rape in 39, 92, 127, 143–4; right to marry 105
Martin, Baron 220
Master of the Rolls 32, 33, 68
Maule, Mr Justice 231
May, Theresa 38
Mead, William 199
Megarry, Robert 72
Mellish, Lord 27
mens rea 136–7
mergers of firms 70
Michael, George 237
Mill, John Stuart 9, 81
Milosevic, Slobodan 9
misfeasance 229
Mitchell, Austin 223
moral purposes of law 5
More, Thomas 3, 5–6, 239
Mortimer, John 59, 208, 209; *First Rumpole Omnibus* 233
Moses, Lord 254
Mubarak, Hosni 9
Munday, Bessie 257

murder 60, 89, 194, 257
My Cousin Vinny (film) 249

names 220–4
Narizano, Nestor 44
nature of law 4–7
necessity: doctrine of 36
Needham, Andrea 197
negligence 175–6; contributory 93; by lawyers 78, 79; manslaughter and 19
Neuberger, Lord 43
no win no fee arrangements 81
noscitur a sociis 141–2
numbers of lawyers 13–14, 61, 66–7, 73

obiter dicta 109–12
O'Brien, Flann 230
Official Referees' Court 98
opening speeches 72; ten classic judgment openings 252–5
Ormrod, Mr Justice 224
overruling precedent 112–13
Owen, Stephen 201

P & O Ferries 20
Park, Peter 54
Parke, Mr Justice 227
Parliament: battle of the law-makers 37–41
partnerships: limited liability partnership (LLP) 69–70
part-time judges 35, 49–50
passing off 221, 222
Patents Court 98
Payne, Cynthia 200–1
peace campaigners 197, 198–9
Pearce, Michael 54
Pearson, Lord 189
Peel, John 237
Penn, William 199
personal injury cases 188–9
Pinochet, Augusto 9, 47–8
police 170; police officers as jurors 206–8
political economy 6
Pollock, Chief Justice 220
precedent 27, 78, 89, 91, 159, 256; Court of Appeal decisions 95–6; distinguishing 113–16; Divisional Courts 97; High Court 97–9; judging system of 126–7; law reporting and 121–4; overruling 112–13; Supreme Court decisions 94

presumptions: against imposing criminal liability without fault 136–7; against Parliament changing the law 136; against retrospective operation 137–8
prisoners: voting rights of 165–6
private law 163
private life: right to respect for 105
private reports 121–2
Privy Council: Judicial Committee 31
profane language 224–6
promissory estoppel 162
proportionality principle 146–7
prosecution of offences 168–70
Pryce, Vicky 187
psychiatric harm 117–20
public image of lawyers 3, 13, 59
public law 163–6
punctuation 138–9, 217–19

QB VII (film) 247–8
Quakers 199–200
Queen's Bench Division 97; President 32
Queen's Counsel (QC) 74, 75–6

racial discrimination 17
rape: marital 39, 92, 127, 143–4
ratio decidendi 108–9, 113
Rattigan, Terence: *The Winslow Boy* 235
Rawlinson, Lord 74
Recorders 32
recuse 229
redundancy 24
Reid, John 38, 139
Reid, Lord 27
religion: freedom of 105
retirement of judges 29–30
retrospective legislation 137–8
Richard I, King 55
Rohan, Paula 70
Roman law 172
rule of law 7–11
Ruskin, John 236
Rwanda 9

Saddam Hussein 9
Scrivener, Anthony 193
seat belts 93
sedition 199–200
Seely, Douglas D. 256
Seinfeld, Jerry 2

sentences: no punishment without law 104
sex discrimination 17
Shakespeare, William: *Merchant of Venice* 233
Sheridan, Ann 222
Shull, Michael 256
Shute, Christopher 19
Simon, Lord 41, 83
Simpson, A. W. B. 6–7, 9, 60, 90; *Cannibalism and the Common Law* 232
single-parent families 18
slavery 11; prohibition of 104
Smith, F. E. 59, 73
Smith, George Joseph 257
social change: law and 17–24
Socrates 185
solicitors 61, 62, 63, 66–7; fusion of professions 65–6, 67; legal claims against 78; rights of audience 65, 67, 68–9; ten classic legal mistakes 255–7; training 68
Solicitors Regulation Authority (SRA) 68
South Africa 10
Spencer, Herbert 9
Spitting Image 258
standards: law as global metwand 15–16
statutes 129–31, 162; interpretation *see* interpretation of statutes; presumption against retrospective operation 137–8
Steyn, Lord 80
Straw, Jack 38
Sullivan, A. M. 218
Summers, Ada 56
Supreme Court 30–1, 39, 93, 94, 243; appointment of justices 33
surnames 223–4
Swift, Jonathan 227

Taylforth, Gillian 237
Taylor, Kevin 201
Taylor, William Francis Kyffin 29
Technology and Construction Court 98
tenancies: homosexual people and succession to tenancies 38, 145
Thankerton, Lord 30
theft 18
Thomas, Cheryl 186
Thompson, E. P. 10
Thompson, William Henry 240
Thornberry, Emily 23
thought: freedom of 105
thought experiments 5

time immemorial 229–30
Times, The 125
Tobias, Anthony 29
Tocqueville, Alexis de 183
tort law 174–6, 221
torture: prohibition of 104
totalitarianism: rule of law and 9–10
trademarks 221, 222
training: barristers 73–4; judges 43–4; legal executives 71; solicitors 68
transsexuality 18, 37, 146
treason 217–19
treasure trove 100
Trollope, Anthony 236; *Orley Farm* 234
Truss, Lynne 217
trusts 176–8
Twain, Mark 203
12 Angry Men (film) 245–6
Twomey, John 187
types of law 157–8; civil law *see* civil law; civil (code) law systems 83, 159, 172; common law *see* common law; criminal law 11, 166, 167–71; equity 159, 160–2; public and private law 163–6; statute law *see* statutes

Ulpianus. Domitius 238–9
Ungoed-Thomas, Mr Justice 177–8
United States of America 7, 13, 36, 158, 197, 244
universal human rights 19

Victim (film) 247
Virgin Group 223

voire dire 230
voting rights of prisoners 165–6

Wakley, Thomas 100
Ward, Lord 253
Warren, Edward 251
Warrington, Lord 196
Webb, Thomas Ebenezer 251
Weekly Law Reports (WLR) 122–3
Wendell Holmes, Oliver 162
Whistler, James 236
William III, King 52
Williams, Glanville 167
wills 35–6
Wilson, Joanna 197
Wilson-Ward, Janet 54
winding-up of companies 99
Witness for the Prosecution (film) 245
witnesses 235–8
women: barristers 73, 74, 75, 76; lawyers 66, 67; magistrates 56, 57; sex discrimination 17
Woolf, Lord 208, 240–1
Wright, Alexander 22
writs 91

Yang, Jason 223
Year Books 121
Young, Stephen 194, 196

Zelter, Angela 197
Zeta-Jones, Catherine 238
Zimbabwe 36, 45